ANYWHERE BUT HERE

ANYWHERE BUT HERE

How Britain's Broken Asylum System Fails Us All

NICOLA KELLY

Elliott&Thompson

First published 2025 by
Elliott and Thompson Limited
2 John Street
London WC1N 2ES
www.eandtbooks.com

Represented by:
Authorised Rep Compliance Ltd.
Ground Floor, 71 Lower Baggot Street
Dublin, D02 P593
Ireland
www.arccompliance.com

ISBN: 978-1-78396-855-8

Copyright © Nicola Kelly 2025

The Author has asserted her right under the Copyright, Designs and Patents Act, 1988, to be identified as Author of this Work.

All rights reserved. No part of this publication may be reproduced, stored in or introduced into a retrieval system, or transmitted, in any form, or by any means (electronic, mechanical, photocopying, recording or otherwise) without the prior written permission of the publisher. Any person who does any unauthorised act in relation to this publication may be liable to criminal prosecution and civil claims for damages.

Picture credit
Page ix: Behind the Fence, copyright © @HejiPH

9 8 7 6 5 4 3 2 1

A catalogue record for this book is available from the British Library.

Typesetting: Marie Doherty
Printed & bound in Great Britain
by Bell and Bain Ltd, Glasgow

For those who arrived on our shores in search of a better life, those who never had the chance and those who died trying.

Contents

Prologue: No Entry *xi*

PART ONE: CROSSING

1. White Cliffs *3*
2. SOS *19*
3. Fortress Britain *35*

PART TWO: ARRIVAL

4. On Solid Ground *55*
5. No Safe Passage *71*
6. Backlogged *91*

PART THREE: DISPERSAL

7. No Room *111*
8. The Black Market *131*
9. Who Cares? *147*
10. Advice Sharks *163*

PART FOUR: INTEGRATION

11. Big Brother State   *183*
12. Raided   *199*
13. When The State Gives Up   *215*

PART FIVE: DEPARTURE

14. Locked Up   *233*
15. Say Goodbye   *247*

Afterword: Home   *261*

A Note on Sources   *277*
Acknowledgements   *281*
Notes   *285*
Index   *327*

Behind the Fence

Prologue: No Entry

In October 2024, I stood on a grassy verge overlooking a beach in northern France, the wind whipping through my hair and sand grains spiralling around my feet. Below, I watched as over sixty people were ushered towards a dinghy, carrying hand pumps and jerrycans of fuel. A chill ran up my spine as I saw a child – probably as young as three; my son's age – gripping his mother's hand and padding towards the sea, with only the moonlight to guide them. Rocking back and forth on the shoreline was the flimsy vessel that was to take them across freezing-cold water to the white cliffs beyond. Thousands of miles, largely travelled on foot, and here they were. Their final destination was in reach.

What is so extraordinary about this sight is how ordinary it has become. In 2018, less than 300 people crossed the Channel by small boat from the camps in northern France to the UK. Sajid Javid, then home secretary, broke off his holiday, declaring it a 'major incident'.[1] The following year, the Foreign Affairs Select Committee warned that closing off 'robust and accessible' passages would force more people into unseaworthy dinghies.[2] And so it came to pass. By autumn 2024, just six years since the first dinghies left northern France, more than 140,000 new arrivals had come to our shores by small boat, fuelling a rise in far-right sentiment and a myriad of failed pledges and plans to stop them. How did we get here?

The UK's asylum system has all but collapsed. A backlog of tens of thousands of claims has swelled out of control, leaving victims of torture, trafficking, persecution and conflict languishing in areas where local people don't want them. Children have gone missing from hotels, exploited into criminal gangs. People have been made destitute and died due to lack of access to medical care, here on UK soil. They've been criminalised, made to stand trial and imprisoned, unable to afford the legal fees to prove their innocence. They have been monitored, followed, harassed and humiliated into leaving the country. And they've been deported back to the nations they fled, despite having narrowly escaped death there.

Creaking under the strain of a poorly resourced, ill-equipped system filled with disenfranchised, disaffected staff – both at a policy and at an operational level – successive governments have resorted to toxic rhetoric and headline-grabbing announcements. Under the Conservatives, the system was deliberately ground down, a crisis manufactured and seeds of division sown for political gain, with strong, eerie echoes of the pre-Brexit narrative on immigration.

Yet, by the government's own reckoning, more than three-quarters of those who claim asylum here are granted leave to remain, considered by the Home Office to be genuine refugees in need of protection[3] – a duty the UK has an obligation to uphold under international law. What's more, asylum seekers are, in the main, welcomed by the general public. The World Values Survey found that the British public's attitude to immigration is among the most liberal and relaxed anywhere in the world, with 68 per cent saying we should allow new arrivals to settle here – the highest of any nation surveyed.[4] So why, if the public perception of migrants is broadly positive, has the government taken such a hardline stance?

PROLOGUE: NO ENTRY

Small boat crossings have become a proxy for the wider debate around immigration, even while the numbers arriving by irregular routes are only a tiny proportion of the overall figures. Asylum seekers account for just 0.5 per cent of the UK population today. We can – and we must – absorb these kinds of numbers. We are not, as many would have it, 'full up'.

Covering these issues day-to-day as a home affairs reporter, it's easy to become lost in the noise. Immigration is one of the most divisive issues in our society. Which side you fall down on – for or against open borders – can tell you a lot about a person. Where they live. Which socio-economic background they may come from. Even which way they voted in the EU referendum. This, unlike many others, is an issue bound up in identity. If you question someone's view on immigration, you are questioning an important part of who they are: their roots, their values, their aspirations. It can be deeply offensive.

When I am asked what I do, where I work or what I write about, I usually pause, take a deep breath and make a face that suggests I am uncomfortable. Having worked for the Home Office as a press officer on the immigration desk during the rollout of the hostile environment policy, and as a spokesperson for the Foreign Office as the Arab Spring uprisings swept through the region, to now reporting on the asylum system for newspapers such as the *Guardian* and the *Observer*, these issues are personal to me. I often question my proximity to them and whether I am the right person to be working on these stories, or if shame and guilt cloud my judgement.

In tackling this subject, I'm frequently asked what I think the government should be doing. Should they stop the boats? Should they be putting new arrivals up in hotels? Should asylum seekers be given the right to work? I usually say it's not my job to answer those questions and my views aren't important. Whether the authorities can, or will, is what I focus on. My role is to report, not to opine.

To that end, this book is not about policy, politics or politicking; it's about people. At its heart are the stories of those affected by the broken, sclerotic asylum system, many of whom I followed over years, from the moment they arrived on our shores and began to navigate the complex, notoriously hostile process to the conclusion of their cases.

Through their eyes, I have seen this country afresh: its ugly, hate-filled side and its kind, compassionate side too. I have been perplexed, angered and frustrated, found my security compromised, faced legal threats and, at times, felt that this is a society of which I no longer want to be a part.

That is nothing compared to those who have fled for their lives and the lives of those they love, who want nothing more than to find safety and peace and who, despite everything, still hold this country in such high regard. What must it be like to walk in their shoes, to be pushed to the margins, unable to access services, harassed, attacked and constantly looking over your shoulder? This book strives to find out.

Much has been written about the journeys people make along the now well-trodden migration route through Europe, but little is known about what happens when they reach the UK. For the first time, we will travel to the frontline of the asylum system, from the coastguard's control room to the town halls and on to the hotels, the detention centres and the courtrooms where futures unfold, diving deep to understand how the system currently works and what needs to change.

We will see the ways in which the asylum system intersects with other parts of the state – healthcare, education, the labour market, housing, social care – by spending time inhabiting the worlds of an overseas care worker, a GP, a delivery rider and many more. Governments have consistently tried to isolate asylum seekers from other sections of society, but, as we will see, it is not possible to push newcomers to the fringes.

I have structured this book around what could be a linear process – crossing, arrival, dispersal, integration and, for some, departure – but which so often isn't. In part, this is a way to show how the system is meant to operate and where it falls short. At every stage, there are problems left unresolved, lives ruined through chronic underfunding, shoddy mismanagement and sheer incompetence.

The title of this book, *Anywhere But Here*, refers to graffiti I saw scrawled on a wall running parallel to a makeshift camp in Dunkirk, written by a recent inhabitant, but it could be the message delivered by migrant spotters on a cliff in Dover, or the coastguard coordinating rescue missions. It may be the staff working at asylum hotels, getting away with abuse, harassment and humiliation of those they are paid to support. Perhaps it could refer to the Home Office subcontractors turning over tens, even hundreds of millions of pounds a year. It may, of course, be the far-right actors, but it could also be those who simply don't want outsiders in their villages, towns or cities. Most likely it's the Home Office and other central government departments who, through their policies and their rhetoric, are relaying the message that migrants are unwanted, unwelcome. 'Go, anywhere but here.'

People move; people have always moved. Migration is part of the human condition. Throughout the centuries, the UK has experienced waves of immigration; communities which have shaped our national identity and which are now integral to the fabric of our society. Those on small boats are simply the latest iteration of that. How we respond to and absorb those in need is what matters.

We live in a divided society, but there is much that we share in spite of our political views. My hope is that the accounts in this book will appeal to a common humanity and empathy, to see beyond fear, anger and confusion to understanding and acceptance. Quite simply, if faced with conflict, persecution, torture and other forms of extreme violence, what would you do?

In the years to come, many will regard this as a pivotal moment in the history of our nation. By documenting the experiences of those who arrive on our shores from the earliest hours to their final moments, I hope to provide an insight into how our society treats those it has a duty to protect and the ways in which our government, and our institutions, fail them.

PART ONE

CROSSING

1. White Cliffs

'When you leave your home for unknown shores, you don't simply carry on as before; a part of you dies inside so that another part can start all over again.'

Elif Shafak, *The Island of Missing Trees*[1]

A siren sounds, followed by a flash of torchlight. Less than 200 metres away, gruff voices call to each other, beating through undergrowth as they edge closer to the group. Arian can't hear what they're saying because a young boy huddled next to him – he guesses two, maybe three years old – is crying, taking in little gulps of air, while his mother hushes him and whispers prayers, hands open to the sky.

A stern, stout man thrusts a shovel into Arian's hands and tells him, in Kurdish, to dig. Earlier that night, the man, known as Pasha, along with four other smugglers, had buried the inflated dinghy here behind the sandbank. Now it is up to Arian and other young people in the group to uncover it and get it down to the shoreline, fast.

With the voices getting louder, the passengers begin to panic, grabbing fistfuls of sand and throwing it behind them. Gusts of wind carry it back and into their eyes. The smuggler's phone light is flashing around so much, Arian is afraid the police will find them. Then, finally, the boat comes free.

Several of the men in the group go first, launching themselves over the sandbank, then passing the dinghy overhead before resting it on their shoulders, five on either side. The men run into the sea until their chests are covered, with the remaining members following quickly behind them, four carrying fuel tanks.

As Arian reaches the water, he realises the engine has been left behind amid the panic. He takes a breath, sprints back up the beach and over the bank and grabs it between his arms in a bear hug. He concentrates on calming his breath in case the police patrol officers are near, but the outboard motor is heavy – fifty, maybe fifty-five kilos – and he staggers under the weight of it back down to the shore.

One of the smugglers uses a torch on his mobile to attach the engine to the back of the boat, pulling two metal bars down to secure it, then connecting a tube to the tank and making quick pumps on the bellow to get the fuel going. Wooden boards are placed in the bottom of the boat and hand pumps thrown inside. Phones are removed from pockets, wrapped in plastic bags and switched off. Arian is instructed to leave his on; he will navigate.

Another of the smugglers lifts the women and children on board, then sprints back up the beach and out of sight. Two others are in the water, pushing the boat out and forcing the starter cord into one of the passenger's hands. The man resists; he's never piloted a boat before and he can't swim, but somebody has to steer and nobody else is willing. Before he can change his mind, Pasha leans over and pulls the shaft forward. With one sharp yank on the cord, the boat sets off.

It's 10 p.m. when the group of forty-five leave the beach in northern France. The conditions aren't as bad as Arian imagined – windy and cold, temperatures hovering just above freezing, but then he expected that, this being late January. He looks out towards the dark night, the moon guiding them, and wonders at how vast the sea looks from this perspective. Ahead, lights twinkle, blurry in the mizzle. 'Not far,' he thinks.

A twenty-mile stretch of sea is all that stands between the group and their final destination: the United Kingdom. Each of them has travelled many thousands of miles – 4,000, 5,000 for most – from Iraq, Iran, Sudan, Eritrea and further, from Afghanistan and India. It is, they hope, the last time they will have to make a journey like this. The last hurdle.

Arian thinks about the obstacles he's encountered to get to this point. He regularly experiences flashbacks – intrusive, uncomfortable images of beatings, robberies and worse. 'When you lose your life many times, you become not so afraid,' he later tells me.

Within an hour, there's no phone signal and no GPS. The app Arian is using to direct the pilot fails to open and the compass on his iPhone is stuck. The offline map isn't working either. He begins to lose the feeling in his right leg, which, like the other men perched on the side of the dinghy, is in the water for balance.

Choppy waves mean the boat begins to take on water. Wind cuts through soaked clothes like a knife and quickly pushes the vessel off-course. One man tries to scoop water out using his remaining shoe; he lost the other running towards the sea. Another puts his daughter on the side rim of the boat, to keep her away from the cold water. The group shout to him in a mixture of languages.

Arian notices that the little boy he spoke to earlier is now sitting in the middle of the boat in his mother's lap, staring wide-eyed into the distance. People around them are praying loudly and crying primal cries. The engine begins to sputter, straining under the weight of the passengers, before cutting out.

The group remain like this, adrift, for thirteen hours. When they can get a signal, they make frequent distress calls to both the French and the British coastguard, but nobody comes to their rescue. While many are paralysed with fear, unable to speak, Arian resigns himself to his fate. 'I looked out at the ocean and thought "Maybe it is my time."'

Then, at just after 11 a.m. the following day, he hears the sound of a helicopter overhead. A motorised boat pulls up alongside them with a dozen people on board. Arian notices that some are wearing military fatigues and he feels fear ripple through him. Another flashback.

Women and children are pulled up first, dead-weight and slipping. Arian feels a hand under his armpit and another pressing into his navel. He can't stand without his legs collapsing beneath him – maybe it's the cold, maybe exhaustion. His thoughts are confused, but he registers a certain numbness. He should feel elated, relieved to be alive, shouldn't he? Instead, he feels nothing.

It took countless attempts for Arian to set foot on UK shores. In one week alone, he tried nine times to cross the Channel. On a December night, with the temperatures hovering just above freezing, he made three futile attempts. Each time came to the same, crushing conclusion: a police squad discovered the dinghy and stabbed through it, before chasing passengers back up over the sandbank. Soaked through and shaking uncontrollably, Arian huddled in bus shelters or on windswept beaches rather than risk missing an opportunity during the hour-long walk back to the camp.

It was becoming more difficult to cross now that the French authorities were patrolling the beaches. In March 2023, Conservative Prime Minister Rishi Sunak signed off a £500 million package to increase the number of police officers stationed on beaches along the coast of northern France.[2] It was the sixth deal of its kind in under four years. The new measures included sniffer-dog detection teams, night-vision equipment, drones, helicopters, CCTV and border guards with the power to arrest.

A month later, at a camp near Grande-Synthe in Dunkirk, aid workers described to me events that had taken place the night before: a mother had been separated from her two children. They hadn't been able to run from the beach police fast enough. Charity workers spent the next twenty-four hours frantically calling the local authority, hospitals and speaking to eyewitnesses, eventually managing to get her released from police custody and reunited with her children.

Later that evening I drove to a beach nearby, where Arian and many other contacts in the camps told me they had attempted the crossing. The path took me over a dusty train track past nuclear reactors at the neighbouring Gravelines power plant, puffs of smoke bellowing out into the adjacent camps. On the Opal Coast beyond lay a sweeping bay, almost desert-like with its soft, rippling dunes.

Empty as it was, I parked on the beachfront and took a bracing walk towards the shoreline. Oystercatchers and grebes flitted around, gulls soaring and squawking, angry to be interrupted. Fishermen had stationed themselves towards the east of the bay, baiting for cod and whiting, a cold-water paradise. And there, swilling around in a pool of water in the distance, was a strange black object, incongruous with the powder-white sand: a deflated dinghy, its rubber curled up and foaming with a fresh mixture of saltwater and sand. Half-buried close by was a trainer with the sole pulled away.

I paused a while, walking around the boat and contemplating the terror of those who had been in my place hours before, trying to imagine what they must have been thinking as they looked out to the horizon. I shuddered, fearing for the people I had met in the camps who would try again that night.

Before heading off, I posted a tweet with a fairly stark message about the deflated dinghy and how UK funding is being used by the French authorities to control the border. I was flummoxed by the response. 'Bravo the French! Stop the illegals!' one anonymised account cheered. 'Good use of taxpayer's money!' another announced with glee, garnering over a thousand likes. Further down in the replies, I noticed a popular post that made me stop cold. It read: 'Let them drown!'

Returning to the camp after a failed attempt to cross only exacerbates the distress. Many find that their tents have been slashed through, with the poles broken and any remaining belongings removed. These evictions, which take place every twenty-four to forty-eight hours in Calais and slightly less frequently – usually twice to three times a week – in Dunkirk, are designed to deter migrants from settling there. Arrests take place in the camps, too, with the CRS (Compagnies républicaines de sécurité) – the French riot police who carry out the evictions – routinely using brute force and detaining people on no-fixed-abode charges.

While most of those in the camps have experienced violence on borders along the well-trodden migration route through Europe, the humiliation, harassment and excessive use of force associated with these evictions baffles them. 'You are journalist. When they destroy our tents, where do they want that we go?' an Eritrean man slurping his sugary black coffee asked me one gusty afternoon. In truth, I didn't offer him a particularly helpful response. The honest answer is that the authorities simply don't care where they go.

The conditions in the camps are dire. There's no shelter, no mains supply for drinking water, no food, no sanitation. They can't be said to be refugee camps. With no UN presence – no UNHCR, no World Food Programme, no International Organization for Migration – underfunded grassroots organisations fill the vacuum, arriving daily, sometimes twice-daily, to deliver replacement tents, hot meals and bottles of water. When the aid vans arrive, groups run after them, calling out for them to stop and huddling close before supplies run out. Charity workers shout to form a line.

Roadblocks are used as benches and upturned shopping trolleys as chairs. Towards the entrance, groups of Kurds and Albanians have converted their tents into shops, selling fizzy drinks and trading cigarettes for croissants wrapped in plastic. Crows roam around, picking up crumbs.

Behind a barbed-wire fence, there's a water tank on a mound where people wash their faces and refill bottles. Children sprint up and down the hill, some venturing behind shrubbery to a ditch beyond, used as toilet facilities. Their parents run after them, hauling them back and reprimanding them: it's not safe down there, they warn.

SIM cards with ten minutes of free international calls are handed over from the back of the aid vehicles, names scrawled and ticked off. Some take the cards and run to the back of the line to get another one, hoping in the mêlée they won't be noticed. Teenagers linger, trying to assert themselves. A fourteen-year-old Afghan boy travelling alone approaches me to ask if he can use my phone to call his mother. He promised he would contact her every day and it's been three days; she will be worried.

Affable aid workers stroll around, clasping hands and practising salutations in Arabic, Albanian, French. One young man from Liverpool has taught himself Kurdish, impressing groups queuing at the vans; he came to Dunkirk for two weeks and has stayed for six years. Others man the portable shower facilities, chatting over a cigarette. There's camaraderie, genuine friendships and a spirit of openness. I find myself forming easy connections, humbled.

At an activity table for children towards the entrance of the camp, I meet Parwen and her seven-year-old daughter, Shewa, who immediately begins painting my face with hot-pink lipstick and matching eyeshadow. Parwen talks openly about their encounters with the French authorities; a recent memorable attempt to cross had ended with a tear-gas canister landing next to her four-year-old son, Hozan. They had staggered away in the fog, her little boy bawling hysterically in her arms, terrified he had been blinded. When they got back to the camp, their tent was gone. I asked where they had slept. 'Here, on this land,' she says, showing me a picture of her two children standing on barren wasteland, ripped plastic bags attached to the shrubbery behind them. They had endured the harsh winter there and now they were beginning to lose hope.

It's not just tents that get destroyed. Calais-based charity Human Rights Observers showed me video evidence of locals and members of the authorities stabbing through water tanks to deter migrants from settling there, leaving children as young as two without drinking water.[3] One aid worker told me this happens so often that they now tend to carry around five-litre jerrycans of water and fill up bottles individually. Phones – those vital lifelines – are confiscated by the CRS without reason and, with them, the numbers of both their loved ones and their smugglers.

After each eviction, a coach – usually one, but sometimes more – waits on the dirt track beside the camp to take people to Lille, where they can claim asylum in France. Many do attempt to do this: France typically receives more than double the number of asylum applications compared to the UK. (In 2023, 167,432 persons registered to apply for international protection in France, while the UK received 67,337 applications in the same year.[4]) Others choose to make the crossing perhaps due to family ties, or because they served alongside the British military, or gained language skills and an understanding of the culture as a result of our colonial roots in their home country. For those who have tried and failed to secure leave to remain in France or other European countries on the migrant route, the journey continues. Many remain under the control of the smugglers, beginning the perilous return to Calais, Dunkirk and the surrounding areas and attempting, once again, to cross the Channel.

Three weeks after I left the camps, contacts sent me videos and images of a complete clearance.[5] The CRS had entered the site carrying plastic shields and brandishing wooden batons. Bulldozers ripped through the land, hauling up tents, industrial washbasins and shopping trolleys. Saws and hammers razed anything that remained.

Walking single-file along a tarmac road running parallel to the camp, more than 300 people searched for a new place to rest their heads and wait for a chance to cross. Many formed new temporary settlements within 100 metres of the site, while others were pushed out into the forest.

Aware that people scatter in the immediate aftermath of an eviction but return to the wooded areas near the waterfront shortly afterwards, the CRS had recently started hacking down some of the trees to prevent migrants seeking shelter from the driving rain and biting winds. Late one night Parwen shared their location on WhatsApp and sent images of a fire built from scraps of wood, Hozan and Shewa huddled around it, wrapped in blankets. Underneath, she added a crying-face emoji.

Meanwhile, the French state provides nothing, other than funding for the CRS and coaches to bring migrants southwards. Without reaching the UK to claim asylum and with no pending claim in France, they are not officially asylum seekers. They're also not refugees in legal terms, because they haven't been granted refugee status in another country or had their claims assessed and confirmed by the UN. They are considered migrants and therefore not eligible for even the most basic provision.

As I drove away from the camps to begin my safe passage to the UK – a journey everybody there is so desperate to make – I saw the graffiti that stopped me quite literally in my tracks. It read: 'Anywhere But Here'.

*

All this – the conditions in the camps, the evictions, the numerous futile attempts – made Arian even more determined to reach the UK. It wasn't difficult to locate his smuggler in this chain of the network. Like Arian, the facilitators were predominantly Kurdish, from Iran as he was, or Iraq. 'All around the camp, they are Kurdish mafia.'

Arian considered himself a mountain goat, more comfortable with the air at altitude than at sea level. Born in the Zagros Mountains in the west of Iran, his earliest memories are of family walks at weekends, learning to climb sheer rock faces and the perfect, still silence when he reached the top. Tracks were lined with *rivas*, or wild rhubarb, pomegranate and pistachio trees, which his mother would pick, carrying bagfuls back to make a stew with slow-cooked lamb that melted in his mouth. There were grottoes and springs gushing into reflective pools. Stories of brown bears making their way down from nearby mountain villages frequently circulated around his school, giving him nightmares. The call to prayer vibrated among the hilltops, punctuating each day with its soothing sounds. In many ways, his was a typical Iranian Kurdish family: faithful, devout members of Shia Islam and pillars of their local community.

But things were starting to change for Arian. He began watching movies, listening to music and talking to friends about the West, these 'modern, Christian' nations, keen to 'learn and change and improve'. He desired that for himself and decided, after a brief period of atheism, that it was 'better to have a belief than no belief'. He read the Bible and found its verses resonated. The first time he read 'seek and you shall find', a shiver ran up his spine. Arian felt he needed to begin a life beyond his tiny village.

A vast mountainous region stretching from south-eastern Turkey, to Iraq, northern Syria and on to north-western Iran, Kurdistan and its people have suffered decades of deep-rooted discrimination, denied their social, political, economic and cultural rights. Parents are not allowed to register their children with Kurdish names and use of the language in institutions, including schools, can result in prosecution.[6] Civil society activists are frequently imprisoned, tortured and denied a fair trial. Some Iranian Kurds have faced the death penalty for expressing their beliefs.[7]

Following the 1979 Revolution in Iran, Ayatollah Khamenei declared jihad against the Kurdish people calling for autonomy. Ever since, there has been what the Kurdistan Peace and Development Society calls a 'systematic genocidal campaign', with tens of thousands killed in a sustained military operation.[8] Kurds continue to call for representation and protection of their human rights and the creation of a recognised federal state.

On 16 September 2022 widespread protests broke out following the death of Mahsa Amini, a twenty-two-year-old Kurdish woman, arrested by the religious morality police for the way she wore her hijab. While the authorities said Mahsa died of a heart attack, eyewitnesses, including women who were held in police custody at the same time, reported that she had been severely beaten and later died in hospital as a result of her injuries.

Starting in her Kurdish homeland of Sanandaj in the north-west of Iran, Mahsa's death sparked the largest protests the country had seen for more than a decade. Hundreds of thousands took to the streets, with defiant demonstrators removing and burning their hijabs in street bonfires and cutting their hair in protest.

Their actions were brutally repressed. Within the first six months, over 500 people were killed and more than 20,000 arrested. Human Rights Watch reported live ammunition fired into crowds and protesters beaten with batons.[9] In Kurdistan, the regime unleashed alarming violence, with agents wielding Kalashnikov assault rifles firing live rounds, pellets and tear gas, sometimes directly into homes.

Seeing the protests, Arian felt acutely aware of his security. He was, he felt, an easy target: with his sleek, jet-black hair tied back in a ponytail, caramel skin and almond eyes, people often told him he looked more like a Mayan than a Kurd, 'a person from the pyramid temples'.

His younger brother had recently married, and while he, too, had been engaged, it was an arranged marriage, not the romance of which he had always dreamed. Constrained and claustrophobic, the relationship had ended and Arian had piled himself into his studies in aerospace engineering, specialising in rocket propulsion and aerodynamics, his ambition to work with helicopters, aeroplanes, 'anything that moves in the air'. He had always been bright and driven, particularly studious when it came to maths and physics. Now he saw his talents as a way out.

The day the protests came to his doorstep, he felt a tug towards them. This was the way to bring about change, to really fight for what you believe in. Compelled to see for himself, he dressed in black and ventured outside, standing at the side of the road and watching as thousands of people marched past with banners proclaiming 'Women, Life, Freedom'.

He was, as he feared, a visible target. Within minutes, thirty armed police arrived on motorbikes, shooting rubber pellets at him. A dozen thugs grabbed him by the hair and wrestled him to the ground, beating, kicking, thrashing him until he could hardly breathe. He was left, curled up, foetal-like, on the pavement and slipping in and out of consciousness. 'I could not open my eyes, or hear. My body was all black and blue and my face was covered with blood.' Arian knew he needed to get out of Iran.

He spoke to a friend who had also been caught up in the protests. It was easy for them to find a smuggler: it was big business, with so many people sharing their experiences of repression, violence and the dream of a better life. They agreed they didn't need to decide where they would go; they would simply travel over the border and keep moving until they could settle.

With help from his father and brother, Arian gathered together $10,000 cash and brought it to his friend's smuggler, someone he felt he could trust: $5,000 to set up the journey, then another $5,000 to cross over to Greece and travel onwards. Their safety, they were told, was guaranteed. Within days he had said goodbye, knowing he might never see his family again, but certain he couldn't stay.

Crossing the Turkish border by truck and arriving in the city of Van in the east of the country, Arian and his friend were passed on to another smuggler. Hours were spent waiting to connect with the next link in the chain, for money to be released, names crossed off lists and messages sent to facilitators further down the network.

From there to Greece over the river crossing of Edirne, then by boat and truck across Italy and on to France, the smugglers made the journey smooth. It was a well-oiled machine, with a broker, or 'travel agent', in Iran releasing money to smugglers each time he crossed a border. Whenever he arrived, a smuggler held up a phone to Arian's ear to say his name, confirm he was there and that the money could be released. Sometimes an address would then be handed over or he, along with other members of the group, would be taken to a sparse, damp flat with sheetless mattresses on the floor to get a few hours' sleep before the journey continued. More often there was nowhere to stay, nowhere to rest.

Separated from his friend, Arian sometimes travelled with new acquaintances he made along the way, but often he walked alone, slipping under barbed-wire fencing, navigating packs of dogs and sleeping under bridges with only his sodden coat to cover him. Once, when he fell asleep on a night bus, a woman left a half-eaten bar of chocolate on the seat next to him. It was the first time he had eaten in days.

By the time he reached northern France, Arian was so physically, mentally and emotionally exhausted that he considered trying to stay there. He asked around the camps about claiming asylum in France, but the only people who had information, he realised, were the smugglers. He hadn't planned to go to the UK, but once he was in the camps, everybody said the same thing: 'England, it's better.'

It made sense. Arian speaks English, he has committed song lyrics by The Beatles to memory, he follows the Premier League football teams. The island beyond was the final destination. 'After England, there is nowhere. You just try to finish the path.' The camps were inhospitable, the system complex. France would never feel like home. He needed to keep moving.

Smugglers circulate freely and visibly in the camps of northern France, so it didn't take long to find the man he needed to help him cross the Channel. Pasha, or the 'big boss' as Arian called him, was one of the more notorious smugglers: quick to reply to messages, organised and motivated. After several failed attempts in the preceding days, Pasha was determined to get his passengers moving.

Late the next evening, there was a ping on Arian's phone. The message told him to make his way to a supermarket on the edge of Dunkirk, where he would be given the next set of instructions.

He did as he was told, nervously approaching a man speaking Kurdish in an aisle of the minimart. Tonight they would try again. Arian just needed to go to the bus depot close by and wait until Pasha's passengers were called.

As night fell, the depot became a hive of activity, with over a hundred people gathering round. Arian spoke to a small group of Kurdish men busily checking their phones for any updates and discussing the weather conditions. They showed him an app called Windy, which detected the wind speeds, the wave heights and the temperatures in the water. 'Anything over a half-metre wave is too much. Below ten knots [wind speed] is OK, no problem for the boat. Over twenty knots, you die.'

Three hours later, his moment arrived. 'Passengers of Pasha, come!' someone called, and Arian stepped forward, a plastic bag and tattered woolly hat in his hands. The group of passengers were separated into smaller units, told where to go, their turns staggered.

The small groups stayed close to their smuggler, told to walk in silence, no smoking, no light – nothing that would draw attention to them. Arian felt all ajumble: fearful, confused, hungry, cold and under immense stress. As he made his way along the muddy path, stumbling through woodland and over craggy peaks, he wondered if this attempt would fail like so many of the others or if today, finally, he was fated to succeed.

In spite of all he had endured, seeing the white cliffs from the Border Force boat was, Arian later told me, 'like new air, like I could breathe again'.

2. SOS

The sea is calm to-night,
The tide is full, the moon lies fair
Upon the straits;—on the French coast, the light
Gleams, and is gone; the cliffs of England stand,
Glimmering and vast, out in the tranquil bay.
Come to the window, sweet is the night-air!
Only, from the long line of spray
Where the sea meets the moon-blanched land,
Listen! you hear the grating roar
Of pebbles which the waves draw back, and fling,
At their return, up the high strand,
Begin, and cease, and then again begin,
With tremulous cadence slow, and bring
The eternal note of sadness in.

Matthew Arnold, 'Dover Beach', 1851

Though Arian didn't know it, a group of eagle-eyed onlookers were watching him arrive from the clifftops above the port. Among them was Bob Satchett, a gruff, rotund man in his late sixties with a pair of binoculars pressed to his face. Fishing trawlers, cruise liners, passenger ferries and container ships dotted the horizon, a string of tiny, twinkling lanterns in the Dover Strait beyond. Squinting through the mist, Bob could just make out a rescue boat chugging towards the quay below.

'Busier today,' he murmured to the four acquaintances seated beside him on fold-up camping chairs. Nobody spoke, only nodded slowly in agreement. Three identical pit bull terriers roamed around the overflowing bins nearby, cigarette butts buried beneath the frost.

The car park at Western Heights was quieter now that winter had set in and the volume of arrivals had slowed, but this group were the committed, the hardcore, armed with cans of Coke and filming equipment, settling in for a day of what they called 'migrant spotting'.

After he retired five years ago, Bob used to come up here every day to walk his dog, to 'get some peace and quiet'. He had lived in Dover all his life, went to school here, got married, had three kids. Decades of driving HGV lorries across borders, sitting in tedious queues at ports, too much time spent away from home, had taken its toll. His wife had left him and taken the children with her. He never really saw them now they had families of their own. This place, up on the westerly ridge, had become a sanctuary for him, a place he came to meet with friends, often going on for a pint or two at the local pub together once it opened.

On a clear day, Bob could see all the way to France from this vantage point, the soft silhouette undulating in the distance. Turning west, the turrets of Dover Castle rose skywards, its fortified walls still perfectly intact. Walking down the chalk path, he could go right up to the deep, sunken ditches, abandoned gun emplacements and former barracks.

The land here was steeped in history, both national and personal. It gave Bob a distinct sense of pride. Sometimes he would wander among the ivy-covered blast shelters and pillboxes, inspect the crumbling remnants of the gun battery, imagining what terror his grandfather and his great-grandfather must have endured. During the Napoleonic Wars, stretching all the way through the First and the Second World Wars, this had been the defensive frontline, designed to protect Britain from foreign invasion.

Now, though, the threats were out of his hands. He felt exposed, unsure who the newcomers were or why they were here. It was impossible to ignore it when it was down there, 'staring you in the face'. No matter what the government did, the dinghies just kept coming.

Being among a group of like-minded people made Bob feel that bit safer. Sometimes Nigel Farage came up to Western Heights to record his pieces-to-camera. The leader of Reform UK – and, many would say, a major catalyst for Brexit – had made some of his most infamous comments on the clifftops here. What we were witnessing was, Farage told his captive audience, an 'invasion' not unlike other pivotal moments of our history.[1]

Bob was well acquainted with Farage – he was 'not a mate, but someone you see around, every now and again'. Like 'Nige', watching the new arrivals coming in and being given the 'royal treatment' incensed him. Billions of pounds of imports and exports were going in and out of Dover, but locals weren't reaping any of the rewards. If anything, they had become more marginalised. 'You've got to look after your own first' was a constant, tic-like refrain.

Once, not that long before – a couple of decades maybe – Dover had been a thriving industrial town, with many taking jobs at Buckland paper mill a few miles inland.[2] Some of Bob's friends had worked as wardens at the borstal at Western Heights, but then that closed down in 2015, and with it went the jobs. Nothing had come along to replace them, other than the odd bit of work for shipping companies and selling fishing tackle. Rates of debt, homelessness, domestic violence and child poverty had spiked.[3]

Working people needed someone who understood them, who knew the area and could speak up for them. Not only that: they needed someone who could stand shoulder-to-shoulder with strong leaders like Donald Trump and not be cowered. Bob admired that, while Nige had power and clout, he'd kept his feet on the ground.

There were always reporters around Western Heights now, cameramen hauling tripods round the corner. Journalists made him suspicious; you never knew who you could trust nowadays. Bob didn't need to watch the news or read the papers. He could see what was happening with his own eyes. What he couldn't get his head around was why the government didn't just do what they'd promised and stop those bloody boats.

Pushing them back in the Dover Strait wasn't a bad idea, Bob felt, but 'they definitely shouldn't be pulling them in'. Sometimes the migrants were making beach landings then 'scuttling off'. They weren't even being apprehended.

The vast majority of new arrivals – the ones he saw – were being taxied in by the Border Force and the Royal National Lifeboat Institution, the RNLI. He couldn't understand why those agencies did it, why they were doing 'such a disservice to patriots'. Neither of those were the real traitors, though. That charge lay with the agency Bob believed was not only helping migrants but encouraging them to make the crossing: 'them up there in their ivory towers, the coastguard'.

In the watchtower located to the west of Dover harbour's inner walls, phones were ringing insistently. Radios spurted, crackled and gurgled to life. Heavy-duty boots clanged up and down the metal steps overhead.

'Another one coming in,' Tony announced, setting down his cup of tea, zipping up his royal-blue overalls and striding down the gangway towards the Border Force boat below. There was never a dull moment in this job. It was just after twelve, but already it had been designated a 'red day', with tides and weather increasing the chance of boat crossings. The red cross on the whiteboard inside the lookout tower served as a warning to Tony and his crew: they had better be prepared.

Outside, the quay was flooded with long-lens cameras, photographers jostling for position. Teenagers with buzz cuts, drafted in from the Navy to support the coastguard with logistics, wandered around looking confused. Towards the top of the gangway, chain-smoking coach drivers waited to shuttle new arrivals between the car park and the compound a couple of hundred metres away, where the process of claiming asylum would begin.

As the cutter docked, a stream of stumbling bodies made their way up the metal walkway, sodden slate-grey blankets wrapped round their shoulders, grasping the rail to steady their trembling legs. Clambering aboard the buses, they collapsed down into worn seats, sitting staring out of the window, watching as the dinghy they had crossed in was spray-painted with a number and punctured.

It was unusual for Tony to be on the quay that day. He spent most of his time up in the control room at Langdon Battery overlooking the port. It was calmer up there, easier for the coastguard to see what was going on, to manage traffic in the Dover Strait. It was no mean feat: the Channel was the busiest shipping lane in the world. Attempting the crossing by small boat was regularly likened to crossing the M25 at rush hour on foot.

He and his colleagues enjoyed the camaraderie up there. They would joke that the Battery looked like a spaceship, its roof covered by thick vegetation, its windows like a cockpit looking out on to the eastern arm of Dover harbour.

Sometimes they got calls from Beachy Head, urgent warnings of a different kind of crisis. They occasionally saw Channel swimmers, too, embarking on a voyage across soupy, silty water. Tony didn't understand it: people were risking their lives to reach these shores, dying in dark waters. To him, crossing the Strait wasn't about leisure, it was about survival.

The work had changed since the boats started coming in. During a particularly busy shift, Tony and his team might receive thirty distress calls from the same dinghy. There might be forty small boats in British waters at once, or more, each with seventy, eighty, even a hundred people on board. It was difficult to keep tabs on them all.

Tony was a seafarer, a mariner, who couldn't picture himself doing any other work. If you cut him open, there'd be 'saltwater in these veins'. He'd grown up that way. At weekends, he'd go out fishing with his dad on the Jurassic coast, tying the bait, learning to cast the net, then taking the trawl home to cook up for dinner. He hadn't enjoyed school particularly, 'too much sitting around'. As soon as he could, he started work, following in his dad's footsteps, like salmon up a stream.

A decade in, despite many attempts to make a decent living, Tony saw the 'writing was on the wall' for the fishing industry. Shortly after the birth of his first child, he moved his family up the coastline. It was a leap of faith; he didn't know if he'd be able to earn enough to support them.

It hadn't always been smooth, but over the years he'd worked his way up through the coastguarding ranks, feeling challenged, motivated, a vital member of the 'blue-light family'. His leadership style was outspoken, even slightly bombastic, but he had the allure of charisma, which kept his colleagues onside. When it was busy he'd tell his team it was 'all hands on deck', and he lived up to it. Tony was always the last to leave at the end of a shift.

Now, though, instead of answering 999 calls from locals and tourists, his job had become 'massively political'. Hours were spent preparing for a high-profile visit from the prime minister, the home secretary, whoever it might be. He would have to give them the grand tour of the Battery, show them the tracking systems and how the new surveillance technology worked. There was a lot of hand-shaking, head-bobbing, smiling. Often cameras snapped distractingly.

What he couldn't tell those politicians was just how overstretched the coastguard was, how under-resourced. He had been working twenty-hour shifts, often with no breaks. A few hours' sleep, then back to it. The pace was relentless. They were finding it difficult to recruit people. Salaries were poor, the nature of the work physically and emotionally taxing.

He had struggled at times himself. Once, he had carried an unconscious toddler from a dinghy, her limbs floppy and her mother inconsolable. Running towards the medical facility, he hadn't known what to say, how to even communicate. An interpreter couldn't be found. He didn't even know if the child was breathing. The young girl was severely hypothermic, but she survived. Those aren't the kind of images you can forget; flashbacks still came to him frequently.

The previous summer had been a particular low point. With nowhere to put new arrivals, tents had been erected on the quayside. Hundreds of traumatised people were forced to sleep on buses in the car park.[4] For days, Tony and his team had worked round the clock, trying to get clothes, blankets and bottles of water to the bewildered newcomers. At that time, the area was open to the public and visible from Western Heights overlooking the jetty. They had faced torrents of abuse from members of the public while they carried out their work.

As the volume of new arrivals increased, so did the scrutiny. Tony had been pictured helping an elderly man as he limped up the gangway, bent double, badly injured. He had been lambasted by the right, but you couldn't win on the left either. They were never seen to be doing enough. It often felt like a no-win situation.

Sometimes the pressure made his team fractious, snapping at each other. Support was on offer, but it was more rounds of tea and a biscuit than talking about what was on your mind. Coastguards didn't tend to be the 'soft and fluffy type' – they just needed to blow off steam and move on.

All he knew was that he and his team had a job to do. No matter how busy they were, they could never 'play roulette with people's lives'. Whenever they received a mayday call they had to act on it, jumping into gear to assess the level of need, the numbers on board, whether there were casualties. They needed to pull together all their resources, to coordinate and put an effective plan in place. While the coastguard didn't have its own rescue vessels, it could call on the Border Force and the RNLI, and they could task a helicopter, but only if they had enough information.

Sometimes a phone call from a dinghy might be just twenty seconds long, or it was inaudible, or the English was so broken it was incomprehensible. At other times, migrants withheld their locations. The smugglers told them they had to; they couldn't risk their details being traced back to the passengers' phones. What was the coastguard team supposed to do then? They had nothing to go on.

Tony had the sense that those making the calls were often speaking from scripts. The boat was sinking. There were women and children on board. No lifejackets, that sort of thing. All emergencies started to sound the same. He didn't want to appear flippant – none of his team came in with the intention of letting people die – but in extremely challenging circumstances, mistakes could happen.

One incident in particular played on his mind. The coastguard was under investigation following a major disaster in the Channel several months before. Investigators had got hold of call logs, where it was all laid out.

On 24 November 2021, a passenger had called the French authorities to alert them that he and thirty-one other people were on board a sinking boat. 'Please, please, we need help,' the caller urged. Screams for mercy could be heard in the background. 'You are in English waters, sir,' the French coastguard responded, before hanging up.[5]

In the Dover coastguard control room, two members of staff, including one who was still a trainee, attempted to phone the passenger back, but they received a French dial tone. They left it, concluding, after much back-and-forth with the French coastguard, that the boat was not their responsibility as it was likely still in their waters.[6]

Twelve hours later, at around 2 p.m., a French fisherman spotted bodies in the water. All but two of the passengers had drowned, died of exposure or remained missing. Among the dead were twenty-one men, seven women, including one who was pregnant, and three children. It was the worst maritime disaster in the Channel for over forty years.

In the aftermath of the incident, I was put in contact with dozens of relatives and friends who had lost their loved ones that night. 'Please [can you] help us meet with the UN?,' one man messaged late one evening, desperately seeking answers. Another sent me screengrabs of the last contact he had had with his brother. 'He cannot be gone,' he typed.

At a vigil in Parliament Square to commemorate those who had died, a grief-stricken brother took the microphone.[7] 'I want to find out who was negligent,' he told mourners. 'The British and the French, they do nothing. They failed them and left them to drown. Now we hear nothing.'

Among the most devastating stories I heard was from Mustafa, whose son Zanyar had gone missing that night.[8] A senior commander for the Kurdish Peshmerga, Mustafa left work early to speak to me, explaining that he now had two full-time jobs: one was in the military forces, the other was seeking justice for his son.

I was struck by Mustafa's eyes, or perhaps what was behind them. He appeared hollowed out, his grief raw and all-consuming. At certain points, when he described Zanyar or the powerlessness he and his wife felt when faced with the heft of the UK and French authorities, Mustafa could contain his pain no longer and he broke down and sobbed.

On 24 November 2021, Mustafa had spoken on the phone to his son's smuggler, who confirmed that Zanyar had arrived safely and requested immediate payment for the crossing. Mustafa's wife went out to buy sweets for the village, going door-to-door to tell them her son had arrived in the UK. The journey, which had caused her so many sleepless nights, was finally over. Days later, still unable to reach Zanyar after multiple attempts, they began to worry. When news of the shipwreck reached Mustafa, he said it felt like 'a horror movie, like every parent's worst nightmare'.

As we came towards the end of an emotionally charged four hours, Mustafa appeared reluctant to let me go, still struggling to make sense of it all. Why, he needed to know, had they heard nothing from the UK authorities? Why were they being treated with such utter disdain?

The atmosphere at Langdon Battery hung heavy in the days that followed. Tony and his team were being called in for questioning, pressed about what had gone so badly wrong. It emerged slowly, painfully, the truth eked out over days of interviews.[9]

At least four small boats had crossed that night. Hundreds of distress calls were made. Amid the chaos and confusion, the coastguard had sent a search and rescue vessel to the wrong stricken dinghy. That one decision, followed by a catastrophic panoply of others, had proven to be fatal.[10]

The incident brought the coastguard's culture and attitudes into sharp focus. Previous mayday calls had 'turned out to be falsely exaggerated', multiple coastguards told investigators. Some in the unit had become 'habituated' to these kinds of calls, rationalising that this was just another incident of 'exaggerated distress'.[11]

An independent inquiry was launched and training offered to help staff prepare to give evidence in court defending their actions. The 'Emergencies on Trial' course was aimed at providing assurances under cross-examination, at a cost of £19,200 to the taxpayer.[12] This was the first time the coastguard had been on trial; they didn't usually face this level of interrogation. They'd never even been subject to independent monitoring. No regulatory body existed to scrutinise their activities.

Tony worried about the reputation of his unit. Was it as bad as people thought it was? Compared to the death toll in the central Mediterranean, where more than 30,000 people had lost their lives in the last decade, surely people could see that the coastguard was doing a good job, a successful job of saving lives at sea. Was it perfect? No. But they could never save everybody. There wasn't a single rescue unit in the world that could say that. Overworked and understaffed, the coastguard was on the frontline of the crisis and 'making it work out of goodwill more than anything else'.

A couple of miles down the road, at the foot of the White Cliffs, lorries beeped their horns at a modest group of protesters. The winter sun was just rising over the eastern docks when Michael arrived on the picket line, greeting his Border Force colleagues with handshakes and nods. He had ostensibly come out to call for better pay and conditions, but he welcomed the opportunity to vent about the latest diktat from the 'Westminster bubble'.

When Michael had heard what the Tories' next 'mad' plan was he had put his head in his hands, unsure 'whether to laugh or cry'. It was almost an affront, an insult to his team, who had already done so much for so little.

First, they had been given two jet skis to try to block the dinghies from getting through. Then there was talk of a line of Navy vessels at the twelve-mile mark, the meeting line between British and French waters. Now they were being told they needed to push the boats back,[13] physically force them to turn round in the water, in flagrant breach of international maritime law, a convention to which the UK had been one of the original signatories in 1979.[14] Besides being unlawful, did the geniuses at Marsham Street have any idea how dangerous that was? Their cutters would slash right through the dinghies. People would drown in front of them.

Michael was more pragmatic than that. 'A grafter', his team called him. He'd once been a docker, then he'd moved into customs for the Border Force. A civil service job had brought him security: a steady salary, pension, sick pay. Not that he ever took a sick day. A portly, stocky man in his late fifties, Michael liked to lead from the front, speaking up on behalf of his colleagues, all decent, hard-working people. He was always rushing off to one thing or another. Often, it was to find a quiet spot away from Dover port to do interviews with local radio networks. A voice of reason, Michael considered it crucial that people knew what lay beyond the pledges, the plans, all the 'flashy stuff'.

For years, the government had been piling resources in to stop the boats, pulling in military assets and forking out on new ones. Under one programme – Operation Isotrope, as it was known – tens of millions of pounds had been spent on equipment for the Border Force. A procurement document from the Home Office showed that £18 million was allocated to military-grade drones, £35 million on search dogs,[15] £200 million on upgrading the fleet of cutters, though none of those had surfaced yet. Then there were piloted planes, helicopters, land-based radars, all manner of kit, some of it bought from Israeli defence firms, the most sophisticated technology they could get their hands on.

Rishi Sunak had liked to pay visits to Dover, flying down in his helicopter for a few hours to have photos taken on the Border Force boats, talking to the skipper in his comically oversized boots, thanking them for all their hard work.

Funding to the French was stepped up, the *entente cordiale* alive and well. In March 2023, Sunak travelled to Paris to strike a deal with President Macron. Additional border guards, intelligence operatives and surveillance technologies were promised, on top of the half-a-billion-pound funding, which the French could use as they liked. It was a pot of money that was available to them and the UK had no say over how it was spent.

Alongside a team of reporters from investigative unit Lighthouse Reports, I helped to gather video evidence which showed exactly how UK funding was being spent.[16] In one of the videos, a French police boat, paid for by the British taxpayer, could be seen circling a dinghy, creating waves high enough to flood it. In another, a police vessel full of gendarmes rams into a small boat, threatening passengers with a large tank of pepper spray. Other dinghies were stabbed through at sea, forcing migrants, many of whom couldn't swim, to attempt to make it back to shore.

Michael was outraged when I showed him the videos. He couldn't believe any mariner could condone that. If he was coxing, he couldn't follow those orders. He felt uncomfortable even watching it. Tactics like that could lead to a 'mass-casualty event', riding right over the top of the passengers and knocking them unconscious. With foam-packed lifejackets, which didn't self-right, people could easily drown. While he knew of incidents like these in the Aegean, with armed Greek coastguards frequently using violent manoeuvres to push migrants back, this was the first time Michael had ever seen anything like that happening in the Channel.

Everybody knew how versatile the networks were, constantly shifting strategies to thwart the French authorities. As border surveillance increased, migrants were being forced to start their journeys further round the coastline, making longer and more perilous crossings. They were boarding dinghies in estuaries and canals, wading out into the water, despite being unable to swim. Their bodies were being discovered washed up on banks and beaches after attempting to reach the 'taxi boats' stationed beyond the shoreline.[17] How the border police couldn't see what was going on was beyond Michael.

Instead of throwing taxpayers' money at the French, he thought that the government should be putting resources where they were really needed: on the frontline. The Border Force cutters were 'falling to pieces'. They were heavy, aluminium-lined boats – cumbersome and difficult to steer. They were high in the water, too; not designed for hauling bodies out of the sea.

Rescue missions were 'awful, just awful'. Michael dreaded his pager going off. He had to rush to put on all his thermal gear, going out drysuited-up, with boots, a hat, gloves and even then he felt the cold cutting through him 'like a knife'. He and his colleagues would often spend hours at sea, that bone-chilling snap numbing his jaw, his toes, losing all sensation in his fingers.

It usually took a few people to pull a body out of the water. Most of the migrants were exhausted from trying to stay warm, dead weights to lift up. Grips on hands were weak. He found it hard to get any purchase, clothes just ripped away. The more the person panicked and struggled, the more they slipped back in.

Children were the hardest to deal with. Desperate parents raised them out of the water over their heads, shouting, praying. *Please, please, help*, faces fraught with anguish beseeched them. *If you can save someone, please save them.*

There were often currents and strong winds to contend with, pushing them off-course. Thick fog made it difficult to establish a search pattern. Sometimes, when the rain lashed down, the coastguard chopper flying overhead, the sound of wailing was muted, coming to him later while he slept. Visibility was often limited, too, the waves difficult to see over. With phosphorus flames lighting up the search vicinity, he could catch only frozen moments, glimpses of a fixed grimace. Nothing could prepare you for it. 'You just do what you can, try to make the right decisions.'

Michael had given up time with his family during weekends and school holidays to do this work. When he was around, he was drained from night call-outs, guilty that he wasn't as present as he would have liked. With all he had given up, he resented the ways in which frontline rescuers had become so politicised.

Volunteers from the RNLI bore the brunt of it and they weren't even being paid. One of Michael's friends, a power station maintenance worker by day, had recently started helping out with the Dungeness boat crew. He'd even moved house to be within the required three-mile radius of the lifeboat station, jumping out of bed and getting himself out of the door within seven minutes of his pager going off. Soon after starting, a group of far-right 'vigilantes' had spray-painted 'Taxi' over the lifeboat station doors, parroting Nigel Farage's claims that the volunteer crews were a 'taxi service for illegal migrants'. Volunteer crew members had started taking RNLI parking permits off their cars after their tyres were repeatedly slashed. Most of them had been pilloried at the school gates and at their local pubs.

One search-and-rescue worker I spoke to over many years left his job after he was beaten unconscious and hospitalised, recognised for TV interviews he had done. Most frontline workers now understandably chose not to speak out for fear of reprisal.

The Border Force had been brought in to do customs work – detecting drugs, searching lorries, swiping passports – not hauling bodies out of the water. They didn't have a mandate to be doing any of it.

None of this was a coincidence, Michael believed. You could draw a direct line between rhetoric and repercussion. Failing to resource the frontline services was a clear political choice: the government had the budget, they just hadn't bothered to invest in chartering seaworthy vessels that could actually help to save lives. What was needed were RNLI lifeboats, with a paid, full-time crew and launch times of two minutes, not twenty. Or they could have an emergency response vessel on permanent standby in the Channel, like the offshore oil and gas industry did in the North Sea. There were numerous possibilities, but the politics always seemed to come first.

Now Labour had come in, promising a new Border Force Command to break up the smuggling gangs, as if that hadn't been tried before. It all just sounded like a rebranding exercise, similar to the Tories' 'Small Boats Operational Command', but with slightly increased powers.[18] Nothing was going to change. Lives were still being lost in the Channel.

'They've done nothing except slap a slogan on it,' Michael told me shortly after the government had changed hands in July 2024. 'It's all smoke and mirrors with them in their gilded cages in Marsham Street while we're here, actually carrying out these rescues. We shouldn't be used as a political tool – we're civil servants doing operational work. It shouldn't feel political, or be political, but it is.'

3. Fortress Britain

'The way a government treats refugees is very instructive because it shows you how they would treat the rest of us if they thought they could get away with it.'

Former Labour MP Tony Benn

Far from the industrial smog of Dover port, tucked between the regal Gothic spires of Westminster Abbey and the Romanesque columns of the Tate Britain art gallery, sits 2 Marsham Street. Once a laundry yard and latterly housing a coke and gas company supplying coal for steamships, the building had been demolished and rebuilt in the 1970s, adjoining its three concrete towers known as the 'three ugly sisters'. It was at once considered a masterpiece of modernist architecture and a blot on London's landscape.[1] Chris Patten, the last governor of Hong Kong, called it 'a building that depresses the spirit'.

The Home Office moved into 2 Marsham Street in 2005 as the influence of Tony Blair's New Labour was on the decline. The following year, Charles Clarke's tenure as home secretary came to an abrupt ending, as so many do, in the midst of a controversy surrounding immigration. A thousand foreign national offenders, including convicted murderers and rapists, had been released and could not be traced.² Shortly after that, in 2007, the responsibility for prisons and probation was split off from the Home Office and handed over to the Ministry of Justice.

Blunders, gaffes, errors and strains in the system were never very far away. Home secretaries who arrived in the department, typically after a reshuffle and on the back of yet another scandal, were said to be ashen-faced, ill-prepared to tackle the enormous remit of the office they now held. Many viewed it as a 'graveyard for political ambitions', a place where the careers of few aspirational ministers survived.

Through sheer stiff-necked recalcitrance and scrappiness, Theresa May, that 'bloody difficult woman',³ remained at the helm of the department longer than any other. Years before, May had carved out a reputation as a steely power player, an honest broker, taking to the stand at the Conservative Party Conference to tell the stunned crowd that they were perceived as the 'nasty party' and needed to reform their image. In an extraordinary excoriation, she went on to denounce her fellow Tories for making 'political capital out of demonising minorities'.⁴

Shortly after the nasty party came to power in 2010 – the majority in a tumultuous coalition government – then prime minister David Cameron announced that they would reduce net migration to the 'tens of thousands',⁵ a target that would only have been possible to meet if the entire country had been locked down. As long as Britain remained a member of the European Union, offering the right to freedom of movement for all citizens across the bloc, it simply would not be viable to stop people from coming here. That political calculation set in motion a whole new chain of events.

In mid-2012, as Danny Boyle's performers prepared to welcome visitors with an Olympics opening ceremony celebrating Britain's rich, diverse, multicultural heritage, Theresa May announced her intention to crowd out those she no longer wanted in the country. She would, she said, create 'a really hostile environment for illegal migration' for those who had 'no right to be here'.[6]

The phrase May coined became her signature policy, designed to run people out of the country or, at the very least, instil fear in those who sought to remain here. It prevented people, many of whom had been here for decades, from earning a living, accessing a bank account or renting a home. Among local communities, the policies created an atmosphere of inherent suspicion and disbelief in which private landlords, NHS staff, teachers, DVLA administrators, bank clerks – anyone in a position of authority – was turned into a de facto border guard responsible for checking a migrant's paperwork to ensure they were in the UK legally and reporting them to immigration enforcement if not. It was to mark a turning point in our relationship with those who come to our shores.

I joined the Home Office in 2014 as the hostile environment policy was at its height. After five years working for the Foreign Office, living in Brussels and Istanbul, I was promised international-facing work, and put on the immigration and security desk in the press office – effectively the frontline of the department. I quickly realised that this wasn't the outward-facing, warm bilateral and multilateral relations I had come to know from the diplomatic world. It was the complete opposite.

The summer before I walked through the revolving doors of 2 Marsham Street, Home Office immigration enforcement teams had stepped up their activities with raids that deliberately targeted racially diverse, multi-ethnic communities. A pilot scheme was launched, with vans circulating around six London boroughs carrying billboards which read: 'In the UK illegally? Go home or face arrest'. Owners of nail bars, construction companies, massage parlours and mechanics' garages found themselves encircled by uniformed, baton-wielding law enforcement officers, rifling through their paperwork and interrogating them in front of their staff. And, though the Windrush scandal had yet to emerge, blameless, decent, hard-working people who had lived and worked in the UK for decades were being rounded up during dawn raids, detained and deported.

Every day, I woke up with a sense of dread, my stomach flipping and diving as if I had just driven over a bridge. On the train I searched for stories to see how the department's latest announcement had been covered, before arriving at my desk to read through newspaper cuttings – packages of coverage printed out and stapled together by news-desk press officers on the early shift.

At a news conference meeting each morning, I or another member of the immigration desk would set out each story, how it had been covered, which journalist had reported it and whether it was favourable to the department and its ministers or not. It was competitive, brash and macho, with press officers clambering over each other to talk up how well they had handled a conversation with a challenging journalist or successfully killed a story before publication. I hated it.

Ahead of the release of quarterly immigration statistics, there were late nights and frenetic meetings as lines to take were prepared, cleared with policy officials and sent up to the home secretary's private office. The click-clack of heels reverberating around the atrium reoccurs to me when I think about those times. Printers stalling, paper ripping, much cursing. Though there was strip lighting and bright, neon furniture, I can remember only grey: cheap tiled grey carpets, creased grey suits, licks of grey hair.

Sometimes media handling required a level of expertise nobody in the press office appeared to have. One of the biggest stories that passed across my desk was about a rise in the number of so-called 'foreign fighters': British nationals who had travelled to Syria and Iraq to join the terrorist organisation ISIS, or Da'esh. I had recently returned to London from Istanbul, where most of my team had been prominent Syrian opposition figures forced into exile. Familiar with the conflict and the broader regional context, I was asked to handle the story.

At a morning meeting we discussed the British radical Islamist preacher Anjem Choudary, who had been arrested for pledging allegiance to, and declaring support for, the creation of an Islamic Caliphate.[7]

'I mean, Sunni and Shia, what the fuck is that about?' one long-in-the-tooth media advisor joked. 'It's the same religion, isn't it? It's basically the same as Protestants and Catholics,' another suggested, glancing nonchalantly around the room to shoulder shrugs and blank expressions.

The faces of my friends and their loved ones who had been kidnapped, tortured and killed by Da'esh flashed through my mind. My distressed Arabic teacher, distractedly checking his phone for updates after his uncle had disappeared, only to find out weeks later he had been captured and brutally tortured. The Aleppo policeman, murdered just weeks after we had brought him and his colleagues over the border for civil defence training. And later, Naji Jerf, a Syrian film-maker friend who had helped me get footage out of the country to use in TV packages for international broadcasters, was shot at point-blank range in the southern Turkish city of Gaziantep, just streets away from where we had last clinked glasses of sugary tea and laughed together.

By the time many more friends and colleagues met their ends, the guffaws and elbow-nudging at Marsham Street were already behind me, but I continue to reflect on those Home Office meetings with a deep discomfort, as if I, in some way, dishonoured their memory with my silence.

Around the time I handed in my Home Office lanyard and came blinking out into the light, Marsham Street ministers had already started to pull up the drawbridge. With every successive home secretary, immigration and asylum policies hardened and the department seemed to fold in on itself, becoming more defensive, more forbidding, more bullish. Now these former colleagues were invaluable sources, a gateway into a hostile department shrouded in secrecy. Among them was Colin Wright, a tenacious but discreet man with sloping shoulders, a broad forehead and wide-set, hooded eyes.

Wright was a career Home Office official, a loyal servant with over two decades' experience in the department. Caught in the eye of a storm, he was a calm, rational voice, even-handed and clear-headed. If meetings became rambunctious, as they sometimes could, he would steer his colleagues back on course with characteristic poise. Nobody around him could put their finger on it, but they noticed a discernible shift in energy when he walked into the room. Maybe it was how little he said, always seeming to observe; maybe it was a perceived inability to question his own judgements, a certainty in his convictions which grated on some of his colleagues.

Wright was unfazed by other people's opinions, reluctant to spend too much time on internal politics. Nobody knew any details about his personal life – whether he was married, or had children, or which way he voted. Every Friday there was always some excuse to avoid drinks after work. Wright preferred it that way. Civil servants should be non-partisan, he felt. Private lives and views should be kept private.

The one thing he could not abide was sloppiness. He saw a lot of that in his job; inexcusable, unprofessional errors. All correspondence on the small boat crossings ran through him, sent up to his desk in the private office on the third floor of Marsham Street, ostensibly ready for the home secretary's box. Sometimes there were missing pages in submissions, clashes in meeting requests, duplicates, half-baked updates. It took him hours to sort out what information was missing.

Diligent as he was, he refused to close the box until all the documents met his admittedly sky-high standards. 'Getting this right matters,' he would tell his colleagues.

When he had first started in the private office, Wright was surprised by how few of his policy colleagues had a background in immigration and asylum. Many had come from criminology backgrounds, approaching migration through a narrow lens. He hadn't studied migration or worked in the area before, but a thirst for knowledge and a sharp mind had proved useful. It was complex, but he had got himself up to speed quickly; others could do the same.

Home secretaries were coming through the office at quite a rate now. Six in the last seven years; that's got to be some sort of record. When they arrived, delivering the same platitudes in a similar-sounding all-staff speech, Wright had the sense that none of them really wanted the job. He could see why, but he fervently believed that this was a position which should be held with reverence, not overcome by ego.

Watching the new home secretary, Yvette Cooper, settle into the role after fourteen years under the Conservatives, Wright had been struck by a shift in mood across the department. Spirits were higher than they had been previously, a sense that a clean slate might bring about change.

Much of her time in the early days was taken up with briefings – national security and intelligence, how to read and handle top-secret documents, the more urgent matters – but she had also had to get used to the presence of a close, armed protection team. That could be daunting for some people.

Wright admired that Cooper could hold a lot in her mind. That's more than could be said for others before her. Under Priti Patel, the small boat crossings had become almost an 'obsession'.

Inside her impersonal, corporate office, Patel would sit behind a heavy mahogany desk and point at a whiteboard facing her. On it was her list of priorities – around thirty of them – all to be achieved during her tenure. Number 1, top of the list, read: 'Stop the small boats'.

Indicating two Union Jack flags positioned behind her desk, Patel would frequently tell her private office staff: 'We will keep the country safe together.' Wright thought this was the home secretary's way of justifying the work in her own mind.[8]

Outlandish ideas kept passing his desk, cropping up in meetings: giant wave machines, jet ski patrols, floating reception centres. There was always something. Wright had a hunch that these plans were intended to make headlines in the *Daily Mail*. Tabloid coverage was, as ever, courted. There was even a diktat known as the '*Daily Mail* test', instructing staff that any correspondence – emails, WhatsApp chats, internal messages – should be sense-checked to ensure it didn't end up on the front page of the *Mail*.

Chris Philp, the immigration minister during part of Priti Patel's tenure, was 'a law unto himself'. Wright had once been at a meeting in which Philp had ordered the Border Force to turn a small boat round in the Channel. This was his 'hill to die on', his cornerstone policy, and he wanted to see it rolled out before he left the department the following week. But as they attempted to push the inflatable dinghy back, the two Border Force cutters broke. At a meeting into what had gone wrong, Chris Philp was 'spitting with anger', demanding that officials should fix the boats and get on with the manoeuvre. It was like something out of *The Thick of It*.

Bullying allegations had been rife. In February 2020 Priti Patel's most senior aide, permanent secretary Philip Rutnam, very publicly quit over what he described as a 'vicious and orchestrated campaign' against him.[9] One senior Home Office official was said to have collapsed after a particularly fractious meeting with Patel.[10] Others began contacting reporters, telling them they had been instructed to carry out activities which clearly broke the law. At times, it felt to Wright like the department was unravelling, 'collapsing under the weight of the mini campaigns being waged from within'.

He noticed that everything had become about numbers since the boats started coming in. Twice-daily updates from the Kent coast, tallying new arrivals. Morning briefings on the weather, wave heights, wind speeds. Decision makers recruited into posts, offset against the number of those who had left. There was a very high turnover in the asylum space; it was notoriously taxing and politically toxic. Young, ambitious staff tended to want to go to the Foreign Office, to learn languages and travel, not come to Marsham Street with its rigid hierarchy and routine days.

Wright could pinpoint a change in the tenor of the conversation around small boats towards the spring of 2022. By then, Priti Patel had become 'fixated' on processing the applications of migrants offshore, and preferably as far away from the UK as possible. A shortlist was drawn up by the Foreign Office, which had gone out to its network of overseas posts to drum up business. On the list were around thirty countries, primarily East and West African nations. Slidepacks were developed for each of the shortlisted territories, setting out economic modelling for a new runway, schools and accommodation, along with country-specific information on political instability and press freedom. In spite of the facts, Rwanda, that 'safe country', that bastion of human rights, landed the deal. It wasted no time cashing a cheque for £140 million. Many hundreds of millions followed.

Wright couldn't fathom why Rwanda had ever been considered. Six months before the deal was signed, the British High Commissioner had warned No. 10 in a diplomatic telegram that opposition activists there faced 'intimidation and harassment, including detention on politically motivated charges', with some people 'disappeared or killed'. His advice was ignored.[11] Perhaps ministers preferred the narrative, developed over decades through former leaders such as Tony Blair, which held up the autocracy as an example of what could be achieved with hundreds of millions of pounds of aid spend, largely from guilt-ridden countries like the UK, which did little to stop the genocide there in 1994. The stereotype of a miraculous nation built from the ruins up – a safe, prosperous country – was convenient spin for a government intent on sending its unwanted there.

The day the plans were announced, on 14 April 2022, I was, by chance, in Folkestone with my husband and our baby son. The evening before, I had been engrossed in the coverage online. Seeing the front pages on the news stand the next morning, I raced down to the coast to hear from those who had, only half an hour earlier, arrived on our shores.

All of those I spoke to – over forty people, from Eritrea, Iraqi-Kurdistan, Iran, Syria, Sudan and elsewhere – said they followed the UK news and had heard about the Rwanda deal, but they had crossed anyway.[12] The deterrent hadn't worked.

'Do you know how many thousands of miles I travelled to be here? How long I was in the desert . . .? To reach this point, to be here, we all had to make so many sacrifices. A lot of people lost their lives on the sea. I left my country now – I cannot go back to Africa,' a man from Eritrea said.

Others huddled around me, agreeing that they would rather die in the UK than be sent to Rwanda. '100 per cent, people will lose their lives by themselves,' a man from Sudan said. 'Some, they will go up to the hills [the cliffs] here, some they will go to the train, to the sea, to any place. This one [the UK] is the human rights problem, not only in Rwanda.'

Days after the government rushed the Nationality and Borders Act through Parliament, facilitating the removal of small boat arrivals to

Rwanda, the first letters were sent out. Among those who received the slim package of documents was Barin, a man in his early twenties with a mop of dark hair and thick eyebrows shielding eyes which darted around, jumpy and ill at ease. The week before, Barin had been taken from his asylum hotel to Brook House immigration removal centre. Early in the morning, a guard knocked on his cell door, handing him a brown envelope without any explanation. Inside was a fact sheet titled: 'I'm being relocated to Rwanda – what does this mean for me?'

Barin was confused. For days, rumours had been circulating among the Kurdish detainees suggesting that he and some of the others he had arrived with were about to be released and taken to a hotel. He didn't even know where Rwanda was – somewhere in Africa, but where exactly? – and he hadn't heard of the government's latest scheme. Lying on the sunken mattress in his cell, Barin stared up at the ceiling, not knowing what to do next.

On 14 June 2022, a van arrived with six immigration officials, who handcuffed him and put shackles on his ankles. He wondered why, if he was being taken to a hotel, they were putting these on him. He felt his blood suddenly run cold and he fell unconscious. A 'use of force' form filled out by custody staff shows that he was then stretchered to an escort van with a medic present and driven eighty miles to Boscombe Down airport in Wiltshire.

When he regained consciousness, a police officer told Barin, through Google Translate, not to resist when they arrived at the airfield. 'I can't move, how can I resist? Please stop this,' he typed back. On the tarmac he could see the plane, its lights on, its engines whirring. Two men, also handcuffed, were being escorted on board.

Inside the plane, immigration enforcement officers put restraining harnesses on deportees, tied tight across their bodies. One man, hyperventilating and banging his head, was held face-down on the floor of the plane. Another, who had been found in his cell cutting his wrists with sharp slices of a broken drinks can, was also brought on board. 'Pain-inducing restraint' was used to seize and hold him there, documents showed. Muffled cries, shouting and praying could be heard towards the back of the plane.

Shortly after 10 p.m., an announcement came from one of the officers on the tarmac. Barin's ticket had been cancelled after an eleventh-hour injunction had been granted by the European Court of Human Rights. One by one, the men were taken off the flight. Barin returned in a convoy to Brook House, arriving just before dawn, bewildered and exhausted. For the next sixty-five days, threats to deport him continued. 'It was a psychological fight,' Barin told me by phone months later, his case still pending at the time. 'We thought we would be sent at any moment. When we got out, I decided I cannot live in this fear – I need to try to move on.'

The air inside Marsham Street was thick with tension in the days that followed the grounded flight. On one side of the floor, asylum policy officials scrambled to get paperwork together for parliamentary aides. On the other, Priti Patel prepared to make a statement to the House, not wanting to appear as embarrassed as she was. It was scandalous, she said. Very surprising. Disappointing. 'It's time we kicked those bastards into touch,' one Tory MP said of the ECHR on the party's parliamentary WhatsApp group.[13]

While the political storm rumbled on, an internal one was brewing. The Rwanda deal had become a flashpoint for many in the department. Nascent rebellion movements started from the inside: just a few organisers at first, but then it rapidly expanded. One team printed posters of Paddington Bear being flown off to Rwanda, pinning them up around the tea rooms and coffee points in Marsham Street and visa centres across the country. Peterborough, Liverpool, Sheffield: requests were coming in thick and fast. Stickers were stuck to cabinets and printers mirroring the banners from protesters outside: 'Refugees Welcome!', they exclaimed.

Internal Home Office meetings were held, giving staff the opportunity to raise their concerns surrounding the Rwanda plans. 'Shame, embarrassment and anger is what I and many others feel,' one person said in screengrabs later leaked to me. Another despaired: 'It feels like working in Germany in 1937.' Senior members of the department were particularly fearful of speaking out against the Rwanda deal in case they were 'cut out of the loop'. Many already had been.

Dissent was quickly quashed. When one junior Home Office official attempted to address some of the language used to describe asylum seekers, such as 'stocks and flows', they were reprimanded. 'Junior colleagues need to learn how to raise issues,' they were told. Complaints were not condoned.[14]

'It's like a part of you dies walking in there,' another said, a notion entirely familiar to me. What people said in the pub was very different to what they said in the office, a former colleague reminded me. 'In the pub, we'll all say, "Obviously these policies are shit, but what's the alternative?"' There was a feeling of powerlessness; that it wasn't worth sticking your head above the parapet. 'The machine will grind on, whether you're on top or under the wheels,' my source said. 'You've got to just keep your head down and power on.'

Wright was concerned about his own lack of accountability. For the first time in his career, he began to question whether he could, in all good faith, serve ministers so intent on a policy direction that he strongly opposed. It had become a toxic place to work, febrile, tense. Colleagues clashed more than at any other time he could remember.

A senior official for whom he had a deep respect had a new role lined up elsewhere in the civil service but had been blocked from leaving by Suella Braverman. They were seen as 'too much of an asset'. Worse still, they couldn't fill the job. Nobody wanted it.

On hearing this, I wrote to the official to request a comment. Within an hour, I received a sharp rap on the knuckles from the department's press office, who called me up to ask what I was planning to do with the information, but not denying it.

There was a 'two-pronged attack' on the media: so-called 'client journalists' fed stories by the department on the right, and those snubbed on the left. During a visit to Rwanda, shortly after Braverman had taken the reins, only tabloid press cherry-picked by the home secretary were invited along, with clear rules and guidelines to follow.

'First Rwanda asylum flights this summer,' the *Sunday Express* splashed, with a picture of Braverman laughing manically outside a detention centre in Kigali, before asking for interior design advice.[15] The *Mail on Sunday* celebrated the home secretary's successful visit to 'one of the world's safest countries'. None of the media outlets critical of her position – the 'usual suspects', as Braverman called them – had been invited on the taxpayer-funded trip to provide scrutiny of any kind.

Later, having got itself into another mess, the Home Office sacked David Neal, the independent chief inspector of borders and immigration, for disclosing unauthorised information to the media, a tactic he had resorted to after fifteen of his reports had remained unpublished. 'Just because the reports might be inconvenient, it shouldn't mean that they are suppressed,' he said, although that is exactly what ended up happening. 'There is a role in public life for people who speak truth to power.'[16]

By mid-2024, after a humiliating defeat in the Supreme Court, two more Bills railroaded through Parliament, and a desperate bid to get one plane, any plane, off the ground, public perceptions of the Home Office's competence had plummeted. YouGov polling showed that 85 per cent believed the government was handling immigration badly, with 52 per cent (a number with significant meaning on this issue) stating that the government wasn't taking a strong enough stance on small boats crossing the Channel.[17]

Chaos abounded and the optics worsened as figures emerged soon afterwards showing that 12,300 people had reached UK shores in the first half of 2024: the highest on record.[18] The numbers continued to climb and the Conservative government was powerless to stop them. It was an open goal for the opposition.

Shortly after arriving back from another extended trip to the camps of northern France, I met Stephen Kinnock, shadow immigration minister at the time, for a coffee at Portcullis House. I was discombobulated to be back in a formal setting, walking the corridors where decisions made directly affected those I had come into contact with days before.

Earlier that morning, Kinnock had been busy preparing a speech on Labour's five-point plan and he wanted to test whether I could recall all five pledges off the top of my head. I got to point four. 'You're someone very well briefed on these issues,' he said. 'If you can't remember them, how are we going to get through to the electorate?' Communicating their agenda to the general public was, he said, a real concern. I felt that the archaic model of a five-point plan was four points too many.

Labour had got the handling of immigration issues over the last two decades badly wrong, which had damaged the party's reputation. In 2004, the European Union had voted in favour of an eastward expansion, opening the doors to millions of citizens from countries including Poland, Romania and Bulgaria. Fearing an anti-migrant backlash, then home secretary David Blunkett took out a week-long series of front pages in the *Sun*. 'Halt the asylum tide now', one headline read. 'Draw a red line on immigration or else', another warned.[19]

In 2010, Gordon Brown was caught on-microphone describing a lady who challenged him over immigration as a 'bigoted woman'.[20] Then the red mugs, those god-awful mugs, during the Ed Miliband 2015 leadership bid pledging 'Controls on immigration'.[21] The party had never quite got the tone right, something Kinnock was aware they would need to correct.

In the general election of July 2024, Labour won an overwhelming majority, sweeping to power on the promise of change. Stephen Kinnock moved to the Department for Health and a new team was brought into Marsham Street, keen to show they were gripping the small boats issue and fixing the broken asylum system. The Rwanda plan was scrapped on day one, with Kigali offering no refund for the £270 million already handed over. Recruitment for a new Border Security Commander began. Proposals for a 'security pact' with the EU got underway and a meeting with European leaders was held at Blenheim Palace, focused in part on migration. Meanwhile, there was no discussion of safe routes or an expansion of humanitarian visas, despite broad support.[22] During Labour's first week in office, four more people lost their lives in the Channel.

'Criminal gangs are making vast profit from putting lives at risk,' Yvette Cooper warned, following news of the drownings. 'We are accelerating action with international partners to pursue and bring down dangerous smuggler gangs.' A new three-word pledge had been born: 'smash the gangs'.

Back on the Kent coast, record numbers of boats were arriving. Among the 701 people who set foot on dry land during Labour's first fortnight were the Qadirs: Parwen, her husband Dara, her daughter Shewa and her son Hozan, the Iraqi-Kurdish family I had first met in the camps near Dunkirk.

'We are in UK!' she typed, with a photo of her children smiling, sitting on tatty chairs in a hotel lobby. Underneath was a large red heart, followed by a crying-face emoji. I jumped in the car to meet them.

PART TWO
ARRIVAL

4. On Solid Ground

*'I always remember, I'm the hope of my family,
Maybe you're the hope of your family too?
Let's shine together
Like the moon in the dark.'*

'Welcome to London: Instructions for new arrivals'[1]

The first glimpse Parwen had of the UK was underwhelming. Through the dawn fog, the Dover cliffs looked more grey to her than white; different to the Google images she'd searched late at night during the long wait in the camps near Dunkirk. A few times, squinting out to the horizon from a vast, sweeping bay in northern France after another failed crossing, she had pointed at the undulating silhouette of the land ahead, telling her two young children that was their final destination, the place they would one day call home. Now here they were. It was surreal, almost dreamlike.

As soon as the Border Force cutter appeared alongside the dinghy, Parwen leaped up, scrambling to lift her children over to the officers. She was yanked back down by other passengers. 'Stay still, don't move,' one man shouted in Kurdish, panicked. 'If you jump, we all die.' She fell back into her husband Dara's lap and he attempted to soothe her, placing a hand on her back. After eight hours at sea, sitting low in the middle of the boat, her legs were stiff, unable to straighten from the knee. She registered a dull, low ache across her forehead, pulled taut behind her eyes.

Once the dinghy was secured against the railing of the cutter, an official held out his arm and took seven-year-old Shewa and four-year-old Hozan aboard, the two sole children in the dinghy, their oversized lifejackets swamping them. Hozan was trembling, his teeth chattering and he was barely blinking. Parwen repeated his name, wrapping him in her arms, murmuring softly in his ear: 'Everything will be good, we are safe, we are safe.'

Border Force officers gave each of them a grey blanket and a wristband with individual numbers on them. Shouting over the whistle of the wind, one of the men instructed the passengers to hand over their phones. 'No phone,' Parwen told the officious woman standing over her. Like most of the others on board, she had thrown it into the sea: a security precaution ordered by the smugglers to ensure their numbers couldn't be traced. Dara, who had been using his phone to navigate the boat, felt obliged: 'You say nothing, you just give to them.' It would be returned to him once it had been checked.

The couple were then instructed to give the officers their wedding rings; when they asked why, an unsmiling, unblinking man repeated the command, before turning to Dara and pointing to his *tasbih*, traditional Kurdish prayer beads worn around his neck, which he solemnly parted with for the first time in over twenty years. These would be returned once they had passed through immigration control, they were told, though it would be days before their possessions were relocated.

For two hours the cutter barely moved, inching forward towards the shoreline, with radios sporadically sounding alerts near them. Finally, the Dover harbour walls appeared in sight and they were taken off one by one, Parwen struggling to balance, stepping out of the boat with her son propped against her hip. Though she was shaken and unsteady, the moment her feet touched solid ground Parwen felt a rush of adrenaline burst through her. She gasped, looked up to the sky and let out a mournful moan from deep inside her, for all that she had lost and for fear of all that lay ahead.

The situation for new arrivals at Dover port had improved significantly by the time the Qadir family set foot on UK soil. In autumn 2021, during a visit to Tug Haven, the processing site on the quayside, a watchdog found families with newborn babies, including one as young as two weeks old, sleeping on floor mats so close to strangers they were 'practically touching'.[2] On the car park site next to the jetty, new arrivals were found asleep on double-decker buses. Among them was a sixteen-year-old girl with diesel burns on her legs, still in the wet clothes she had crossed in, her untreated wounds stuck to the fabric.[3]

David Neal, the independent borders inspector, wrote that the conditions were 'inexcusably awful'.[4] A senior manager had told him that identifying particularly vulnerable people who required safeguarding 'went out the window' during busy periods. Neal said it was even worse than that: there was no sign whatsoever that safeguarding procedures were being followed, even when it was quiet. More than 200 Vietnamese nationals who arrived by small boat in 2021, showing clear indicators of trafficking, had simply disappeared.

Tug Haven was closed and a newer area opened 200 metres away: Western Jet Foil. That site quickly became mired in controversy too, with ground staff repeatedly warning that there was a heightened risk of attack. The area, they said, had been left too exposed to the general public.

Though nobody listened, they were right: on 30 October 2022, an admirer of the prominent far-right activist Stephen Yaxley-Lennon (better known as Tommy Robinson) got into his car and drove more than 100 miles. He parked up outside the site and threw three petrol bombs over the fencing before killing himself at a petrol station nearby.[5] The next day, Suella Braverman stood up in Parliament to declare that the Conservatives were the only party serious about stopping the 'invasion on our southern coast',[6] adopting the language of neo-fascists up and down the country.

While they were aware of what was being said about them, the Qadirs didn't pay much attention to it. One thing did confound them, though. 'The UK, your Blair and his friend Bush, they make war in our country – now they don't want to help us. Why?' Dara mused one day, characteristically cautious and considered.

Dara had never really known life without conflict. The day he was born, his father had been on the frontline fighting in one of the bloodiest, fiercest battles of the Gulf War. He was unable to return for more than two months. Days after Dara turned twelve, as the West waged its 'war on terror', his father headed back to the battlefield as a commander for the Kurdish Peshmerga, training and later fighting alongside the British and American coalition forces.

When the threat of invasion was looming in 2003, I was in my first year of university; an impassioned, politically engaged, if slightly idealistic, English student. Behind the bar in the student union, where I was working shifts, we discussed the front pages. A team of UN weapons inspectors led by Hans Blix had visited Iraq and found no evidence of Saddam Hussein's alleged 'weapons of mass destruction'.[7]

We made rudimentary banners, bought loudspeakers and boarded buses bound for London, flooding the streets along with 1.5 million others, chanting, urging the government not to go to war. It was the first protest I had ever joined and I was exhilarated. Nuns, toddlers, actors, lawyers: everyone was there. Jeremy Corbyn gave a speech, then actor Tim Robbins. Even the *Daily Mail* had printed maps for out-of-towners, showing something akin to support. In the end it changed nothing, but its legacy still looms large, with few political demonstrations galvanising as much support since.

A decade on, I moved to Istanbul to act as a media advisor to Ahmed Jarba, the imam-turned-leader of the Syrian National Coalition. The West – primarily the US, Canadian and UK governments – had stepped up support for the coalition in the hope that it would become a legitimate transitional government to oust the then-Syrian President Bashar al-Assad and his henchmen. I was among the resources thrown into the mix.

My colleagues and I worked late into the night in hotel lobbies, huddled around laptops until two in the morning, then waking four hours later to prepare for the day ahead. I sat in on meetings with foreign policy analysts from the US, military intelligence operatives from the UK and diplomats visiting from Canada as they pored over maps marking the position of the regime forces, opposition-held areas and the unstable locations that were likely to be taken next. Networks were multiplying rapidly and splintering into newer, deadlier factions, taking gas fields, dams and conducting prison breaks.

Strategies were drawn up for when Assad was overthrown, largely based on the flawed model of a transitional council supported by Western powers in Libya, which had ultimately led to a failed state. Brits, Americans, Canadians plotted and planned. Syrians were in the room, but they were bit players in the future of their own country.

Tensions mounted and the Syrian National Coalition, too, fractured and divided down ethnic and religious lines. One afternoon, at a meeting in a hotel outside Istanbul, as I darted between huddles of Syrians, attempting to agree messaging before journalists' enquiries came flooding in, President Jarba was punched in the face by one of his advisors. Protocol, the logistics and security team, hastily created an exit route from the building and piled Jarba into a bullet-proof car before anyone could see his swelling face or hear the raucous riot unfolding in the hotel conference room. It was chaos, it was war and the West was powerless to stop it.

At a vote designed to pave the way for military intervention, David Cameron said that this was a 'judgement issue'. Public confidence had been badly damaged by the 2003 war in Iraq, he told the Commons. Unless Britain acted, Assad would continue to act with impunity, killing and maiming his own people. He needed to be stopped. 'People talk about escalation; to me, the biggest danger of escalation is if the world community – not just Britain, but America and others – stand back and do nothing because I think Assad will draw very clear conclusions from that,' Cameron said.[8]

The government lost the vote. Britain had acted on shaky evidence in the region only a decade before; it would not make the same mistake again.

I watched the British government unravel on a Syrian friend's laptop, in his basement flat on a winding lane in Istanbul's European quarter, the warm, salty breeze from the Bosphorus blowing in through the windows. Around me, a dozen Syrian and Lebanese colleagues spoke rapidly, translating for some and analysing for others. I was the only British person there. The vote was seen as critical: they knew that without UK support, the US, Canadians and the French would be unlikely to act. The lives of their loved ones, trapped inside Syria, were at stake.

There was shock, disquiet and anger when the news came in. 'You let us down,' a seething friend muttered, reflecting a betrayal by the West not unfamiliar to those in the Arab world. I felt a deep sense of shame and embarrassment.

Meanwhile, President Obama was left isolated. He had previously said that Assad's use of chemical weapons would cross a 'red line' on whether the US took military action. 'That would change my calculus,' he told a packed room of reporters at a White House news conference, to the surprise of his advisors.[9] But when, on 21 August 2013, more than 1,400 people were killed following a sarin gas attack in the Damascus suburb of Ghouta, his calculus didn't change. Obama had ordered the Pentagon to prepare for attack but, at the last minute, he blinked.

While the West and the Syrian National Coalition scrabbled around for solutions, ISIS, or Da'esh, filled the vacuum, ripping through Syria and on to Iraq, raping, torturing, killing. Its militants moved to the north-west corner of Iraq, taking the Kurdish towns of Sinjar and Zummar and forcing 40,000 Yazidis, a minority group of predominantly Kurdish descent, to run for their lives.[10] Girls as young as eleven were kidnapped, bought and sold as sex slaves. Elderly women, too old to be sold, were buried, often still alive, in mass graves.[11] Barbaric atrocities followed, shooting, immolating and beheading people held captive. Those who weren't captured fled over borders, surviving on aid support, sometimes for years, living in makeshift camps and plotting journeys to the Western countries which had failed them.

One night in spring 2023, I attended a 'Stop the War' event in Preston run by a group set up in the wake of the US–UK invasion of Iraq. In the prayer room of a mosque on the outskirts of the city, with badges and leaflets laid out on trestle tables, academics and activists discussed the war in Ukraine and the inaction of the West in Afghanistan, which the Taliban had retaken nearly two years previously. One person raised their hand, keen to highlight the plight of the Kurds, now coming to the UK in ever greater numbers by small boat. 'Nobody ever asks why,' she mused perceptively.

Just around the corner, attempting to get their children to settle in a run-down hotel overlooking a noisy A-road, was Parwen, singing

ARRIVAL

Kurdish songs to lull them to sleep, soothing them with soft, sweet memories of their homeland.

As I sat in the stuffy prayer room listening to the well-meaning voices rallying against the UK's legacy of violent imperialism, it occurred to me that British foreign policy had, finally, come full circle. Was the so-called 'small boats crisis' the inevitable consequence of intervention and inaction, the reckoning Britain needed with its past?

Waiting in the draughty, dank marquee at Dover port, with people in uniforms milling around, a painful memory intruded on Parwen's thoughts. A few years before, she had listened as Dara, then a middle-ranking member of the Peshmerga, had been interrogated outside their house in Iraqi Kurdistan by volatile men dressed in black clothes not dissimilar to the UK's border officials.

From the front room of their house, Parwen had heard her husband being beaten, the butt of the gun cracking across his skull, as he screamed for mercy. She was helpless to protect him, wrenching her howling children away from the window; Shewa can remember specific sounds and smells from that day. Now here they were, in a land far from home, about to face more invasive questioning from the authorities.

Leaving her home city of Hawraman, nestled against the border with Iran, had been a tumultuous time for Parwen. She had never lived outside her community, never visited the Iraqi capital Baghdad, never crossed a border before. Adventure wasn't her calling; Parwen longed for stability, finding tranquillity in the plaiting of her daughter's hair, visits to the local market to buy strawberries and neighbours stopping by for her nutty, spiced *qazwan* coffee. She always had the table laid, ready to greet guests, with ornate plates of dried mulberries, nuts and *hurma* dates. In the summer, when the town reached more than fifty degrees, the heat bouncing off the looping lanes near their house, the family would visit Ahmad Awa, a gushing waterfall high in the mountains, where Shewa and Dara swam in the cool lake below. In the winter, she laughed as her husband, back from his ten-day stints away, built snowmen for their daughter and played shin-deep in snow.

While Parwen and Dara had learned some English at school, neither of them were fluent. They were unlikely to ever need it, or so they thought. But now, standing in this impersonal, soulless compound, she felt a world away from home. The language barrier made her vulnerable and confused, reliant on her young daughter, who had absorbed the language from YouTube videos and songs from Disney's *Frozen*.

Eventually, immigration officials called the numbers on their wristbands and they shuffled forward to spell out their names, dates of birth and nationality through an interpreter. Polaroid photos were taken of each of them, facing forward and to the side as in a police line-up. Then, like cattle, they were herded through to another booth for medical assessment.

After more than a year moving between the camps of northern France, often sleeping on the ground with no shelter, no blankets and no dry clothes, the Qadir family were ridden with complex health conditions. Dara's front teeth had been broken when he had fallen in the woods, tripping over a tree trunk and slamming down while fleeing the French riot police. The children both had scabies; Shewa had scratched her skin so badly it had bled and scabbed over. Parwen had a sty which she thought was so ugly that she continually pulled her hijab over her eye like a hood. And that was just their physical health. The mental scars would take a lifetime to heal.

The previous years had taken their toll. During the crossing from Turkey to Greece, their over-capacitated fishing trawler had taken on too much water and sunk, dragging Parwen's mother and ten others down with it. In a video filmed by some bystanders, Parwen can be seen in a rocky inlet, crying out a primal scream and beating herself over the head as she watched her mother drown. By the time the Greek coastguard reached them the boat had broken into fragments; there was nothing anyone could do.

Believing they were being taken to secure housing, the family gave themselves up to the police, who arrested and detained them for two months in a makeshift prison on the outskirts of Athens. Photos stapled to the detention facility paperwork show the children smiling broadly, while their parents stare ahead at the camera, washed-out, gaunt and shell-shocked.

After their release and desperate to get out of Greece with its cruel, cold authorities, its barbed-wire fencing and its gut-wrenching memories, the family gave everything they had to a smuggler. Within only a few days, they had barrelled their way through Italy from south to north and on to the camps near Dunkirk. There they would stay for months, enduring a bitter winter, countless evictions and more than fifty failed attempts to cross the Channel.

Among the many people I have met in the camps over the years, the Qadir family really got under my skin. Shewa was bright, resourceful and a mirror image of her mother, always trotting along beside her. 'We are like glue,' she said one morning with her LA twang. They shared the same effervescent energy, giggle and mischievous sparkle in their eyes. Shewa's favourite game was to hide and jump out at me; my job was to react as dramatically as possible, though it often did genuinely take me by surprise. Now, though, sitting in front of an immigration officer in Dover and representing her family at just seven, she felt the weight of responsibility to help her family navigate another system, another culture, another language.

Before long, they were moved swiftly along the conveyer belt at the quayside and handed tracksuit bottoms and long-sleeved T-shirts to change into. Parwen asked if there was a headscarf she could have; she had lost hers during the crossing and felt deeply uncomfortable without it. She was told there was nothing left.

Gathering plastic bags of wet clothes, they boarded a coach at the exit and took seats towards the front, the children pressed up against the windows. It didn't occur to any of them to ask where they were going. 'I did not care,' Parwen told me later, tutting, shaking her head and laughing with relief. 'Just as long as it was far from the sea.'

Close by in the port compound, Jamal, a timid teenager from Afghanistan, was being shown a chart with numbers on it. He pointed to '16' and told the immigration official he had a digital copy of his *taskira*, or identity card, saved on his phone. If he could just access it, he could prove his age. The official scanned him up and down and laughed, telling him he had arrived by boat and must have known what he was doing. He then made an on-the-spot guess that Jamal was twenty-two.

Moved aside to a private room, the teenager was placed on a rickety chair, where his appearance was mocked. One official indicated towards his chin, suggesting that Jamal had a beard and could not possibly be the age he stated. He felt irritable but unsure of his footing, naturally deferential to uniformed guards. 'I tell them many times, let me show my ID, then you will believe me, but they don't allow this.' That immigration official wasn't the only one: in an earlier case involving another Afghan boy, a judge found that the Home Office was using an article from Gillette to show the age at which young men typically start shaving, as if that proved the child was lying.

Back out in the compound ten minutes later, Jamal watched as a female friend he had travelled with was escorted out of the door to another area, known as the Kent Intake Unit. Unlike him, the girl had had her age accepted. From the KIU, she would be linked up to the local authority and brought into the care system, assigned a social worker, foster carer and a place at college. Most children would never reach that point. Jamal, like so many others, would have to ask for help from the council further down the line to reassess his age, if that opportunity ever arose. It's unlikely that the local authority would have the budget or the capacity to ever make the checks.

By the time Jamal's friend had passed the brief visual assessment to confirm she was indeed a child, the KIU was already a horribly austere place. Robert Jenrick, the former immigration minister, had ordered the removal of all cartoons painted on the walls of the reception centre, arguing that the pictures of Mickey Mouse and Baloo were too welcoming and sent out the wrong message.[12] The Home Office later revealed that some of the lone refugee children at the KIU were as young as nine.

In a further degradation, the Conservative government announced that it would X-ray children's teeth and wrists to assess their ages.[13] MRI scans, too, would be taken of their knees and collarbones. If a child refused to undergo medical tests, the Home Office threatened that it would damage the credibility of their statements and may affect the outcome of their claims.

Campaigners raised the alarm, saying that children had left accommodation and care settings in other European countries after being threatened with similar tests; they had simply disappeared. Medical experts, including the Society of Radiographers and the Royal College of Paediatrics and Child Health, warned that the tests were both unreliable and unethical. The government pressed ahead anyway, bringing the new legislation into force in January 2024.

Among aid workers, there was growing disquiet that hundreds of children – possibly thousands – were being wrongly assessed and could face removal to Rwanda before childcare professionals had a chance to assess their ages.[14] The main issue was that the Home Office wasn't keeping track of the numbers of people arriving in Dover who stated that they were under eighteen. Nobody was. Without the broader picture, it was impossible to say where they'd gone, whether they were in adult hotels, in detention or had disappeared.

Jamal, meanwhile, was moved towards a group of adults. He had been separated from the friends he had made along the way and had no phone to contact his parents. Nobody knew of his whereabouts. The safeguarding risks were plain to see.

Three miles inland, a collection of marquees in the grounds of a former army barracks was to be Jamal's next temporary resting place.

The town of Manston burst into the public consciousness in autumn 2022 when it was discovered that nearly 4,000 people were being held there unlawfully for up to six weeks, despite a twenty-four-hour maximum stay rule. Public health concerns quickly began to emerge, with rats running around the site and the spread of Covid-19, MRSA and scabies.[15] In spite of the obvious risks of cross-contamination, mats were placed close together on the floor, or they got stolen, leaving people to sleep on flattened cardboard boxes or rows of airport chairs.

Portaloos overflowed into the marquees, and blankets were used to keep the driving rain and biting winds out. Later, an Iraqi-Kurdish man, Hussein Haseeb Ahmed, originally from a town near the Qadir family, presented to the medical team with symptoms of diphtheria. He was given paracetamol and sent back to the overcrowded marquee. A week later, he was hospitalised and died.[16]

There followed at least two documented cases of people attempting to strangle themselves using seatbelts in an unlocked van parked outside the marquees. A pregnant woman suffered a miscarriage after she was separated from her husband, 'apparently punitively', and left to look after her five children.[17] Several hundred unaccompanied children and age-disputed teenagers, some as young as fourteen, were discovered to be staying there and there were reports that staff were selling drugs on the site.[18] Shortly after protests erupted outside Manston, a coach took around fifty asylum seekers to London's Victoria station, dropped them off and drove away, leaving them to wander the streets with no food or water for the night.[19]

A few weeks later, during a disastrous appearance at the Home Affairs Select Committee, Diana Johnson, the committee's Labour chair, asked an embattled Suella Braverman: 'Could you tell the committee how the Home Office got itself into this mess, with up to 4,000 people being detained at Manston? Whose fault is it?' Braverman stuck to her well-rehearsed line: 'I will tell you who is at fault. It is the people who are breaking our rules, coming here illegally.'[20]

For the Qadir family, the three days they spent at Manston felt like months. Parwen couldn't sleep, disturbed by the noise and people talking, shuffling around throughout the night. Without any functioning showers there was an acrid, stale smell of sweat which lingered on their clothes.

Each morning at dawn, Manston was abuzz with activity, with tiny triangular cheese sandwiches and bottles of water handed out. The children played tag, running around the perimeter of the marquee over the mats where people slept; Parwen shouted at them to watch where they were going. Often the children fell asleep in their mother's lap during the daytime in an exhausted slumber – too alert, or perhaps too afraid, to close their eyes at night.

For Jamal Manston was, to all intents and purposes, an open-air prison. He resented being monitored and followed, with security guards everywhere he looked. One official repeatedly told him that he was under arrest, a criminal without any protection, 'just under his control'.

Like everybody else held there, his phone had been taken away from him without explanation – it was 'like an arm or a leg was missing' – and he knew his family would be unable to sleep until they heard from him. He felt it was like 'one big refugee camp', with no access to a lawyer, a social worker, or any information. There was no medical support, no grassroots organisations or NGOs helping as they had in the camps of northern France, even though many people asked for assistance.

After three long days, Jamal was called forward, fingerprinted and interviewed again. Multiple times, he was asked a variation on the same question: why did you travel to the UK by small boat? The answer was always the same: there was no other way.

5. No Safe Passage

'A child refugee is someone who waits.'
Valeria Luiselli,
Lost Children Archive

The small boat route was not the first way Jamal had tried to reach British shores. Month after month, he had wandered the same central reservation near the entrance to the ferry port in Calais, waiting to jump aboard a slowing lorry. Some days more opportunities arose than others. Striking workers helped. Queues of freight vehicles bunny-hopped along, the tailback snaking for miles, drivers unaware that the rear doors of their trucks were swinging open.

Once, he slipped on a wet back step, rolling on to the motorway into oncoming traffic. He still bore the wounds: a thick, raised scar on his forearm and a vicious, oozing gash on his calf, not fully healed months on.

After several close calls, Jamal moved on to the lorry park to try his luck there. He waited until night fell to dart between the vehicles, methodically testing the locks on the rear doors of each one. He'd almost made it once, sitting huddled in the back of a truck among stacks of wooden pallets with two other wide-eyed stowaways, heart racing, exhaling misty puffs of air. When he heard a sharp bark outside, he readied himself to run. As the doors creaked open, Jamal sprang out of the back and sprinted towards the barbed-wire fencing nearby.

Sniffer dogs were everywhere, pulling on their leads, noses out front, hauling border officials along behind them. Nobody could figure out how to put them off the scent. One of Jamal's friends, a fellow Afghan, had attempted to wedge himself between the cabin and the trailer of the lorry. As it set off out of the parking area, he felt a sudden pressure and the nauseating snap of a bone. He had almost been squeezed to death as the vehicle turned a corner.

Others tried climbing underneath the lorry, clinging to the rear axle, facing the high risk of falling on to a motorway at speed. Cutting through the canvas at the top was a less perilous tactic, but it could easily set off the carbon monoxide detectors or the heart-rate monitors at the port.

Charities had started handing out leaflets around the camps with a list of dos and don'ts, issuing words of caution. 'The moving mechanisms can injure and crush you,' the leaflet stated. 'They can heat up and burn you. Lorries can be refrigerated: there is a risk of hypothermia. There may not be enough air: there is a risk of dying of asphyxiation.'[1]

Jamal had heard what happened to those Vietnamese people in 2019. Thirty-nine of them suffocated inside the back of an airtight lorry container, starved of oxygen. 'Maybe going to die . . . can't breathe any more, dear,' read an unsent message found on the phone of one of those who perished.[2] The idea of it scared him, but he was a realist. Jamal knew his life was in danger with every attempt, but the overground journey was short – not least when compared to other stretches on the route so far – and it was free.

During the pandemic, lorry crossings had all but ground to a halt, the parking area like a ghost town. He had wandered around but there was nothing. Tired of waiting, with no end in sight, Jamal decided to travel south to Lille to begin the asylum process in France. Some months later, friends in the camps began messaging, telling him of opportunities to cross by boat. Jamal returned north to try again, curled up in a spare seat, dodging train ticket conductors.

For the smuggling gangs, the pandemic had been a boon. With freight routes closed, a bottleneck of migrants had been created, all potential customers with no other way to cross. Exploitation in the camps became rampant. Women were forced to give their bodies in exchange for a roof over their heads and shelter for their children. Men became facilitators, arranging logistics, assembling boats, burying outboard motors and running the dinghies down the beach. Teenagers – children – were being recruited to run errands and act as lookouts and informants. For those who had used up their money getting to this point, the gangs were their only way out of squalor and desperation.

After returning to Calais, Jamal was offered the chance to start afresh, working for a smuggler known as Tava as a runner and all-round dogsbody. 'They tell me, if you work hard, you get a place in the boat, this is how we pay you.'

Tava was a stringy, skittish man with wiry dark hair and a nasal voice. A tiny cog in a slick, well-oiled machine, he had spent several years working a specific patch on the periphery of the camps around Pas-de-Calais, protected by armed men. Nobody went into his area and he kept away from others.

Tava was well versed in the UK immigration system, which he saw as porous; 'so many gaps', easy to game. He gave his customers the same instructions: all they needed to do was call for help from the British coastguard at the right time and they would be rescued. From there to a four-star hotel after a week or so. Then the interview, 'very, very important one'. Making a political case for asylum was good; better than a humanitarian one. They can't make you go back then.

Though he appeared outwardly confident, a nervous twitch betrayed a certain insecurity, an awareness of how quickly his security situation could be compromised. Rival gangs had sprung up, touting for business among the same groups, in similar territories. It was driving down the average price: he used to get £5,000 per client; now it could be as low as £1,500, maybe even £1,000. There was a reason this place was called The Jungle. Only the strongest survived. To Tava, his job was all about survival: 'You do what you need to do.'

Jamal had the same ethos. In exchange for more than eighteen months of unpaid labour in the camps, he was finally offered a free journey, boarding a dinghy bound for Britain. A fresh start was, at last, in sight.

A hundred miles north-west of Calais, a diminutive figure dressed in faded jeans and a black top headed out to a nearby park in his Mercedes saloon. It was mid-spring and the bluebells in the woodlands of Wanstead Park were turning their heads towards dappled rays of sun, a heron swooping low over the flatlands.

To his neighbours, Hewa Rahimpur lived a fairly simple life, selling sweets and tobacco from a kiosk close to the park. Locals described him as 'like gold', an affable, gregarious guy who laughed easily and settled well among Ilford's close-knit community. His landlady, who owned a hairdressing salon on the high street, was particularly fond of him: he was a reliable tenant, trustworthy, always paying rent on time and keeping on top of the bills.[3] Nobody could have imagined what he was doing behind closed doors.

As Rahimpur swung into a car park at the flatland's edge, two plain-clothes police officers approached the vehicle, apprehended him and locked his arms behind his back before placing him under arrest. Onlookers gawked, whispering, wondering: *What is going on?*

Unbeknownst to Ilford's community – or Rahimpur – at the same moment police officers were marching over farmland at a smallholding in Osnabrück, a rural area in western Germany. Bursting into a run-down barn, they discovered more than sixty inflatable rubber dinghies and 900 lifejackets stacked high, some falling out of their plastic wrappers. To the side, buried amid the loot, were a range of firearms.[4]

Having located the middlemen, the police seized their phones, downloading a treasure trove of messages. They had hit the jackpot. WhatsApp exchanges revealed the key players in the supply chain stretching west to Belgium and north to the Netherlands. There had been particularly frequent contact with one UK-based number, traceable to Ilford: Rahimpur's stomping ground.

The kiosk owner's expansive pan-European smuggling network began to unravel before him. Officers from the joint operation discovered that he was the highest-ranking member of an organised crime group which had brought 10,000 people to the UK by small boat over an eighteen-month period.[5] Rahimpur had been the linchpin responsible for a vast network which procured dinghies from Turkey and outboard motors from China, stored them and planned the onward logistics to get the equipment over to the coast of northern France.

An astute broker, Rahimpur had advertised his services on Facebook, laundering and filtering finances out to the rest of the twenty-strong gang. He, like all other smugglers, used the *hawala* system, whereby a migrant pays a handler in their home country, with instalments released each time they cross a border. No physical money is ever exchanged or transferred, making it labyrinthine for police officers to track transactions. It was a system largely based on trust and honour, familiar to European law enforcement officers across the migration route.

It had taken six months and 900 officers to find Rahimpur. Europol, Interpol, the National Crime Agency, national police services from multiple countries and many other organisations were involved. It was one of the largest joint operations ever conducted to uncover a smuggling kingpin.

Catching Rahimpur had been a significant moment for the UK authorities, but it also revealed the extent to which the people-smuggling trade was being directed from British soil. Finding those at the helm was like finding a needle in a haystack, like a game of 'whack-a-mole', as one law enforcement source told me. As soon as the authorities got one, another popped up to fill the gap. All the technology in the world couldn't break them.

British law enforcement had eyes on much of what was happening in northern France. Joint intelligence cells operating out of embassies in capital cities across Europe. Surveillance technologies. Downloads from phones. 'Debriefs' with migrants. Social media campaigns targeting people before they left. None of it was stopping the boats. With every new approach, every new policy, the smugglers simply adapted their methods, outsmarting the authorities at every turn. Now they had a foothold in Britain. They could be operating from anywhere.

Some members of law enforcement told me they had tired of the government politicising the issue. It was always the same resolute statement: 'We will smash the business model of the evil people smugglers.' Now Labour were saying the same thing, suggesting they would invoke anti-terror laws, powers which nobody in the enforcement community had called for. Only recently, three Bills had passed through Parliament and anti-terror laws hadn't been raised in any of them. It appeared more presentational than practical.

What was required, a senior official suggested, was closer cooperation with the European Union and recognition that the small boats issue wasn't going to be solved at a UK–France level. That relationship had 'never been warm'. There had always been reluctance from the French to have British border officials on the ground in their jurisdiction, always a sense that the UK had a 'second-hand role' in the wake of Brexit.

The UK now needed to establish shared intelligence-gathering and improve cross-border prosecution rates. It had to regain access to systems lost following the UK's departure from the EU, such as Eurodac, the database where fingerprints were registered. That would help British agencies to see whether somebody had already made a claim for asylum elsewhere in Europe or had a criminal conviction. Returning them to their country of origin was then more likely. These were the kinds of tangible actions that would shift the dial.

Several members of law enforcement lamented that ministers, no matter how well briefed, seemed to have little to no understanding about how the gangs operated. Some appeared to 'gloss over' the detail. Even the former home secretary Suella Braverman had been shaky on the rules of the asylum system and the ways in which border security worked.

One poor performance was particularly telling. At a Home Affairs Select Committee session in 2022, Conservative MP Tim Loughton set out a scenario for Braverman. He played the role of a sixteen-year-old orphan from an East African country escaping a war zone who had a sibling living legally in the UK.[6] What, Loughton asked, was a safe and legal route to come to the United Kingdom?

'We have an asylum system, and people can put in applications for asylum,' said a defiant Braverman. 'If you are able to get to the UK, you are able to put in an application for asylum.'

A straight-faced Loughton pressed on. 'I would only enter the UK illegally then, wouldn't I?' After some painfully long pauses and much bluster, Braverman, head bowed, sunken in her chair, indicated to her colleagues, inviting them to save her.

That one clip, which subsequently went viral, revealed colossal incompetence at the very heart of government. It showed that, bar a few limited, narrow schemes to bring people to Britain legally, most, like Jamal, had no choice but to risk their lives crossing the Channel by small boat. And it showed that some nationalities were considered worthy, wanted migrants while others were disregarded simply because they sounded and looked different to us.

At just after 6 a.m. on 24 February 2022, Iryna woke up, her phone flashing on the bedside table. Down the other end of the line, her brother was frantic. On state television, the Russian President Vladimir Putin had just made an early-morning address, authorising a 'special military operation': what any Ukrainian would immediately recognise as a declaration of war.

There had been 'something in the air' for days, a certain sense of tension that Iryna couldn't shake. Her husband Jeremy, a British teacher, had tried to reassure her, but she knew that he, too, was rattled. She had seen him bounding up and down the stairs, preparing the bomb shelter beneath their house. Inflatable mattresses, blankets, cushions, warm clothes, canned foods, bottled water were all stashed in the musty basement, ready, just in case. At night, Iryna had slept fitfully with their two children tucked in the middle, her younger daughter telling her that if a missile struck their home, at least this way they would die together.

Then, there it was: a wailing which rose and fell, an urgent warning to take cover. The girls whimpered, not wanting to make too much noise. Iryna and Jeremy shushed them as they made their way down to the basement. This was their new reality now. 'Life was what happened between one siren and the next.'

That same night, at around the time Iryna, Jeremy and their daughters were seeking cover, I received an unexpected late-night phone call. My source said that British nationals had been contacting them from underground bunkers, bewildered and terrified.[7] The Home Office was refusing to waive visa requirements for their Ukrainian spouses and children, fearing that extremists and Russian agents posing as refugees may try to enter the UK. All those without a British passport would need to submit their biometric data at a visa centre and pass the necessary security checks before onward travel.

From the bomb shelter underneath her house, Iryna searched for information. Jeremy and the children had British passports, but she didn't. When they called the embassy hotline in Kyiv, there was the same automated message saying that the Home Office was 'very busy'. Emails bounced back with out-of-office messages. Embassy staff had already started to evacuate and visa centres, where they could submit their biometric information, were closed. When they found the correct webpage to apply, the site continually crashed. Jeremy couldn't understand why there had been no priority given to Ukrainian family members of British nationals. They had known for weeks this might be coming. What was he supposed to do now, just leave his wife here to die?

Abandoned by the UK government and in a state of utter confusion, Jeremy, Iryna and their two daughters filled backpacks and made their way to Kyiv-Pasazhyrskyi central station, joining thousands of others packed on to the platform, waiting for a train west to Lviv. The girls clung to their parents' legs with one arm, clutching dolls in the other. When the train arrived, the crowds surged forward, shouting and shoving. Guards fired shots of blanks into the air to disperse them amid high-pitched shrieking.[8]

The family sent me messages as they made their way to safety along with the elderly and infirm, carriages packed sardine-like with cages of cats and birds, suitcases with a few items of clothing.[9] Many grasped photos in shaky hands, memories of their loved ones and the homes they may never return to. They still didn't know whether Iryna would be allowed past British border controls.

Just over a week later, Iryna and her family arrived in Britain to outcry from the general public. Headlines in the majority of newspapers were urging the government to waive visas for Ukrainians as all other European nations had already done. While the European Union had welcomed 400,000 Ukrainians, Britain had kept its borders firmly closed.[10]

The protestations that followed prompted a sudden gearshift. Three weeks after Russian missiles first struck Ukraine, a safe route was set up to bring those fleeing the bombardment to Britain. Within the first twenty-four hours of one of the schemes going live, more than 100,000 British families had offered up rooms in their houses. Communities up and down the country came together to organise cake sales, clothes collections, toy donations. They arranged convoys to bring nappies and baby clothes to the border areas. Others flew the Ukrainian flag from their windows and organised language classes for new arrivals. My son's favourite cartoon even had an episode teaching toddlers how to say 'Welcome' in Ukrainian.

Despite obvious initial flaws in the administration of the schemes, the Ukraine response was broadly viewed as a success. It showed how swiftly the government could mobilise if the political will was there and, crucially, how effective compassionate rhetoric could be in shifting the dial, influencing public opinion towards those fleeing violence in an overwhelmingly positive way.

By June 2023, Ukrainians didn't feature in the Home Office figures for small boat crossings at all because they already had adequate protection: a legal route to safety. By stark contrast, Afghans, whose nation had been retaken by the Taliban, were the top nationality for those seeking to reach the UK by small boat. The double standards were plain to see.

Batoor, a mild-mannered, softly spoken man in his early thirties, had felt an immense sense of pride in his work for the British mission in Afghanistan. Walking through Kabul to lecture at the university, ambling around its lush green gardens, had brought him great joy. Though the country was still mired in corruption, Batoor had enjoyed relative freedom, travelling to the southern provinces to lead workshops for the British Council, with security staff to protect him. As a public intellectual he felt he could criticise political figures, 'explaining what was in my heart and my mind'. All told, his educational contracts allowed him to earn a decent living, the flexible hours offering quality time at home with his wife Mina and their baby daughter Najwa.

On 15 August 2021, Batoor was on his way into the university when a colleague came rushing out, warning him to go home immediately, that the Taliban were on the periphery of the city. He brushed it off, attending his class undeterred. 'This is an academic place, not a political one,' he told his colleague.

Moments in, the dean of the faculty entered the lecture theatre, telling everybody to pack up their belongings and leave without delay. Outside the university gates, traffic jams wove down the street towards the airport. A friend called him: foreign troops had started their evacuation missions. Everybody was leaving without a passport or a visa; he should do the same.

Dressed in a formal suit and a tie, Batoor worried that his Western-style clothes would make him a target. He kept his head down, running home past the Taliban's white flags flying on the roadside. Hawkers had set up tables, ensuring all citizens had one. Religious songs blasted out of loudspeakers as Taliban fighters drove around on motorbikes, Kalashnikovs strapped across their bodies. Reaching his flat, Batoor heard bullets hitting the wrought-iron balcony outside. The Taliban were shooting into the air with jubilation.

He had known that this might be coming. The final Western troops had just withdrawn and the Taliban had been preparing to launch its attacks on Kabul, encroaching into government areas. Much of the rest of the country had already been seized, provinces collapsing like dominoes, fighters encircling military bases.

While President Ashraf Ghani had promised he wouldn't let Kabul fall to the Taliban, later that day he fled over the border to Uzbekistan, saying he wanted to avoid bloodshed.[11] Pictures circulated of Taliban commanders sitting behind Ghani's desk inside the presidential palace, flanked by armed fighters.[12] Meanwhile, smoke rose over the US embassy compound where staff were destroying confidential documents and lowering the American flag.

Less than a month later, on the twentieth anniversary of the 9/11 attacks, the Taliban flew its flags over the palace, marking its resurgence. The economy was already on the verge of collapse, with famine looming amid crushing poverty.[13] Secondary schools closed their doors to teenage girls in a rollback of rights dating to the late 1990s. Harsh Islamic punishments – stonings, amputations, public executions – returned.

Batoor felt a familiar sense of foreboding. He had been a boy when the Taliban had last held a grip on power in the late 1990s. Then there was nothing: Kabul was 'like a graveyard, rubble everywhere'. The city's 'beautiful, modern buildings' had been destroyed. Its streets were empty of people; Batoor remembers only dogs barking, nobody walking around.

Now, having worked for the British Council for several years, he knew with certainty that he would be blacklisted, considered an infidel by the Taliban. An affiliation to the West was tantamount to a death sentence. When Batoor started to receive death threats, the only option was to immediately go into hiding, separating from his wife and child for their protection and moving from house to house under cover of darkness.

Not long after that, Najwa, then just two years old, became seriously ill.[14] Mina was forced to treat her at home, banned under Taliban law from travelling without a male chaperone. Over the days that followed, Najwa's health severely deteriorated.

By the time Mina had made it to the paediatric hospital, carrying her daughter's tiny, ailing body, it was too late. There was nothing the doctors could do. Najwa's medical records show she died from acute septicaemia, liver failure and cardiac arrest. Batoor was not able to attend the hospital or go to his daughter's funeral. 'If I had not been in hiding, I would have been able to help. I am to blame.'

In fact, it was the British government that was to blame.[15] It had pledged to support Afghans like Batoor – those who had been loyal to the British mission, working as teachers, interpreters, security guards, human rights defenders, women's rights advocates, putting their lives on the line – but when it was time to go, the British government and military simply turned their backs and left. For the tens of thousands of Afghans like Batoor, it was a devastating betrayal. 'They left us here to die.'

I raised Batoor's case at a House of Commons Foreign Affairs Select Committee hearing in October 2023 as part of an inquiry into the UK's withdrawal from Afghanistan.[16] I had been invited to give evidence about the government's two resettlement schemes, which were intended to bring Afghans who had worked directly for, or alongside, the British government and military to safety in the UK.

Walking into the Palace of Westminster was an oddly disorienting experience. I had made my way through the same security gates every day during a brief stint at the No. 10 press office, en route to the twice-daily press briefings with the prime minister's spokesperson. Then, a dutiful if slightly jittery civil servant in my mid-twenties, I listened closely from the back of the poky, stiflingly hot briefing room, high up in the Gothic spire of the central tower, as lobby hacks quizzed my impressive boss. Now, though, I was in the chair, and I felt the weight of responsibility to speak up for those Afghans who had been so badly let down by the government.

I waited outside the committee room with Andrew Kidd, the kind, compassionate former head of UK Aid based in Kabul, and we discussed the questions that may come up. Before we were invited in, a clerk came out to say that the committee members would like to ask us about the situation in Israel and Palestine. Two weeks prior, on 7 October, Hamas had broken through the border wall, massacring 1,200 people and capturing 240 hostages. Israel had responded with brute force, waging a campaign of annihilation, with President Netanyahu threatening: 'The enemy will pay an unprecedented price.'[17] Within a month, Gaza had been decimated by relentless bombardments, killing over 13,000 people.

Like Afghans, Palestinians too would end up abandoned by the UK government, with the Home Office refusing to create a safe route to Britain despite considerable public pressure. Hundreds of Palestinian families in the UK resorted to crowdfunding tens of thousands of pounds for the evacuation of their loved ones.

While Andrew and I understood that the situation in the region was front-of-mind, it gave us a strong indication that Afghanistan had already slipped down the government's list of priorities.

Seated in the committee room, I knew I only had ten to fifteen minutes to answer questions and I had three key points I wanted to make. At the top of my list was what seemed to me to be an important and obvious link between the failure of the two resettlement schemes and the number of Afghans who, with no safe route open to them, had been forced to take small boats across the Channel. Not only were they the majority nationality crossing by dinghy, those who had drowned in the Channel were also predominantly Afghan.

While the government had fudged its numbers to look as though it was reaching its target of 20,000 people resettled in the UK, the facts told a different story. At the time of the hearing, a little over one hundred people had been brought to Britain under one of the schemes. (Only forty-one people had been evacuated through one pathway of the Afghan Citizens Resettlement Scheme and sixty-six through the UNHCR.) Meanwhile, Afghans who had served with, or worked for, the British mission were facing torture, kidnapping and, as in the case of Najwa, death.

There appeared to be a sense of apathy and intransigence within the government. While 540 civil servants had been moved from the Foreign Office and the Home Office to work on the Ukraine resettlement schemes, only seventeen were assigned to the two Afghan schemes. 'There is no sense that Afghanistan is any kind of priority,' a source within the Foreign Office's South Asia Directorate told me. Personal data was leaked, putting people's lives at risk. Application forms got lost. There was initial contact, then the line of communication went dead.

Many Afghans tried to cross to neighbouring countries, from where they could be assessed and resettled through the UNHCR, but the costs were prohibitive. Exploitative agencies charged $2,000 for a passport, with a further $1,500 for a visa: impossible for people who hadn't worked after two years spent in hiding. For those who did make it over the border to Pakistan or Iran, an enormous backlog of cases meant they were forced to languish in temporary accommodation while they waited to learn their fate. Corruption and nepotism remained common complaints, with bribes solicited by officials. Then Pakistan announced that it would begin rounding up Afghans and deporting them back over the border, straight into the hands of the Taliban.[18]

Sitting in the wood-panelled Select Committee room in the Commons, some members looked as though they could fall asleep.

ARRIVAL

One sat on his phone flicking through the *Telegraph*. Another left to take an extraordinarily long phone call, still lounging back on the bench outside fifteen minutes later. Others seemed more interested in the politics behind the chaos, a chance to gather evidence of Tory Party failure.

'When we were pulling this session together, the Foreign Office said that the Home Office needed to be alongside,' said Labour MP Liam Byrne. 'The Home Office was approached, but they said that the topics fell to the Foreign Office, the MoD and the Department for Levelling Up . . . The Levelling Up Department was then approached but they said it was the Home Office's job. And the Home Office said that these topics were not their responsibility. It sounds like an episode of *Yes Minister* but it's not funny.'

After we had given evidence, I waited in the chairs behind, listening to the next session with Foreign Office Minister Lord Ahmad, who had reportedly been on holiday when Kabul fell to the Taliban.[19] The committee put my points on small boats and the failed resettlement schemes directly to him.[20] 'It is not the Foreign Office that makes decisions on immigration,' he said. 'I am not sidestepping it, but it is for the Home Office to answer that.' Despite being invited, nobody from the Home Office was there to argue its case.

Afghanistan was yet another issue to be palmed off, ping-ponged between Whitehall departments. Britain had intervened militarily, then withdrawn all support to catastrophic effect. What was left in its wake was a vacuum the Taliban had inevitably filled. If not with the British government, where, I wondered, was the accountability?

Stopping the boats remained one of the Conservative government's key pledges, with little to no regard for the human consequences. Not only had it squeezed and stalled all but a few narrow safe routes; it was increasingly providing funding to overseas governments to prevent migrants from reaching the UK's border. The department responsible was the Home Office.

Working with reporter Hannah Lucinda Smith, we discovered that within Marsham Street there was a small, secret unit, 'like a mini Foreign Office', made up of around a dozen staff known as Home Office International Operations, or HOIO.[21] Its remit was to fund, equip and train border guards, including national police forces and coastguards, to cut migrants off 'upstream'. After Brexit, with no mechanism in place to return migrants, the HOIO had started to increase its activities, embedding its staff in embassies, high commissions and consulates around the world.

In Ankara and Istanbul, Home Office staff had begun to outnumber Foreign Office staff. Some diplomats begrudged their presence: they were seen as 'adversarial', rather than 'collegiate and cooperative' international negotiators, I was told by a Home Office source. Turkey was viewed as a nexus on the migration route, a key choke point to prevent Afghans and Iranians from crossing the border into Europe and travelling to Britain.

The Turkey–Iran border was known to be particularly violent. In one case, a two-year-old Afghan girl died in her father's arms after being brutally pushed back to Iran. His fingers were later amputated after they froze burying his daughter's tiny body in the snow.

Another Afghan man had been arrested on the Turkish side of the border alongside his wife and six young children. He and his sons were separated from the female members of the family before being stripped down to their underwear and forced back through a cutting in a barbed-wire fence. Turkish police officers then fired live rounds at the feet of his children as they ran away.

At around this time, a photo emerged of the UK's deputy ambassador at a ceremony, handing over nine patrol vehicles to the Turkish

National Police in Van, on Turkey's eastern border with Iran.[22] The vans were funded by the British government, redirected from the overseas aid budget, which had been slashed under Boris Johnson.

Funding 'upstream' migration programmes not only helped to prevent migrants from reaching British shores, it also allowed the Home Office to build 'soft-power credentials', said a departmental source who sat in on HOIO meetings. The government would offer its expertise and provide local border forces with evidence, showing where gangs were situated. 'It'll probably be along the lines of: "This is a route smugglers and illegal migrants use to get to the UK, we need to do more to stop it." The Turkish government will then respond by saying: "This is what we need to be able to do that," and then we fund it, basically.'

Interviews with migrants on arrival in the UK also helped. Information gathered was passed on to the Turkish border police and coastguard to 'put an operational plan in place to stop it'.

I contacted the head of Home Office International Operations, Nick Fowler, who agreed there was value in people knowing about the 'important work' of his team. Fowler suggested I attend a security conference the following week, where he would be a keynote speaker. I would, however, need to run it past the press office before he could speak to me. Shortly after that, our courteous exchange stopped. I received a snappy call from the Home Office media team, who offered a short, innocuous statement on the ways in which 'mutually beneficial close working' with international partners helped to tackle 'socially damaging issues' such as immigration. They would not, on this occasion, be providing any access to Nick Fowler or anyone in his unit.

With routes squeezed and more limited resettlement pathways, in early 2024 many people began turning to overground travel again. Lorry crossings increased. One man was electrocuted after climbing on top of a Eurostar train. Far from stopping the boats, the government had simply displaced migration, funnelling desperate people another way.

It couldn't have looked worse for the Conservative government during an election year. By summer 2024, nearly 120,000 people were waiting for an initial decision on their asylum application. Average waiting times stood at around eighteen months. Hotel costs had risen to more than £8 million a day. The UK was, once again, adrift.

6. Backlogged

*'Give voice to what you have learned:
describe the pains of your suffering race,
the abuse and agony that became commonplace
while the world's eyes were turned.'*

Saharawi poet Nadgem Said Oala[1]

Shadi thought the asylum system was like a maze. 'You go in, then you can't find your way out again,' he would say with a broad smile, eyes crinkling lightly at the edges. A striking, smooth-talking man in his early thirties, Shadi had the good fortune of making his way through the process with immaculate English, learned from a secondary-school teacher in his native Sudan, an echo from the days of empire.

Timing had been everything to Shadi. Just days before Brexit, on 31 December 2020, he had navigated the dinghy carrying him and his fellow fifty-five passengers into British waters, marking the end to an arduous ten-year journey. Though the odds had been stacked against him, he had never lost heart. More than once, he had told himself he would reach the UK. He just needed to be patient, 'to keep the faith'.

Arriving at Yarl's Wood immigration removal centre in Bedfordshire, he suddenly felt himself floating out of his body, light-headed and uncharacteristically thrown. Staring at the ceiling of his cell that first night, lying statue-still 'like a mummy', his mind raced. Was he about to be deported?

Britain had a tradition of respect for human rights, a history of law and order. He had read and learned so much about it back in Khartoum. His father even remembered British missionaries and colonial administrators strolling around in their beige safari suits. This was meant to be the land of freedom, of decency and honesty. He wasn't a criminal, so why was he being treated like one?

Any chance to sleep was interrupted by howls of distress from neighbouring detainees, banging on doors, shouting out from their nightmares. The clanging of boots on metal steps followed as guards came to reprimand them. Then the sickening metallic crunch of the key in the lock. He told himself it would all be fine. He had always managed to land on his feet, somehow.

After a restless night of tossing and turning, Shadi woke to find himself in a ball on the floor. Like so many others, after nine months in flimsy tents on the barren wasteland around Pas-de-Calais, he couldn't sleep in a bed, preferring to be grounded by the solidity of the earth beneath him. Relief washed over him when the morning buzzer went off, the heavy-duty door to his cell creaking open. Outside he saw red alarm buttons spaced no more than twenty metres apart, too many to count. There was netting all around, secured between the landings to catch those who protested or attempted to self-harm. Guards counted detainees in and out: numbers, never names.

Shadi kept his head down, following orders, gulping down some slop for breakfast. He only made eye contact when he got to the exercise area outside. Barely anybody was moving, bar a handful of people attempting to carve out a space for sit-ups, jogging on the spot to release pent-up nervous energy. Others appeared spaced out, their eyes glazed over. He overheard a group of Arabic-speaking men nearby, the familiar sounds muffled behind their masks. Standing towards the edge of the group was Basam, a timid Yemeni man, peeking out from under a thick, furrowed brow and a mop of curly jet-black hair. Shadi felt the urge to protect him, as he had his five younger siblings in Khartoum. Together, they approached the duty guards to ask if they could access their phones, speak to a solicitor, maybe call a charity, but were met by shakes of the head, stonewalled.

Four days passed in the holding facility before Shadi was brought to one of the administrative offices, fingerprinted and interviewed by a Home Office official online. The man on the other end of the video call appeared jaded, ticking off questions as he went, the interpreter barely grasping what was said over the patchy internet connection. Shadi was asked if he had any health conditions they should know about. Any diseases? Any scars? 'I said, "I'm like everybody else here – we are all sick, we are all traumatised."' Later that day, without any explanation, he was handed a plastic bag, told to gather what few belongings he had and escorted to a taxi waiting beyond the security gates. Already inside was Basam.

Driving southwards in silence, afraid to speak to his friend and not knowing whether to trust the driver, Shadi was alarmed to see motorway signs for Dover. Were they being brought back to France? Shortly before the junction for the port, the car veered uphill to a provincial town with neat rows of residential buildings and leafy cul-de-sacs. Barbed-wire fencing and security guards came into view and beyond he could see red-brick, single-storey dorms, each with tiny, blacked-out windows.

Napier barracks had opened to asylum seekers only a few months before in the midst of the second national lockdown. The Home Office move caused uproar among Folkestone's local community, with many complaining they hadn't been consulted by the council about the plans. Well-attended online meetings were held, with the opportunity for residents to put questions directly to councillors.² Couldn't they be housed elsewhere? Surely they should be immediately deported? What action was being taken to control the border?

Napier was a historic site, considered 'the birthplace of the modern British Army'. The site had once been a staging post for the Duke of Wellington's troops, and latterly a training ground and a resting place during the two world wars before servicemen headed across the Channel to the Western Front. It was inappropriate, locals warned, to place asylum seekers there.

It wasn't long before the right had co-opted the narrative. Shortly after the barracks came into use, Nigel Farage jumped on the historical bandwagon, filmed roaming around, stirring up fear and anti-migrant sentiment by claiming that Napier would soon become Britain's version of The Jungle in Calais.³ A group of far-right nationalists followed his lead, filming through the fencing. In one video uploaded to a Facebook group, a protester jibes at a new arrival: 'We don't want rapists like you around our daughters.' A prominent YouTuber racked up over 100,000 views by illegally flying a drone over the former military base, describing asylum seekers as 'terrorists', verbally attacking security guards and making a range of inaccurate statements about asylum law. Kent Police were called to disperse the crowd several times.

As their taxi pulled up outside the security-heavy gates, Shadi and Basam were hurled straight into the furore. Beyond the barbed-wire fencing they found residents on hunger strike, sleeping outdoors on the basketball court to protest against the conditions. Fears had escalated when Covid ripped through the dorms. It later emerged that half the residents – 197 of nearly 400 people – had tested positive.⁴ At breaking point, a man then set fire to one of the dormitories.⁵ Those who remained at the site were left with no electricity, heating or potable water, with many drinking from bathroom taps. It was, aid workers told me, 'a pressure cooker about to explode'.

One Sunday morning I took a train to the nearest station, looping up lanes and ambling through woodland to reach the barracks, there to speak to locals and asylum seekers caught up in the commotion. Near a military graveyard overlooking a vast bay, charity workers handed out parcels containing mini tubes of toothpaste and hand sanitiser. Seeing my notepad and dictaphone, an apprehensive Shadi approached me to ask what I knew about the Home Office waiting times. Weeks into the process, he wanted some sense of agency over his future. Helpless, I mumbled about the system being chronically under-resourced and the lack of political will. Lest I dampen his spirits, I hesitated to describe how far the situation had spiralled out of the government's hands.

At that time, early in 2021, as the UK was emerging from its third national lockdown, asylum processing had ground almost to a halt. Around 46,000 people were waiting more than six months for a decision on their claim and the queue was growing rapidly. Whenever I asked the Home Office what their staff were doing to expedite outstanding claims, they blamed Covid. The picture that emerged was of a system completely overwhelmed – not by new arrivals but by gross mismanagement. Eighteen months later, the backlog had nearly quadrupled, reaching 166,000 unprocessed claims.

With both the left and the right on their backs, the government needed to act. 'We expect to abolish the backlog of initial asylum decisions by the end of next year,' Rishi Sunak promised MPs in the House of Commons in December 2022.[6]

A slew of wild plans followed. In one, the government set up a three-day 'hackathon', convening academics, tech experts, civil servants and businesspeople to come up with ideas to reduce the backlog.[7] First prize was a ceremony with the prime minister at No. 10. One idea mooted at the competition was whether AI could be used to transcribe thousands of hours of asylum interviews to analyse trends, a suggestion which sparked concern among lawyers, academics and campaigners. The government had committed to looking at the 'face behind the case', to genuinely consider the plight of the individual before them. Was this, critics asked, a U-turn on that pledge?

Another idea, which had more legs than the Silicon Valley-esque solutions, was a questionnaire, removing the requirement for asylum seekers from five countries with high grant rates to attend a face-to-face interview.[8] The day before the questionnaire was announced, I sat in on a briefing call with the Home Office alongside around twenty-five other home affairs correspondents from across print and broadcast media. 'Let's just call this what it is – it's an amnesty, isn't it?' one reporter asked. Officials dodged the questions, skirted around the subject and talked up their latest strategy to tackle the insurmountable problem.

It was, inevitably, doomed to fail. The form needed to be filled out in English; those who had no understanding of English would have to use Google Translate. Answers were invariably gobbledygook. Forms got sent to previous or incorrect addresses. Applicants struggled to fill out and return the paperwork in the allotted twenty days, the threat of their claim being withdrawn hanging over them. Meanwhile, the number of new arrivals spiked. For decision makers struggling to get on top of their unassailable caseload, it wasn't worth the stress. Many simply downed tools and left.

Nestled between Canada Docks on the River Mersey and Anfield football ground sits a drab, glass-fronted oval building known as Redgrave Court. Every morning for the last thirty years, local Scouser Kay Hopper has followed the same routine, buzzing through the processing centre's security doors just after seven before making a cup of strong tea you could stand your spoon up in. Piled up on her desk were tens, hundreds of training manuals, some now decades old. She often still referred to them while planning sessions for new cohorts of asylum caseworkers.

A stout lady with mid-length hair which she pinned back with clips, Kay had gentle, watery-blue eyes which she tried to disguise with a brusque manner. She cared deeply about doing a good job, about appreciating how critical their roles could be to an applicant's future. 'Life or death decisions', she called them.

Trawling through considerations on individuals' asylum claims wasn't meant to be part of her job, but they were on their knees now. There weren't nearly enough recruits, and those who did make it through the training left six months later. It was the worst she'd ever known it to be.

The Home Office had started to hire decision makers through high-street recruitment agencies.[9] One she could almost see from her desk: a branch of Brooks, where kids, straight out of school, 'totally green . . . never worked a day in their lives', seemed to walk out, take a few tests and move straight into their office. Some of them had barely held down jobs in supermarkets – Aldi, Lidl, Tesco, always the same on their CVs – stacking shelves, or in customer service roles. Sometimes there were former teachers, retired police officers or social workers. They were better, but not one of them had an understanding of the asylum system and how complex it could be. What the Home Office needed to appreciate was that, yes, they needed 'bums on seats, just not arseholes'.

On Kay's watch, nobody started making decisions on asylum claims until they had been through the training modules. There was one on the 1951 Refugee Convention, another which looked at templates for best practice. She had tried to set up an academy, running a course with involvement from senior decision makers, getting the 'young ones' to shadow the experienced caseworkers, running scenario exercises, that sort of thing. But then they started bringing through sixty new recruits a month. There was no chance to consolidate any of the training. Within days, some of them were being rushed through the basics and then put in front of people who were all, in some way, severely traumatised.

Kay noticed that the quality of decision-making in Bootle had dropped. Sometimes she saw transcripts from interviews and shook her head. 'You haven't even asked them the most basic questions,' she'd tell her junior staff. Levels of written English among the caseworking team were so poor, she knew that a judge wouldn't accept their decision; she'd have to redo the whole thing herself. Hours were spent sitting with new recruits, talking them through it. If it's somebody from Eritrea, ask about the calendar system, the currency. If they're a teacher from Iraq, ask about the education system there. A taxi driver from Egypt: ask what a car licence plate looks like. It wasn't rocket science.

At times, some of her juniors showed a callousness that made her wince. 'What is it about men's backsides that attracts you?' one decision maker asked a man persecuted for his sexuality. 'When X was penetrating you, did you have an erection?' Some of them seemed intent on humiliating the applicant, framing questions in a way that was designed to catch them out. They were usually fired, but not always.

The number of cases getting overturned in court spoke volumes about the quality of interviews. She saw that there was a direct correlation between the incentives for caseworkers and the drop in calibre. A decade before, the Home Office had downgraded the position of its decision makers, meaning an immediate and significant cut to their salary. That made getting the right people in – qualified, motivated staff – even more of a challenge. It was a very highly skilled job but it just wasn't being given the respect it deserved.

Targets made it even more pressurised. They were 'busting a gut' to try to finish a case and boost productivity levels to meet the government's demands, but mistakes kept getting made. Needless to say, turnover was now the highest of any function across the Home Office. 'Worst job I ever had,' one former decision maker said on a student forum. 'Don't do it – it will ruin your life,' another warned.[10]

Kay felt there was an 'art' to decision-making. With commitment and engagement, you could learn so much about the world around you. What it was like growing up in another country. How different it could be, how difficult. Why they had left, whether through choice or not. You could also learn about the human psyche. What does someone look like when they're lying? How can you determine when somebody was, without a shadow of a doubt, telling the truth?

It was unimaginable what some of them had been through. Once a Syrian man had walked into the interview room, pulled up his top and pointed at a thick scar, still raw red, slashed diagonally across his abdomen. He had waited two years for his interview and many more for sanctuary. The last few days preparing for his interview had tormented him, he told Kay. Nights spent lying awake, anticipating questions and thinking through his answers. Then, when he showed up, there was a Sudanese interpreter who spoke an entirely different dialect of Arabic to him. The workflow team hadn't been able to find another interpreter at short notice and she had been forced to postpone the interview. The man had sobbed with anguish. All she could do was hand him a tissue.

Even after years of doing this – first at a junior level, then climbing higher to more complex cases – Kay never felt adequately prepared to deal with the consequences of the decisions they made. One day a desperate man had self-immolated outside the processing centre after a refusal. She could still see the flames licking off his shoulders, up to his ears. She had heard of others, too, who had seriously self-harmed after being denied status, children who had tried to take their own lives. Hearing those stories was what kept her up at night. That was her motivation: to 'do right' by these people.

ARRIVAL

Empathy was what lay at the heart of decision-making. There was country guidance to provide caseworkers with context, though it wasn't always easy to digest. Some staff had started referring to Lonely Planet travel guides for potted histories to help them prepare for substantive interviews.[11] Though it embarrassed her to admit it, Kay had done that too.

A case had come up of a man who had fled Western Sahara. She had never heard of it before, looking it up on Google Maps to check where it was. There, marked on the map with a dotted line, was a disputed, divided land, 'Africa's last colony', where displaced families had set up informal camps decades before. It was, and it remains, one of the most protracted refugee crises in the world.

I had long been fascinated by Western Sahara, and in February 2018 I travelled to the refugee camps to present a radio documentary for the BBC World Service, landing in a military airport in Tindouf, south-west Algeria, before daybreak.[12] I found a people entirely abandoned by the international community, forced into the desert when Spanish settlers had left in 1975 and Moroccan troops had moved in from the north. Western Sahara was now divided into two territories – the Occupied areas, still controlled by Morocco, and the Liberated Territories.

A five-hour drive from Tindouf along parched, cracked desert flatlands, past prickly shrubland and the odd lonely-looking acacia tree brought me to a wall, known by Saharawis as the 'Berm' or 'Wall of Shame', which separated the two territories. Over 7 million landmines had been planted either side, killing or maiming anybody who attempted to cross.[13] Everywhere I looked, the carcasses of burnt-out cars and artillery shells dotted the landscape: remnants of the war.

Further north-eastwards over the Algerian border lay the refugee camps, where more than 165,000 people lived, surviving on subsistence from the UNHCR.¹⁴ I stayed there for a week with Zorgan, an amiable, hospitable man who had spent the last five decades living in exile.

At night, under an inky-black sky blanketed by stars, Zorgan sang songs of love and loss, reading stories from his ancestors to his children and opening up his home to musicians, keen to keep traditional Saharawi songs alive. During the daytime, I would sit on the cushions lining the perimeter of their mud-brick house, chewing on white bread spread thick with Dairylea cheese and listening to the sandstorms whistling from beyond the metal-sheeted doors. I felt peaceful, held by the silence.

One afternoon, over several glasses of sugary green tea, Zorgan told me of the gunfire raining down from the mountains above as Moroccan troops entered his village, driving him and his family from their home.¹⁵ For eighteen days they had drunk water from a stream and slept in a valley, huddled together behind rocks as Moroccan helicopters circled overhead, lights beaming down on them. Zorgan's father, who stayed to fight alongside the Polisario Front, the nationalist liberation movement, was then captured by the Moroccan forces. He later discovered his father's fate: he had been thrown alive from a helicopter.

Zorgan, his mother and nine siblings continued on, crossing the border into Algeria. Deep in the Sahara, they set up temporary shelter by tying clothes to sticks and butchering camels to survive. 'I found myself in the desert, starving, with nothing. One person was always in my mind: my father. We had lost everything.'

I imagined an indigenous Saharawi sitting in front of Kay, who, despite her best intentions, had no idea what those like Zorgan had experienced, what oppression and brutality their people had faced under Moroccan occupation, and what that individual would have sacrificed to reach Britain's shores. I tried to track the applicant down, but navigating the complexities of the labyrinthine system proved fruitless. I could only reach dead ends.

As decision waiting times increased, I was contacted more by people with nowhere else to turn. I would tell them I couldn't speak to the Home Office on their behalf – that is, after all, not my role – and that I tend to work on longer-term investigations, exposing abuse, nepotism and failings within the asylum system. What I rarely covered were individual cases. I would usually redirect them to the Home Office, Migrant Help, contacts within charities and aid organisations or put call-outs on Twitter to link them up with a lawyer, if they didn't have representation already.

Handling individual cases is, journalistically speaking, highly complex. The rules surrounding source protection mean that I must always be careful not to identify those who speak to me. Added to that, there is a clear duty of care for those who take the time to talk to us, alongside safeguarding considerations, consent, dealing with trauma and ensuring that vulnerable contributors have the support they need, before, during and, crucially, after interview. Even if somebody waives the right to anonymity, which people do surprisingly often, I always explain that there can be ramifications for speaking to a journalist. Sometimes it can help and sometimes it can hinder.

The Home Office press office are particularly obstructive when it comes to stories about an individual's case. Each time I approach them for a right to reply – a legal requirement for each article – they tend to roll out the same line: that they require the applicant's full name, nationality, date of birth and case number for 'internal purposes'. I'm reticent to give them these details, walking a fine line between protecting highly vulnerable people and knowing that sometimes, giving the department this information, with the consent of the individual involved, can tip the balance in their favour.

During the pandemic, I was contacted by Thia Malan, an NHS consultant anaesthetist, who had spent over twenty years caring for critically ill children and babies.[16] Her husband, Peter, a South African national, had been told by the Home Office that his spousal visa application had been rejected because he was not from a majority English-speaking country. 'We are not convinced you can prove knowledge of English,' the department said in a letter to Peter, an English teacher with a degree in English literature.

When we spoke on the phone, Thia was at home on extended leave from work, under enormous strain following months on the Covid ward of a major London hospital, returning early in the morning to an empty house. 'I keep having these dreams where I'm trying to scream but not being heard, like everything is closing in on me,' she said, her voice wavering and cracking. Thia and Peter were convinced he had been given the wrong English language test for his visa application, which would have flagged up red on a decision maker's screen. They gave me their permission to hand over all the necessary details to the Home Office, which had, for days, stalled before sending me a comment for a piece I was writing. Within two days, their case had been expedited. Within a week, Peter had been granted a visa. And within three weeks, the couple were reunited in the UK.

While this was a great result, and showed the power of the media to hold government to account, it also revealed how utterly flawed the decision-making system was. Tens of thousands of other families had been left in limbo, part of the mounting, spiralling backlog, separated for months at a time during the global pandemic. I was being contacted more and more to cover their stories, but, if I did, where would it stop?

Sometimes, the lines became more blurred. In mid-2022 I was contacted by a Syrian interpreter who had worked in Turkey at the same time as me. Ali had translated for the Foreign Office and Mayday Rescue, a humanitarian organisation that supported the Syrian Civil Defence, better known as the White Helmets. He had arrived in the UK two years before on a tier-2 skilled worker visa, staying near Liverpool, where he claimed asylum. From there, in the midst of Covid, his case fell down the priority list. Panicked, he contacted me from a train station, telling me he didn't know what else to do. 'Even though I was vetted by the Foreign Office, the Home Office still asked for an accent expert to double-check I'm Syrian. Why would one part of the British government trust me to translate highly sensitive material but not trust another branch of the government that I am who I say I am? It makes no sense.'[17]

Ali's mother had recently been arrested and interrogated in a regime prison in Syria; he and his family had become targets due to his work for the British government. 'She is now too terrified to speak to me, worried the line is being monitored. She's traumatised and feels she is being watched . . . and I have no security here, which makes it even worse.'[18]

With his consent, I gave the Home Office Ali's details so they could conduct their 'internal investigations'. Four days later, as I was picking my son up from nursery, I had another call: Ali was on his way to his solicitor's office to pick up a grant letter from the Home Office. He had five years' leave to remain.

As overjoyed as I was for him, I couldn't help but feel a pang of anger, injustice and guilt for all those I couldn't write about. I felt strongly that this was not how a functioning system should operate.

An immigration barrister later told me that, when accessing his client's Home Office files, he saw a box which needed to be ticked: 'Media interest: Yes or No?'. Kay acknowledged that this was standard practice. 'If a journalist has asked about an individual's case, it'll come into the senior caseworker's inbox and we'll say: "This is high-profile", so the case gets looked at quicker.' While I and many others had our suspicions, it was strange to hear them confirmed.

*

One day in summer 2023, I turned my phone on to find a message. 'I just got my leave to remain. Finally.' It was Shadi, in shock. He had waited two and a half years for his decision. The first line of the letter from the Home Office, which he screen-grabbed and sent me, read: 'Unfortunately your application for refugee protection has been refused.' With his heart in his mouth, he read on, the words swimming around on the page. 'However your claim for humanitarian protection has been accepted.'

A colossal war was ravaging Sudan, the largest humanitarian and displacement crisis in the world. Millions of families had fled over the border towards Chad, South Sudan and Egypt amid airstrikes, drone strikes, tanks and heavy artillery fire.[19] Those who escaped told of street battles raging through suburbs and villages, with snipers shooting as people ran for cover. There were widespread war crimes, massacres, sexual violence and the burning of homes. In Darfur, devastated twenty years prior, at least 10,000 people were deliberately targeted in a campaign of ethnic cleansing waged by the paramilitary group, the Rapid Support Forces. In the West there was a muted response, a sense of a savage conflict in distant lands, dubbed 'the forgotten war' by international media outlets.

Watching the destruction of the Republican Palace in downtown Khartoum and the shelling which had demolished Souq Omdurman, where he had often shopped with his mother, Shadi had never felt so far from home. His family had been scattered across the region and beyond, his nephews and nieces divided from their parents. Some were in South Sudan, others in Oman, separated when they needed each other most. Meanwhile he was safe and he had some form of international protection, albeit not the refugee status that would have allowed him the Convention documents to travel to see his family.[20]

Though he tried not to think too much about it, he couldn't help but notice that many of his Sudanese friends were also being denied refugee status and given the slightly inferior grant of humanitarian protection, which fell under a different legal framework. Perhaps the

Home Office thought people from Sudan wouldn't face serious harm if they were returned, or maybe it was because he and his friends had arrived before the outbreak of conflict. They would never know.

Shadi wondered whether he had been given 'HP' because of his 'tribe'. He was Nubian, a distinct ethnic group that could trace its history back to the pharaohs. When the war broke out, his father had fled to Dongola in Sudan's north, an ancient land dotted with hundreds of pyramids, sandstone sculptures rising from the earth, their spectacular columns etched with inscriptions from Tutankhamun.[21] Here, one of Africa's earliest civilisations had risen up, its kings, known as 'Black Pharaohs', ruling the vast territory stretching from Aswan in southern Egypt to modern-day Khartoum. Dongola had been the capital of medieval Nubia, a fortressed kingdom with palaces, churches, domed tombs or *qubbas*, a major stopping point for caravans of camels transporting ivory between Sudan and Egypt.

In the 1950s, during the days of the British empire, the region's vital life source – the Nile – had been dammed, flooding the Nubians' homelands in southern Egypt. A gigantic man-made lake, Lake Nasser, was created. On a reporting trip for the BBC in 2017 I visited Kom Ombo, a sprinkling of villages on the northernmost edge of the lake, where tens of thousands of displaced Nubians had been forced to relocate, scavenging for scraps to survive.[22]

A stone's throw from the border with Sudan was Abu Simbel, a magnificent village rich in agriculture. There, I went out fishing for tilapia on the lake with a local musician, Fikri Kachif, and wandered with him around the breathtaking thirteenth-century monuments built for Ramesses II, relocated stone by stone after the original land had been submerged.

In the evening, I sat with Fikri under the date palms looking out on to the lake.[23] He pointed to the distance, where Sudan meets Egypt. Though the land was rich in gold, limestone, clay and granite, Fikri worried that Nubians were becoming further marginalised, pushed away by foreign investors seeking to plunder their resources.

Now that Sudan was in the midst of war, Abu Simbel was to be the next destination for Shadi's father. Fleeing over the border on rough terrain, he had just one last checkpoint to pass through, where he was asked to show his passport. Volatile military guards asked him where he was from, immediately identifying him as a darker-skinned Nubian. They removed him from the car, beating and racially abusing him, accusing him of being part of the paramilitary Rapid Support Forces. When they were finished, they left him in a ball on the side of the road. A local family brought him to their home, tending to his wounds. A few days later, Shadi's father boarded a ferry, crossing the Nile with conflicting feelings of betrayal and relief.

Shadi had told the asylum decision maker all of this – that, as a Nubian, he and his family were at heightened risk, that his father could have been killed, that they had faced generations of persecution – but it had been swiftly passed over. These, seemingly, were not grounds for a grant of refugee status. He was instead asked questions from a stock list on Sudan: the names of roads, the biggest building in Khartoum. Why, he wondered, did these people not get taught about the lands they had once occupied, as he had learned about Britain? Why did they not know of all the suffering Sudan and its people had endured?

Meanwhile, Britain's debt of honour accrued. The Home Office said it would not consider a bespoke pathway for those fleeing Sudan to reach the UK. Amid brutal conflict, Shadi would remain separated from his family, unable to travel or be reunited with them for many months, possibly years, to come.

Something else about Shadi's grant of status drew my attention: the timing. I had noticed that long-awaited decisions were being pushed through at a much faster pace. Though at the time nobody at the Home Office would confirm it, I heard from numerous caseworkers that so-called 'legacy cases', of claims made before 28 June 2022 like Shadi's, were being rushed along to meet Rishi Sunak's target of clearing the backlog by the end of 2023.

Not only was the Home Office granting legacy claims en masse, it was also withdrawing them from the system entirely. Over the course of 2023, nearly 25,000 asylum claims were withdrawn – a quarter of all applications – after the department accused people of absconding, missing asylum interviews or failing to respond to questionnaires.[24] All those who arrived through irregular routes after 20 July 2023 – the day the Illegal Migration Act came into force – would be automatically deemed 'inadmissible', their claims never assessed in the UK and with no possibility of being granted leave to remain or becoming British citizens.

Among those still in the backlog were the 175,000 people waiting for an initial decision, and the tens of thousands languishing in hotel rooms, desperate to move on with their lives. They were sitting ducks for attacks from the far right.

PART THREE
DISPERSAL

7. No Room

*'The ache for home lives in all of us. The safe place
where we can go as we are and not be questioned.'*

Maya Angelou,
All God's Children Need Travelling Shoes

Just off an industrial estate on the outskirts of Liverpool, between an Amazon distribution hub and a tangle of congested A-roads, stands a four-star spa hotel. Incongruous with its surroundings, The Suites had long been a popular location for lavish wedding receptions and weekend breaks at knock-down prices.

It came as something of a shock to Scouse cabbie Chris when one day he had a call from the receptionist there to tell him they would need to cancel his daughter's wedding celebrations. They offered a full refund and told him they would be closing their doors to the public for the foreseeable future. Nobody could tell him why, but word gets round quickly in Knowsley. It wasn't long before Chris had heard exactly what had happened: they were moving asylum seekers into The Suites. It was 'locals out, immigrants in'.

He was fuming. Not only had his daughter been let down; this was going to floor his business. Chris had been shuttling people to and from the hotel for years. There was a cost-of-living crisis, energy bills had skyrocketed, housing was in a mess. Times were already tough enough for the community. Knowsley didn't register on many people's radars, but they all knew the realities. This was the second-most deprived local authority area in England, home to over 150,000 residents, including more than 1,500 who relied on food banks.[1] Hotels had provided employment for hundreds of people in hospitality, cleaning and transportation, hard workers who earned an honest, decent living. And it wasn't just that one either. Four other major hotels in Liverpool's city centre had shut down for migrants too.

A month later, a WhatsApp message pinged through on one of Chris's group chats. It was a video of what looked like a fifteen-year-old girl being harassed in the street. The message below said that the man accosting her was an asylum seeker staying at The Suites hotel. Chris thought it was disgusting, coming in here, approaching our schoolgirls in the street. Anything could happen to them. Imagine if that was your daughter; he'd wring the guy's neck. More videos and voice memos followed, then an invitation to join a peaceful protest outside the hotel that Friday evening. Nobody else appeared to be listening to local people, the message read. They needed to 'make them listen'.[2]

It started off peacefully enough. Shortly after 6.30, a small gathering convened at the gates, but the crowd grew rapidly. People started rattling the metal fencing, kicking and punching it. One man had brought what looked like grenades – canisters that exploded on impact – which he threw over the fence towards the windows of the hotel. A man with a sledgehammer started smashing the bonnet of a police van. Then there were flames whipping up the side of it, lit fireworks going off.[3]

Inside the hotel, Iranian-Kurdish arrival Arian had been unpacking his belongings, settling in for the third night at The Suites since being dispersed north-west. Hearing commotion in the lobby, he made his way downstairs to find a crowd gathered around a fellow Kurdish man who had returned moments before. Rocks had been thrown at him as he entered the security gates, he told the group. Another man described how he had been chased on a moped and verbally abused near a petrol station shop that morning.

Peering out the windows, the residents could see a group – already 400, 500 people – near the perimeter fencing, shouting something like 'Get them out'.[4] Arian wondered whether the cries were directed at the hotel staff, instructing them to relocate the residents, or if it was aimed at them, to get them out of the hotel, the area, the country.

Across the car park he could see flames. Rioters were attempting to break down the metal fencing to get into the property. Hotel staff locked and bolted the doors, warning Arian and the growing number of perplexed, frightened residents in the lobby not to go outside for their own safety.

For more than four hours the mob, led by the neo-Nazi fascist movement Patriotic Alternative, whipped up hatred against those staying inside. Riot police outside were targeted with missiles, kicked and threatened. Among the protesters were three teenagers, including one boy of thirteen who was later charged with violent disorder.[5] For Chris, it had all got a bit out of hand; he had made a sharp exit before it got 'too messy'.

Two weeks after the Knowsley riots, I went to meet Arian at the gates of the hotel. A handful of security guards were patrolling the perimeter wearing stab vests, comms radios clipped to their jackets.

Arian and I ventured towards the city centre on the bus, winding through Everton past abandoned buildings and a branch of Home Bargains where he liked to buy cheap sugary snacks. A group of five teenage boys clustered around us, kicking Arian's feet and flicking his hair. Several times I asked them to stop. When they persisted I felt the heat rising, burning in my body. We got off and waited at the shelter, huddled under our hoods. One bus drove past us, then another, and another. All of them appeared fairly empty. 'This is normal for us,' Arian told me with a shrug. 'Buses never stop for foreigners.'

Later in the week, I was put in touch with someone who had worked at The Suites and some of the other hotels in the area. My contact had been employed by Serco, the Home Office subcontractor awarded a ten-year, £1.9 billion contract to manage asylum accommodation and support across the country.[6] I was warned that this source had never spoken to a journalist before and was particularly nervous, but they felt compelled to speak out about what they had witnessed.

What followed was an extraordinary series of revelations. My contact said that during one particular shift, they had seen senior Serco staff chase an asylum seeker diagnosed with schizophrenia into his hotel room, then kick and rattle the handle and shout abuse at him from behind the locked door. 'You've got someone with paranoid schizophrenia being told: "If I see you outside, you'd better run", then kicking his door to intimidate him and laughing about it when he got distressed,' they told me, still outraged. 'It's verbally and psychologically very, very aggressive behaviour. The power dynamics are stacked against the service users.'

Other staff, former and current, came forward to speak to me. One told me that on the night of the Knowsley riots, a senior Serco staff member had said he 'wanted to be there', allegedly claiming that if the protests took place outside their hotel, they would join in. The source said that racist language such as 'sand niggers' was routinely used by staff to address residents in the hotels, with some denying children water and food outside mealtimes. Anyone who requested support was told to 'fuck off and call Migrant Help'.

Over the weeks that followed I corroborated these accounts, and many more, with a growing list of sources. I was sent contracts and other documents, messages, photos, and I had the full names of the perpetrators, dates and locations of the alleged incidents.

Following the advice of my editor at the *Observer*, I gave the list of names to Serco. It wasn't long before legal threats started rolling in. A senior legal director at the paper was contacted, stating that Serco had not had a fair opportunity to respond and that the company had not been made aware of the allegations we proposed to publish. (I had been in contact, with clearly set-out allegations, for over a fortnight.) The company refuted all the allegations, stating that it had 'rigorously investigated the claims . . . and found that they are without foundation'. No complaints had been made by any asylum seekers through any of Serco's 'comprehensive, robust and independent complaint procedures', the company said.

Despite strong pushback, my editors still wanted to run it. They believed there was a strong public-interest argument in letting readers know about the conditions and treatment of those inside The Suites and other hotels in Liverpool. I was buoyed up.

On the Saturday morning ahead of online publication, I reread the copy, mulling over what the ramifications could be. Did I have complete confidence in my sources? Had I got hold of all the supporting evidence I could to verify what they had told me? Did I have dates, names, locations exactly right? I nervously painted furniture outside, repeatedly checking my phone. At 3 p.m., a breaking news alert popped up.[7]

There was immediate condemnation from the general public. Then, two weeks after publication, I received a message from one of my sources to say that all but two of the alleged perpetrators had been fired. The others had meetings and were also likely to be let go.

Serco was still on my tail, asking me to remove posts on social media and issue corrections to the copy, which would serve to weaken the reporting. 'Can you confirm that X is still working for Serco?' I emailed back. 'It is correct that this individual has left the business, however the reasons are unrelated to the claims that you have made and the connection that you have made in your tweet is invalid,' came the terse reply.[8] They couldn't say more because all of the individuals I named had already been fired. My posts remained online.[9]

The Knowsley riots marked a gearshift in the way asylum hotels were targeted. A wave of far-right attacks followed. In the area around The Suites hotel, police recorded fifteen attacks in the weeks after the riots, leading to a curfew for residents after dark.[10]

One of the more virulent piggy-back riots was in Skegness, a downtrodden seaside town in Lincolnshire suffering the effects of years of austerity, cuts to public services and an acute housing shortage.[11] When I visited over a busy Easter weekend, the pleasure beach promenade with its funfair and donkey rides had queues round the block. There was an abundance of mobility scooters and arcade slot machines, Funland bingo halls and fudge factories lining the beachfront. It was a town of faded grandeur – perhaps more faded than it ever was grand – still wholly reliant on British tourism to survive.

At the North Parade hotel on the beachfront, manager Julianne told me that the protests in Skegness, which had gathered around a hundred local people, had unnerved some of her customers. 'My regulars have started calling me up to ask if it's safe to come in the summer. I tell them, "You came here last year when they were here and there were no problems." My problem isn't the migrants, it's the media who are making it seem like there's an issue when there isn't.'

Just down the road at another hotel, manager John agreed that any dent in his profits was down to perceptions, rather than the new arrivals themselves. 'Some of my regulars say, "Oh, Skegness isn't the same town it used to be", when it is. We've got 150 people maximum in four hotels across the whole town. It's not that much, is it?' The four hotels housing migrants were 'repos', or repossessions, which had been out of use long before they were converted into asylum accommodation.

I had my own concerns about some of the media coverage surrounding the hotels, largely because of the way in which it exposed vulnerable people to increased risk in an already turbulent climate. Irresponsible coverage had started to appear more frequently. In one broadsheet article, a child was photographed in front of their hotel, with the caption identifying them by name, age and country of origin. Calls to take the photograph down were refused.

Far-right violence surrounding the hotels continued to blight the next government. On 29 July 2024, less than a month after Labour had taken the reins, a mass-stabbing incident took place at a Taylor Swift-themed dance class in the Merseyside town of Southport, leaving three children dead and eight seriously injured. Racially fuelled riots swiftly followed, after a surge of misinformation appeared online, claiming that the seventeen-year-old suspected of murder, Axel Muganwa Rudakubana, was an asylum seeker who had arrived in the UK by small boat.[12] (He was, in fact, born in Cardiff.)

Less than two hours after mourners gathered in Southport to honour the children killed in the brutal attack, hundreds of rioters flooded the streets of the town, throwing bricks at a mosque, attacking police and setting cars on fire. Two days later, more than 200 far-right extremists surrounded an asylum hotel in Aldershot, chanting racist abuse and throwing objects in what Hampshire Police called a 'mob-type' riot. Images of seven people were released to the public in a bid to identify those engaged in criminal activity[13] amid calls to strengthen security outside mosques and hotels housing asylum seekers.

By the following weekend the violence had spread across the country. In Rotherham, thugs set fire to a hotel, launching petrol bombs and fireworks and attacking police vehicles nearby. Children and asylum seekers with disabilities were told to remain inside the premises.

Two asylum seekers later said that they had to put fires out themselves, while the majority of staff working for the Home Office subcontractor Mears were evacuated from the building. The same day, in Tamworth in Staffordshire, a mob smashed their way into asylum accommodation wielding bricks and missiles. The hotel walls were left covered in racist graffiti.

A contact at an asylum support centre in Liverpool got in touch with me to say it had been forced to close its doors temporarily after decades supporting the local migrant community. Rioters had gathered outside the centre, preparing to attack those going in and out. When I tried to reach them by email, I received an automated reply. 'Do not come to the centre,' it warned. 'It is not safe.'

I too became exposed to some of the far right's hate. Over the course of a particularly difficult weekend, while looking after my sick child, I received a stream of messages on social media, then emails, then WhatsApp messages. The language used in many of the messages ('libtard' featured prominently) was right out of the Trumpian white supremacist playbook. One of the more sinister emails told me they knew where I lived and where my son went to nursery and would harm him, then 'come for you and fuck you up'. Based on advice from the police, lawyers and editors, I took measures to protect my family, but it wouldn't be the last time I got caught in the crosshairs.

The risks I faced were nothing compared to those of the hundreds of lone children placed in hotels for adults. In October 2022, ministers admitted that they had no idea of the whereabouts of 222 vulnerable children the government was meant to be protecting.[14] Three months later, it emerged that dozens of asylum-seeking children had been kidnapped from a single hotel in Brighton and exploited into criminal gangs, including county lines drug trafficking.[15]

The scandal caused outcry from across the political spectrum and led to a coalition of charities launching legal action against the home secretary and Kent County Council, the local authority which has a duty of care to lone asylum-seeking children who arrive by small boat.[16] 'There is a serious possibility that a criminal offence is being committed by hotel owners contracted by the Secretary of State to manage what are de facto unregistered children's homes,' said one of the charities, ECPAT. While the challenge rumbled on, a hundred more children were, once again, unlawfully placed in adult accommodation.[17]

By January 2024, that figure had ballooned: one report showed that over 1,300 child asylum seekers might have been wrongly identified as adults and placed in unsupervised adult accommodation.[18] Among them was unaccompanied Afghan teenager Jamal.

Arriving at a hotel near Warrington on the banks of the River Mersey, he was given his room number and handed an armful of folded sheets and a blanket. Upstairs on the third floor, a light blinked in the corridor and there was shouting and a discernible thud from behind one of the closed doors. Finding the room, he knocked, calling out, his heart racing. Inside were two bunk beds shoved against the walls either side of the room. His three roommates were all Kurdish men in their late thirties, maybe early forties, who spoke the same language, loudly, and throughout the night. Jamal mentioned this to the manager downstairs, reiterating that he was still just sixteen. He was warned that if he refused the room he could face destitution. Despite clear safeguarding concerns, there was no other choice.

In one particularly cruel asylum hotel, inspectors found that managers had gathered dozens of children together, forcing them to play a sick little game. Whoever correctly guessed the next person to leave for a foster care placement would win.[19] What they won was unknown. Those forced to remain in the hotel were understandably crushed, the rejection weighing heavily on them. As part of the same inspection, it was found that staff in at least four asylum hotels had failed to have regular DBS checks, as was required by law. At least 147 children across these hotels chose to run away and disappear.[20]

Social workers and charity staff despaired. Every day they were making safeguarding referrals, which often went unanswered. Local authorities, under pressure and with budgets slashed, didn't have the capacity to visit children, whose age might have been obvious to them if they had. A reassessment simply took too long and cost too much money. 'Councils tell us they know someone's under eighteen, but they can't do anything about it,' one youth support worker told me. 'We need to be properly resourcing local authorities to provide safe, secure accommodation rather than lining the pockets of the private-sector companies running them.'

Kent County Council, which was overwhelmed by the rising numbers of age-disputed children arriving in their local authority areas, batted cases away to the Home Office. But, the department said, it didn't have the mandate to be caring for children: that fell to the Department for Education. Why was the department for immigration enforcement taking decisions on the care of children at all? Meanwhile, hundreds of vulnerable young people were left in freefall, with nobody at a governmental level willing to take responsibility for them.

'There is no asylum accommodation strategy at the Home Office,' David Neal, the beleaguered watchdog told the *Financial Times*. 'They don't identify the lessons, they don't learn the lessons. The Home Office doesn't want to change.'[21]

The over-reliance on so-called 'asylum hotels' had quickly become a major political issue. Before the pandemic hit in spring 2020, most asylum seekers had been placed in houses and flats while they waited for their claims to be processed, but the social distancing guidelines meant that local authorities were mandated to broaden their range of accommodation structures. At the end of March 2020 there were around 1,200 asylum seekers with claims pending in hotels. Six months later that figure had skyrocketed to 9,500 people. By the summer of 2023, more than 50,000 were housed at over 400 hotels around the UK, at a cost of more than £8 million a day.[22] Alongside the optics associated with the boat crossings themselves, polling consistently showed that hotel use was one of the government's most contentious policies, drawing widespread condemnation among swathes of the general public.

While the dispersal process had always been unfair to asylum seekers and the communities in which they were placed, it became clear that the spread of asylum hotels across the UK was politically skewed. 'They've got to be in non-Tory areas,' a Home Office official told me over coffee one winter's day. 'It's politically toxic – she [Suella Braverman] doesn't want them anywhere near Tory seats.' Many deprived communities, already struggling following years of austerity and cuts to public services, felt that they had simply become dumping grounds for migrants.

The decision about where to house new arrivals wasn't only a political calculation; it was a budgetary one too. Ministers were at pains to show that they were doing what they could to keep costs low. Accommodating asylum seekers in cheaper parts of the country was the answer.

But where was all the money coming from? As half the world's population, including more than a billion children, struggled to survive on less than $2 a day,[23] and in spite of Britain's commitment to spend 0.7 per cent of its GDP on aid, one-third of the international aid budget was diverted towards asylum hotels. 'The government must put the UK's aid budget beyond the reach of the Home Office,' the International Development Select Committee warned.[24] 'The world's poorest people are being short-changed while other government departments raid the FCDO's [Foreign, Commonwealth and Development Office] aid budget.'

The three Home Office subcontractors providing asylum accommodation – Serco, Mears and Clearsprings Ready Homes – laughed all the way to the bank. To the year ending January 2024, Clearsprings boosted its profits from just over £60 million to £90 million.[25] Mears adjusted its profits before tax to £43 million,[26] while Serco's underlying operating profit increased to £270 million.[27]

Hotel providers, meanwhile, were looking for ways to cut costs to ensure maximum profit margins for them and their shareholders. One hotel near my house in south London, which I have visited frequently over the last few years, cut back its staff to eight rather than the fifty-plus they had before they closed their doors to the public. There were no cleaners, no waiting staff, few reception staff and one security guard hired by the subcontractor G4S, who sat watching YouTube videos as people signed themselves in and out. Meals were brought in from external companies three times a day. The pared-back hotel staff have very little, if anything, to do.

Where profit trumps all, conditions were predictably poor. Food was often inedible – it is by far the most frequent complaint I have heard over the years. I have been sent countless photos of the meals on offer: chips for lunch, chips for dinner. Raw chicken. Undercooked, cold burgers. No fruit or vegetables for months at a time. When apples were brought to one hotel, some had maggots crawling in them. Children refused to eat and pregnant women got sick. A consultant obstetrician called me, concerned that expecting and breastfeeding mothers were becoming malnourished.

Critics and campaigners repeatedly called for a phased withdrawal from hotels, diverting the money from profiteering private-sector companies and individuals to local authorities, but their warnings fell on deaf ears.

In Dickens' industrial novel *Hard Times*, Preston – or 'Coketown' as he names it – is a 'sulky blotch' of red-brick warehouses and tall chimneys, 'a blur of soot and smoke'.[28] Its oppressed workers, or 'Hands', are seen as useful tools to keep industry going and there is a certain dull, monotonous thrum to the language, 'a rattling and a trembling all day long'. Shortly after a visit to Preston to meet striking workers, Dickens described the streets as being 'inhabited by people equally like one another, who all went in and out at the same hours, with the same sound upon the same pavements, to do the same work, and to whom every day was the same as yesterday and tomorrow'.[29]

I walked through some of the streets Dickens described with Dave Savage, an affable, ebullient man and a prominent member of Preston's arm of the Trades Union Congress. He showed me the foundry where his dad used to work – 'backbreaking work' – employing 7,000 people before Margaret Thatcher closed it down in the mid-1980s. 'That was it, he was thrown on to the dole.'

Then British Aerospace came in, building Tornado jets for the RAF; it was a moment of hope, offering jobs to thousands of people, 'skilled work, properly paid'. That quickly disappeared too when in 1990 the aerospace plant was closed. 'This closure will have a devastating effect on the Preston area,' Labour members said in an early day motion.[30]

It did. Now there were few places left to look for work in Preston except for call centres. 'Reading out scripts, Ts and Cs, that sort of thing.' Staff turnover was high and rising. Young people left for other cities where they might be able to find better – and better-paid – jobs. 'That's the lived experience of so many people round here.'

Preston still had thriving workers' clubs, which Dave and many of his friends often drank at. Politics was a bit of a 'dirty word' there – there wasn't anyone, from any party, that really listened, understood and represented them. What did politicians know about normal, working people in post-industrial towns? 'Nothing, they know nothing. They're all millionaires. They belong to the Westminster world.'

In this context – with a severe housing shortage, high unemployment, poor infrastructure, soaring food bills, record high NHS waiting lists – new arrivals were not always welcomed. Years before, during the so-called Syrian refugee crisis of 2015, Dave had heard that the English Defence League was planning to visit Preston to take to the streets and protest. He and other union members had organised a counter-protest, with 1,000 people showing up. 'Multi-nationality, multi-faith, with food from all over the place. It just goes to show, we can mobilise against them.'

Housing was now the major issue in Preston. The terraced, two-up, two-down houses around the foundry had long since been sold off to private landlords. The energetic great-grandmother who ran the BnB I stayed at told me her son had bought up cheap properties years before and rented them out to Serco. It was good money. After basic refurbishments, he hadn't had to do anything else. Any complaints were made through the Migrant Help advice line for asylum seekers; the landlord pocketed the bulk of the profits.

But supply wasn't keeping up with demand. What was available was often crumbling, low-quality accommodation, inappropriate to the needs of the occupants. In the winter of 2024, the Qadir family were moved into self-catered accommodation on the edge of Preston. I went to visit them, a forty-minute bus journey from the town centre past boarded-up pubs and shuttered-up shops.

Parwen had bought glasses for tea and tiny china cups for coffee, a tray and little silver bowls for the many sweet treats she had made. The children busied themselves, giggling and chatting as they drew pictures, Blu-Tacking them to the walls to cover up the stains. In the living area, Dara showed me a large mushroom growing between the floorboards and the wall. Migrant Help hadn't answered their calls and the council had been slow to respond. Dara had tried to cut it away, but all he could do was watch as the damp worsened and the fungus grew back again.

Others messaged me to say that their boilers had broken, there were leaks, there was mould. For a while, I became a conduit between local councils and families who had been ignored. One Syrian family had had their windows smashed; they went for over a week with draughts and driving rain coming in through the tape, fearful of their security. Councils, many facing bankruptcy, had few resources to handle the number of cases on their desks.

Even if new arrivals managed to forgo a pleasant, safe living environment, many were eventually moved on. At a drop-in run by the British Red Cross on the outskirts of Preston, slightly to the east of Blackpool Tower, I met a Nigerian man with five children, one of whom was critically ill. His child had been receiving treatment at the local hospital, while his other children attended schools nearby. Out of the blue, the family had received an eviction notice from Serco. With no explanation, they were told they were being moved to a different home in the south of England. 'We know the doctors here, we know the teachers,' the distressed father told me. 'We've already had to move three times. How can we settle in one area and start our lives if we keep being moved?'

The problem was, every time the Home Office looked at alternative accommodation arrangements there were setbacks.

In August 2023, as part of its 'small boats week' to show the government was committed to moving asylum seekers out of hotels, the department announced it would send up to 500 men on to the *Bibby Stockholm* barge in Portland, Dorset. The barge had been intended to cut the costs of asylum accommodation and move hundreds out of expensive hotels, but embarrassment followed when, just four days later, a deadly strain of legionella was detected in the water system. All those who had been moved on were swiftly moved off.[31] The empty barge sat moored in the port for over two months, at a cost of almost £300,000 a week.

Meanwhile, an inspection of the *Bibby Stockholm* by Dorset and Wiltshire Fire Service found that lives could be put at risk because there were too few fire escapes and air vents.[32] The barge was dubbed the 'floating Grenfell', in reference to the fire that had engulfed Grenfell Tower, a residential London tower block, on 14 June 2017, killing seventy-two people. Then the local mayor, Carralyn Parkes, brought a legal challenge against the Home Office to the High Court, claiming that its use of the *Bibby Stockholm* to accommodate asylum seekers was in breach of planning rules. (She later lost her case.[33]) Further incompetence was exposed when new figures emerged, showing the average cost of a room on the barge was 10 per cent more than a hotel, despite the subcontractor's best efforts to cram more people in by putting bunk beds in each room to double the capacity.[34]

Local Dorset residents began contacting me, inviting me to join closed Facebook groups and WhatsApp conversations. Members of the 'No to the Barge' group were particularly active, sometimes with hundreds of comments a day. Often the posts were logistical, spreading the word about protests taking place down at the port or sharing articles, but more typically the online content was a place to vent their frustrations. 'Not long before there's a rape on the barge,' one woman raged. 'I'm sorry if I appear ignorant, but are they all criminals?' another asked, to which respondents answered with a resounding 'yes'. At a packed-out local council meeting, which I watched livestreamed on the Facebook group, many backed a vote of no confidence in Dorset Council, with outraged audience members standing up, pointing and accusing the authorities of 'lying to [our] faces'.[35]

A month later, Leonard Farruku, an Albanian asylum seeker, was found dead in a shower room, in a suspected suicide. Shortly after the news broke, I attended an event in the House of Commons, where one of Leonard's friends, who had been placed on the barge at the same time, was speaking. Ali had had serious concerns about being moved to the *Bibby Stockholm*, believing that the situation could 'easily go awry'. Ali identified as non-binary and had already faced multiple instances of verbal and racial abuse. 'I didn't need another thing to survive,' they told the audience, which included several Labour MPs. 'I had already survived enough.'

Every day, those on board the barge went out for a walk. When they returned they were searched and asked to walk through security scanners. While residents were free to come and go, the checks and heavy surveillance made Ali feel as though they were being detained, 'like it was the most legal way of putting us in jail'.

Leonard hadn't been the only person who was suicidal that night. Another man had reportedly been calling out for help but was told by guards to keep quiet. The next day, after Leonard's body had been discovered, Sarah, a member of the catering staff, was on pot-wash duty in the kitchen. She described hearing chefs laughing and saying: 'That's one less Muslim to feed.'

There were, she added, 'constant racist undertones' among the staff working on the *Bibby Stockholm*. At one point, she was pulled aside by the manager and warned that she was putting herself at risk for speaking to the residents. 'They look at you like you're meat,' she was told. Sarah was later let go from her position for what she believes was being 'too friendly, talking to the residents'.

At a local level, the town had become divided by the new arrivals. It was, one community member speaking at the Commons event said, 'the most serious threat of racial tension anyone in Dorset can remember'. Far-right activity elsewhere in the country – Knowsley, Skegness – had spilled over into their area, with groups travelling down to Portland to harass asylum seekers whenever they left the barge. One man had been accused of being a rapist while out for a kebab at a Turkish takeaway restaurant. Schoolchildren had huddled around the port, whispering and shouting taunts at the passing migrants.

Dorset Council had been provided with funding from central government to run activities for the men on board, but nothing had ever seemed to materialise. In fact, no money had been saved, only lost. Then, in July 2024, Labour announced that the barge was to be closed, adding that it would have cost £20 million to keep it open. The move was widely celebrated. The Tories' headline-grabbing plans had been in nobody's interests: they hadn't served asylum seekers, or local communities, or the government.

At around the same time as the barge was moored on the South Coast, the Home Office was facing yet more controversy elsewhere in the country. Two former RAF bases – one in Wethersfield in Essex and the other in Scampton in Lincolnshire – had been secured to house new arrivals, leading to further legal challenges and protests.

In April 2023, a gathering in Scampton, which featured speakers such as the Patriotic Alternative member Alek Yerbury, unsurprisingly ended in clashes. 'We have shown [the Home Office] that if they are not prepared to resolve this problem, we will do it ourselves,' he told the baying crowd.[36] The historic site should be protected, the protesters argued; the Red Arrows and the Second World War Dambusters squadron had once been based there. A group predominantly made up from people beyond the local community set up a camp outside the site, where they remained around the clock for months on end. Eventually, Labour closed the site, stating that, at a cost of £122 million, it didn't represent value for money.

Meanwhile Wethersfield airbase, where 500 men were placed three to a room in metal containers, was encircled by security fences, with no pedestrian access or public transport to the nearest town. Gunshots could be heard from the rifle range nearby. There were multiple claims of security guards assaulting asylum seekers. Five people attempted to take their lives there. One man was only allowed to leave when his wife delivered a stillborn baby.[37] By the winter of 2023, Médecins Sans Frontières, which operated in conflict zones and refugee camps, began its first programme in the UK, holding weekly surgeries on the site.[38]

Internally, the department was struggling to come up with other options. 'A lot of scrabbling around looking for anywhere that isn't a hotel,' a former colleague messaged one evening. 'We've basically been told to look at where government already owns buildings/land, where it wouldn't cost anything or take up social housing stock.' A report from the National Audit Office then found that more than £1.2 billion was being spent on alternative accommodation sites – £46 million more than the cost of hotels – with a capacity of only 900 people.[39]

Hopeless and desperate, many languishing in hotels and military bases turned to precarious work on the black market. One security guard told me they regularly saw residents being picked up at the asylum hotel where they worked and taken to car washes, warehouses, to work as cleaners, or, he claimed, drawn into sex work. Exposed and vulnerable, in desperate need of an income while they waited for a decision, many felt they simply had no other choice.

8. The Black Market

> *'The biggest migration problem is not that there's too much of it, but that . . . there is simply not enough of it. The rationale for migration this century is clear: it is essential to help us survive environmental change, poverty and global inequality.'*
>
> Gaia Vince, *Nomad Century*[1]

Kewser dreamed of making it to Britain to work as a radiologist. A vivacious medical student in her early twenties, behind the wide smile and that mischievous sparkle in her eyes lay a steely determination. This wasn't some pipe dream. She had made a promise to her father; a promise she intended to keep.

On the barren wasteland of Loon-Plage near Dunkirk, Kewser was the sole female in a sea of male faces, but she was more than capable of handling herself. 'My brother, my brother,' she said, indicating to a friend nearby, before whispering: 'He's not really my brother, but I say that so I'm safe.'

Though still only twenty-one, she appeared older, wise beyond her years. She had had to develop a thick skin to make it this far. In November 2020, a bloody, brutal civil war had broken out in her native Tigray, the northernmost region of Ethiopia. The government's federal forces, backed by local militia and troops from neighbouring Eritrea, had launched a fierce military operation against the ruling Tigray People's Liberation Front.

A campaign of gang-rape, sexual slavery, enforced starvation, torture and massacres against the civilian population ensued. In the village of Adi Gosha, over sixty people were rounded up, taken to a bridge, lined up in rows and shot dead. Human Rights Watch and Amnesty International described the atrocities in Western Tigray as an 'ethnic cleansing campaign' carried out through 'crimes against humanity and war crimes'.[2]

Dansha, the lush, verdant hill village where Kewser had grown up, was under siege. Schools were closed, hospitals bombarded, humanitarian assistance blocked. Kewser's father, a doctor, had offered livestock and crops from their smallholding to Eritrean troops to be allowed to reach the medical facility where he worked, but masked, volatile men had prevented him from passing.

In times of war, agriculture can be a safety net, providing food and an income, but now it put the family at increased risk. Troops moved farm-to-farm, slashing the throats of livestock and destroying machinery and production equipment. The small plot of land where Kewser and her family lived had already been battered by extreme weather conditions. Now, with roads blocked, no seeds or fertiliser could get through. As their crops began to fail, she worried that the threat to their lives wasn't only from the conflict. Desperate, crippling poverty would lead to starvation before the troops got to them.

Northern Ethiopia had long been on the fault line of conflict and climate change, but it was only in the mid-1980s that the world began to notice. On visiting the camps in Tigray, the BBC's Michael Buerk infamously described the scene as a 'biblical famine, now, in the twentieth century'. Though the West blamed failing rains, it was a combination of politics and cyclical droughts and flooding which drove more than a million people to early graves.

THE BLACK MARKET

In April 2016, I spent ten memorable days with members of the Borena tribe, an agro-pastoral clan near Yabelo, an eight-hour drive from Addis Ababa.[3] On arrival in the village of Adegalchat, I was brought to a conical hut and placed ceremoniously on a wooden bench. In front of me sat the village elder, Sanou, a wizened yet regal man in his mid-seventies. Minutes later a bleating, bucking goat was brought in, laid at his feet and promptly sacrificed. 'This is how we know when the rains will come,' he told me, adjusting his coronet and inspecting the intestines of the now quite still goat.

Sanou was known as an *uusa lalani*, or reader of entrails. His analysis was relied upon by the local community to determine where and when famine would come, to ready themselves to move their livestock on and find pasture elsewhere.[4]

Prolonged dry spells had had a severe and lasting impact on his *kibele*, which depended on the sale of livestock to survive. 'When drought comes, we all suffer the same. These are the only periods when everyone – no matter how wealthy or poor – feels the same impact,' said Sanou. At the time, more than 10 million people across Ethiopia were thought to be in immediate need of aid assistance, according to the UN's Food and Agriculture Organization.[5]

As is so often the case, women and children were at particular risk. The lack of access to food and water meant children were forced to leave school to help their mothers find these vital resources. On a smallholding nestled among parched terraced fields, twenty-year-old Tume Yarco Deeda described her daily tasks: bringing the livestock to pasture, carrying heavy jerrycans of water from a nearby well, collecting hay, preparing food and looking after her children. Drought meant she needed to walk further to find food and water. She spoke of the women who had given birth on their way to the well. An aid worker later told me that many of them likely never returned.

Kewser had never known her mother, who died in childbirth at around her age. She was desperate to avoid the same fate. Bright and capable, she saw a life beyond her rural village. The outbreak of conflict – and the likely secondary impact of poverty and famine – was the push she needed to escape.

There are a multitude of reasons why someone might seek to leave their home, though only a fraction actually set out with the UK as the final destination in mind. Conflict and persecution provide clear and obvious grounds for international protection, as laid out in the Refugee Convention. There are those fleeing dictatorships, corruption and the associated brutality. There may be daily injustices – harassment, prejudice, stigma – which, over time, grind a life down. Others may be reuniting with family members, hoping to integrate into communities and establish networks of connection with their homelands.

Then there are the 32 million people worldwide who were displaced due to the devastating effects of climate change in 2022 alone.[6] The vast majority of this group tend to identify themselves as political refugees rather than environmental migrants, a category not covered under the Convention.

Those with no grounds for international protection may be labelled an 'economic migrant', a pejorative term typically used to describe those who seek to reach wealthier countries to earn money and improve their outcomes. In many quarters of the media around the world, this group are viewed as less deserving of protection – 'scroungers' as some would have it – taking jobs from locals: a notion rejected by many – indeed most – economists.

'Immigration adds to both labour supply and labour demand,' wrote Jonathan Portes, a former Cabinet Office Chief Economist.[7] 'If an immigrant gets a job, they will earn money, most of which will be spent . . . The business they work for will see profits rise; that money, too, has to go somewhere. There is no necessary reason to think unemployment will rise.'

As soon as Kewser arrived in Britain, she wanted to work, or study, or volunteer, or do anything that would allow her to play an active role in society. She had the skills to do so: native-standard English, straight As, charm and charisma in abundance. Learning that she was not allowed to work for at least the first year after applying for asylum – that there was a ban – filled her with anguish. It felt to her as though she was standing on the 'outside looking in'.

At her asylum hotel near Leeds, she whiled away the days waiting for her weekly top-up: a meagre £8.90, some of which would be used to buy phone credit to call her father back home in Tigray. Sometimes she cried before he picked up, letting the emotion out so he wouldn't hear a waver in her voice and ask her what was wrong. Most of the time, she focused on the positives – she would soon be able to attend college, she was practising English every day – sounding upbeat, convincing. He was already going through enough at home; she didn't want him to worry about her.

One day, a friend staying at the same hotel told Kewser that she could find work on the black market. It was an easy way to make money while she waited for her decision, which may be two or three years away. She could then send some of it back to her family; that's what most people did. There were cash-in-hand jobs in cleaning or in chicken and chip shops. She could work as a nail bar technician, an air conditioning engineer or on a construction site. Or, more straightforward than any other, she could be a delivery rider.

All she needed to do was go on Facebook and look for Deliveroo or Uber Eats groups. From there, she could rent an account for £50, maybe £60 a month from someone who had registered with a passport and right-to-work papers. She could borrow a delivery bag too, and a helmet, lights for a bike, even an e-bike or moped if she wanted to get around faster and make more money. Everybody seemed to be doing it. Within a couple of weeks, she was riding all over the city, committing road names to memory, moving, earning, free.

Aware that the ban on the right to work had pushed many migrants like Kewser underground, in the summer of 2023 I shadowed a delivery rider to see how it worked.[8]

Shortly before midday on a muggy Friday, I sat with Shaffi, a British-Bangladeshi rider, on some steps in Soho, fuelling ourselves with biscuits and crisps before our shift got going. Around us were thirty or so other riders, jostling to find the optimal position ahead of the lunchtime rush. All of them were undocumented workers or asylum seekers from Brazil, India and Bangladesh, with a few Albanians among the group, too. Most didn't speak English, but then, they didn't need to.

As noon rolled round, Shaffi loaded up Deliveroo and Uber Eats on his phone. Within seconds, the first order pinged in.

Filtering, tucking, weaving our way through traffic, we arrived at Nobu, one of London's top-end Japanese restaurants, to pick up the order. Stapled to the bag was a receipt for £84: sashimi and crab rolls. With the clock ticking, we cycled through Mayfair, nipping along back roads and side passages, past a Ferrari dealership and the glitzy shop windows of Gucci and Louis Vuitton.

The extravagant lunch was for an intern at a large American asset management company on Berkeley Square. We lined up alongside a row of riders as, one by one, a trickle of twentysomethings appeared, all chinos and gilets. We were told the desk meals were chargeable to the company, which is worth billions, and would be written off against tax. Shaffi got a total of £3.15. There was no tip.

At a palatial penthouse just off Savile Row, we dropped off another order to a concierge. This one was for a young Saudi man: dinner costing £192 from the high-end Chinese restaurant Hakkasan, a stone's throw away. Deliveroo would take £35–40 of the order, while the restaurant got £150. Shaffi received £2.90. No tip again.

Though the riders were seemingly invisible to their customers, the Home Office had spotted a trend. At around the time of my shift with Shaffi, the department announced a series of crackdowns on delivery riders who, they suspected, were largely undocumented migrant workers and asylum seekers banned from taking on jobs. Immigration enforcement officers hovered around hotspots such as the one in Chinatown, demanding insurance paperwork from them. If they couldn't produce it, their vehicles were impounded and the rider was detained; some had been deported. (The Home Office said that in 2023 it arrested more than 380 food delivery riders, following an agreement with three major apps to tackle unlicensed workers.)

During a brief lull in orders, a Brazilian rider showed me a video of his friend being handcuffed and hauled away in a police van. 'They're all plain-clothes immigration police,' he said. 'There's a waiting place up on Tottenham Court Road where we all used to go, but they're always there now, so we tell each other to avoid it.'

While their stories rarely made headlines, some riders had even been killed.[9] Outside Deliveroo HQ, a glass-fronted building in the City of London, I attended a vigil for a Brazilian rider who had been knocked down in a hit-and-run incident and died at the side of the road in a pool of his own blood. Union representatives spoke about his case, seeking justice and compensation for his devastated family. At the side of the group, sitting perched on a moped, was his friend Afonso, still in disbelief.

Like countless others, the two friends had lived a precarious existence, staying in cheap sublets with no protections, where predatory private landlords wielded all the power. These unregulated, overcrowded houses or flats typically crammed bunk beds into one room

– as many as would fit – with mattresses on the floor beside them. At its worst, some people slept in kitchens and bathrooms.

One case had come to the public's attention which highlighted the conditions riders were living in.[10] An e-bike battery had caught fire in a flat in Shadwell, killing one of the residents trapped inside. Eighteen Bangladeshi delivery riders were found to be living in the two-bedroom flat sharing single beds. Each person paid £100 rent a month to a private landlord. 'This was worse than slums in Bangladesh,' one of the residents told reporters. 'In slums you might be sharing with two to three people but I had eight people in this room – sometimes more than ten.'[11]

On the edge of the formal economy, delivery riders, nail bar workers, car wash attendants, hospitality staff, cleaners, security guards and so many others were being forced into precarious existences with low-skill, low-paid work. Unregulated sectors, unregulated accommodation: these invisible grafters, working superhuman hours for less than minimum wage, were putting their lives on the line to provide a service lauded during the pandemic, then quickly forgotten again. Policy had created a market for labour exploitation – what some described as modern-day slavery on UK soil.

When Grace saw the advertisement for vacancies in Britain's agricultural sector, she felt it was an answer to her prayers, 'a call from God'. The single mother had struggled to make ends meet in South Africa. Now here was an opportunity to pick fruit in the English countryside for six months. It wasn't a long period away from her children – they would stay with her mother – and it sounded idyllic. Pictures showed sunshine on the fields, beaming smiles of women who looked to be the same age as her. She wondered if they, too, wanted to provide more for their children, to give them a better life.

After completing a short online form and submitting her identity documents, Grace received a notification from a UK government-sponsored recruiter: her application had been successful. She would need to fly out within the next two months. Several others from Johannesburg were doing the same. They would be met on arrival and taken to their new employers, where they would be housed on-site. She would earn around £500 a week, quickly paying off the loan she had taken out for her flights. Ignoring the niggling doubts of her mother, who warned it was too good to be true, she prepared to leave.

On the day of departure, her two children wept, fearing they may never see her again. She told them she would return before the end of their school year, but this time with money. They would, she promised, 'never struggle again'.

On arrival at the farm in England's West Midlands, the reality of the situation hit Grace 'like a bullet'. She was given a number to which she would be answerable throughout her stay. Picking strawberries inside oppressively hot polytunnels, she felt she might suffocate, or become dizzy and faint. Whenever she asked for a break, Grace says verbal abuse was hurled at her. Often, her pay was docked or her hours cut short. Then she was handed a bill, told she needed to pay back the cost of her accommodation and food. She would never be able to work enough hours to cover all those costs. When she approached her manager to raise her concerns, they threatened that the Home Office would be informed and that she would be deported.

Grace didn't know it, but the Home Office was already aware of multiple complaints of debt bondage on Britain's farms but had chosen to turn a blind eye. 'No allegations were investigated by the Home Office,' the immigration watchdog wrote in a report which looked into the seasonal worker scheme.[12] 'When serious concerns have been raised by workers themselves, they did not act promptly or seriously.'

Though the department routinely blamed Covid, the labour shortages crippling the economy were down to Brexit. Before 2019, tens of thousands of casual workers had come from across Europe to pick fruit and harvest vegetables, but now, with the end to freedom of movement, the government needed to look further afield. Seasonal worker visas increased from 2,500 in 2019 to over 47,000 in 2023.[13]

Meanwhile, economists warned that post-Brexit Britain was 2 million workers short. A disgruntled Boris Johnson compared the UK's reliance on overseas workers to a heroin addiction, saying that businesses had been allowed to 'mainline low-wage, low-cost immigration' for too long.[14] Nevertheless, employers increasingly searched overseas to plug gaps across the labour market and reduce fiscal pressures from the UK's rapidly ageing population: a constant push and pull, boom and bust.

For its part, Labour made vague promises in its election manifesto – better enforcement of labour laws, crackdowns on employers and agencies abusing the visa system – all long-term projects which would do little to ease job shortages. A proposal from the European Commission for an EU–UK youth mobility scheme to increase freedom of movement was ruled out by the party in 2023, so politically toxic was the suggestion in the wake of Brexit.[15]

Britons looked on, watching a country in freefall, its economic, political and social decline irreversible. Why, many began to ask, did we not just employ asylum seekers who were already here? Local businesses, MPs said, were 'crying out for staff'.[16]

Attitudes began to shift. A YouGov poll found that 81 per cent of Brits believed that asylum seekers should be allowed to work after six months, with 73 per cent saying that lifting the ban on the right to work would help new arrivals to integrate better into local communities.[17] In the World Values Survey, the UK was the least likely to say that immigration causes unemployment for Brits, with migrants filling important job vacancies.[18] Was this yet another sign of a government out of touch with its citizens?

At an event in the House of Commons, I heard Lord Harrington, the former minister of state for refugees (a role scrapped after Harrington left), speaking about the ban on the right to work, which he described as 'mad'.[19]

Among the panel were asylum seekers who had been given opportunities to volunteer on allotments, rewilding projects and clearing rubbish from beaches across the UK. Through these local projects they had integrated, learned new skills, improved their English. The benefits to their mental health were enormous. 'It helps the local English people understand that we can be helpful for this country and build good relationships with others,' a lawyer from Zimbabwe told the packed room.

After the panel discussion I got talking to Lord Randall of Uxbridge, which was, at the time, Boris Johnson's constituency. He explained that he was part of a cross-party group which had looked at the evidence from other European nations, spoken to businesses, trade unions, grassroots organisations and new arrivals and reached the consensus that asylum seekers should be allowed to take on jobs within months rather than a year. I suggested it would make sense, given labour shortages, to allow people to work sooner rather than force them underground or into jobs where they would face situations of extreme exploitation. A complete lifting of the ban wouldn't be palatable to ministers, I was told.

Far from the heady heights of Westminster, Kewser was spending all her spare time figuring out how she could complete her medical training, her sights firmly set on becoming a diagnostic radiologist. She trawled through universities and colleges online, looking at the myriad requirements to specialise. She would need to restart her training, then take a further two-year foundation course after that. The costs were astronomical: for a British student it cost £9,000 a year. For an international medical student, fees and living costs could amount to as much as £300,000. She was an asylum seeker living in a hotel, surviving on less than £9 a week. The reality started to sink in slowly, painfully.

Six months after arriving in the UK, Kewser was now allowed to apply for courses at colleges in and around Leeds. First she would have to pass an entry-level English language test, then she could apply for Access Courses and take her GCSE English exams. Finding the patience was difficult. She wanted to finish her training, to work, not sit in a class studying English, a language she was already proficient in.

She made a list of GPs' clinics and phoned around NHS trusts, volunteering to work in administration, as a porter, anything to be in a care environment, to learn practical skills.

One man was particularly kind. He was Indian and had come over as an international student several years before. It had been straightforward; he had been encouraged to apply and he was able to bring his wife and children too. He had needed to show he could cover the costs of the course and to sustain himself and his family – more than £700 a month for living costs alone. The difference between them, Kewser realised, was not only their status, or the way in which they arrived. It was about the finances they had to make a future in Britain, finances she could never acquire.

International students had long played a vital role in the economy, with one study estimating that this group alone contributed more than £42 billion.[20] Universities actively courted overseas students to help balance the books, subsidising British students, who were loss-making and whose fees had been capped. Not only that: once they completed their courses, they would become high-skilled, highly educated workers with excellent levels of English. They would be more likely to integrate and to raise children who, like them, were bright and focused and high-earning. These were the 'good immigrants' who were wanted, who contributed and gave back to society.

But as net migration levels rose to record highs, the Home Office saw the student route as a place to make easy cuts. In spite of the fiscal arguments from economists and universities nationwide, the Conservative government consistently viewed students as a way to hack away at the figures, which had been increasing for more than a decade. In 2023, nearly half a million sponsored study visas had been issued, 140,000 of which were for dependants.[21] The law was swiftly changed, cutting visas for spouses and children of students, who Suella Braverman said, were 'piggybacking . . . not contributing' to the economy.[22]

By early 2024, universities were struggling to stay afloat, in what some vice-chancellors called a funding crisis.[23] Courses were cut, tutors made redundant. Early admissions of foreign students were down 37 per cent.[24] Chinese, Indian and Nigerian students, who had made up more than half the admissions, chose to go elsewhere. To Braverman, the international reputation of these centres of excellence mattered little. 'What we've got to accept is that some universities may go bust,' she told the BBC. 'I don't think that is necessarily a bad thing.'[25]

To me, the student visa route was about more than just business and economics. It was the reason I left government communications to report on the Home Office.[26]

Back in 2014, at around the time I joined the department, a scandal emerged. An undercover investigation for BBC's *Panorama* showed proxies sitting English language tests for students seeking to extend their visas.[27] In the film, around thirty pupils are seen in a test centre. Next to them are paid cheats telling them the correct answers. The students then walk to the front of the room to have their picture taken as evidence of their attendance. Theresa May, who was home secretary at the time, was shocked when she saw the footage, pledging to crack down on abuse in the system.

Inside Marsham Street, the news set the hares running. There were heated meetings between officials, special advisors and press leads. ETS, one of the major companies that ran the tests, had their contract immediately suspended. When the Home Office asked ETS for a list of alleged cheats, they made the necessary checks. The results came back: 97 per cent – almost all – of the English tests taken between 2011 and 2014 were suspicious, while 58 per cent of candidates had definitely used deception, they told the government.

Almost overnight, 35,000 international students had their visas revoked. A further 22,000 were told that their test results were 'questionable'. Despite having paid enormous sums to get Master's qualifications at some of the most elite institutions in the world, they were immediately thrown out of their universities.

Without the right to remain in the UK, some of the accused students – around 7,200 – returned to their home countries, where, a decade on, many live in shame within their communities. Some were forcibly removed, while others stayed here and continue to fight for justice, desperate to clear their names but unable to work, pay rent or even get a bank account. Some have faced homelessness or were unable to attend parents' funerals without the paperwork or the means to travel. And others took their lives, unable to see a way out.

In Marsham Street's frenetic press office, I was told to clear my workload for the day and focus on getting messages drafted and cleared. With others on the immigration desk, we proactively called reporters to brief them on background. Playing it down was paramount, though a briefing from officials had suggested that the numbers of students 'gaming the system' could be the 'tip of the iceberg'.

How many people could be involved?, I was asked. What are you doing about them? How will you make sure this doesn't happen again?

I stuck to the agreed background messaging, sounding embarrassingly robotic. Some of the reporters I spoke to told me of specific students who could prove their innocence, but who had been unjustly penalised. One journalist, who I had always got along well with, asked me if I believed that what I was saying was true. 'No,' I admitted, 'but I know what I need to do now.' Shortly after that, I left the civil service.

A decade on, I stood apprehensively outside No. 10 as a group of around forty students prepared to hand in a petition to the government, calling for some semblance of justice, a chance to retake the test or wipe their immigration records clean.[28] All of them believed that they had been 'easy targets' who would go quietly back to their home countries once their visas had been revoked. 'Enough is enough,' one man said, his friends patting him on the back. 'We are not criminals.'

Among those I met was Tanvi, a drawn woman in her mid-thirties with long dark hair framing her lined face. As I scribbled down notes from the students huddled around me, all vying to get their story out, she appeared quietly beside me and asked to speak privately. At the edge of the group, she told me that she had been unable to conceive for many years. She believed the stress of all that she had endured and all that still hung over her was the cause.

The English language test had been simple for Tanvi, almost like something a child might do in a reception class, describing a picture with sheep on a farm and white, fluffy clouds in the sky. Once she had completed the test, she didn't think about it again, assuming she had easily passed. She would then be able to continue with her course in tourism management and go back home when her studies were finished.

One morning in late 2014, immigration enforcement came knocking. Tanvi was told to gather her belongings and come in for questioning, hauled out with two officers either side of her. Bewildered and humiliated, she asked why, what she had done wrong. Officers told her that her name was on the list compiled by ETS of those who had used deception to secure a student visa.

Three years later, Tanvi was finally given appeal rights. Her case was heard at the upper tribunal court, alongside a dozen others who, like her, had been accused of cheating. The appeal was refused: she didn't have enough evidence to support her claim. By that stage, the legal costs alone had amounted to over £50,000. In the meantime, she and her husband were left with no savings. At times she feared for the future of her marriage, so strained was it. 'I feel I am living in an open prison. I am just fighting for my existence here, fighting to stay alive,' she told me outside the black gates to Downing Street, tears streaming down her face.

While her case was pending, Tanvi's parents told her she would not be allowed to return to their village. They and others in the community had agreed that they could not welcome somebody who had lied or deceived the British authorities. 'I feel ashamed to face my family,' she said. 'Everyone will ask "What have you done in the UK?" and I have no answer. They think we have done a crime.'

More than anything else – a return home, her marriage, a child – Tanvi wanted the Home Office to 'remove the deception' from her case file, to have her name cleared. Only then would she be able to take 'one peaceful breath' and move forward, rather than always look back.

9. Who Cares?

'Health does not begin or end at a country's border. Migratory status should not be a discriminatory factor but a policy driver on which to build and strengthen healthcare and social and financial protection.'

Dr Santino Severoni, Director of the World Health Organization's Migration Programme

The town of Witney in the Oxfordshire Cotswolds is chocolate-box, picture-postcard perfect. There are wisteria-covered sandstone cottages and wobbly tables lining the cobbled lanes outside quaint tea rooms. Locals gather in pub gardens spilling out on to the River Windrush, enjoying pints of beer from a microbrewery nearby. There's the magnificent St Mary's Church with its ornate stained-glass windows and the Buttercross, built in 1600, around which a weekly fruit and vegetable market still takes place. Just down the road is the old blanket hall, where Witney wool blankets were woven, traded and shipped around the world. It is an affluent, well-heeled community, a rural idyll.

Before the Liberal Democrats' surprise victory in the 2024 general election, Witney had long been a safe Conservative seat, with the Tories consistently picking up between 45 and 55 per cent of the votes.

For fifteen years, from 2001 until his resignation in 2016 in the wake of the Brexit result, this was David Cameron's constituency. He would regularly be found drinking ale at The Eagle Tavern and turning up at social functions to oppose the ban on fox-hunting. It is here, on his doorstep, that 200 of Cameron's 'swarm of migrants' now reside.[1]

A hotel popular with locals had done a deal directly with the Home Office to house asylum seekers there without informing the local authorities, emergency services or the NHS. Residents were outraged they hadn't been consulted about the plans and concerned that background checks hadn't been adequately carried out.

'It isn't what it used to be around here. Witney used to feel really safe, but I wouldn't want to be out on my own, especially down by the river,' a smartly dressed man in beige chinos and a Barbour jacket raged.

'It's always blokes, never women. We can't let our kids run around any more,' said a young father nursing a pint.

A local doctor told me the whole town was 'up in arms', regularly attending town hall meetings to air their grievances. More than a year into the hotel closure, public sessions were still held weekly and were standing-room-only affairs.

What wasn't made clear to the community was that the majority of those accommodated at the hotels in and around Witney were families, and in particular single mothers and pregnant women. Among them was Elira, a shy, subdued woman from Eastern Europe, still in her late teens.

'Everybody says, "She is so young, how will she cope?"' she told me over lunch, picking at a chicken wrap. 'The only thing I knew about the UK before I came here is that a woman who needs help is protected, but it's not really like that. I don't believe anyone – I can't trust anyone any more.'

It was little wonder Elira had lost faith in humanity. Her path to the

UK had been paved with abuse, starting with her childhood sweetheart, a man she had loved deeply for many years. After a short period apart she had reconnected with him on Facebook and they began to meet up, going for walks in the park together. She told him how difficult she had found it without him in her life and he promised he would provide for her, on one condition. He could not, he said, make a comfortable life for them there. They would need to move to Italy.

When Elira told her parents the plan, they warned her not to go, saying they didn't trust this man and that they would disown her if she went against their wishes. As devout Christians, they urged her to get married before she got in any deeper. Elira didn't want to wait. Blinded by love and the promise of a fresh start, she fled.

Within only a few days of arriving in Italy, the man turned cold, telling her she would need to go out and earn money, that he would not be the only one to work. While he would be busy doing daytime shifts on construction sites, she would have to work at night. When she refused his demands, she was savagely beaten.

Fearing his violence and not knowing where to turn, a few weeks later she joined a group of sex workers on the streets, terrified. After she left each client she would return to the damp, squalid apartment they shared with eight others and sob herself to sleep. All the money she earned had to be given to the man she believed was her partner and his acquaintances.

Following months trapped in a cycle of domestic abuse and sexual exploitation, Elira returned to the flat one day to find that another woman had moved in to take her place. A ferocious argument broke out, her feelings of betrayal and heartbreak laid bare. Elira emerged bruised and bloodied.

It was a moment that was to change her life's course. Now she could see that this man was not her lover, he was her trafficker. She needed to get out, fast.

The next day Elira waited until he had left the flat and his colleagues were smoking outside, the door ajar. She took a deep breath, grabbed hold of a few belongings packed in a tattered handbag and escaped, not knowing where she would go but seeing no other way out. Running as fast as she could until she felt sick with adrenaline and exhaustion, she came upon a petrol station shop and asked if she could shelter there overnight. Seeing her desperation, a man working there offered what she described as 'like a life support', putting her in touch with someone who could help.

The next morning, a truck arrived at the gas station and she piled aboard, promising to be silent. Inside were several others, their eyes down and hoods up. Travelling overland towards northern France, Elira began to feel dizzy and nauseous. She didn't know it yet, but a new life had already started inside her.

As Elira was preparing to board a boat bound for Britain, I, too, discovered that I was pregnant. Our experiences of antenatal and postnatal care would be wildly different. While I attended scans and midwife appointments, Elira went into hiding, fearful of contacting the health services in case her trafficker found her.

Access to healthcare had long been an issue for migrant groups, but the challenges were greatly exacerbated by the pandemic. During the three national lockdowns, starting in March 2020, I kept myself busy by coordinating baby clothes donations, driving around south London to drop them off at asylum hotels and hostels. I signposted new arrivals to medical support through charities, linking them up with obstetricians, midwives and birth partners. And I ran English classes on Zoom for a group of new and expectant mums from around the world, a veritable motley crew of women from Vietnam, Bangladesh, Iraq, Albania and elsewhere. We shared our experiences of pregnancy

– the backaches, the insomnia, the nausea – and delighted in the mews and yawns of newborns appearing on-screen. Early motherhood was an experience that bonded us, transcending language barriers.

I kept in touch with many of my students and, when I returned to my desk in late 2021, I heard about a woman named Kemi who had given birth by emergency caesarean section. Within hours of delivery, nurses told her she would need to pay for her care. The bill amounted to over £14,000.[2] Without the correct exemptions, Kemi, who was undocumented, was liable to pay the extortionate immigration health surcharge. When she told the nurses on the ward that she didn't have that kind of money, debt collectors began to phone her, the tone of the calls becoming more aggressive as time wore on.

Many undocumented women – including those who had been trafficked like Elira – avoided seeking medical care altogether, afraid that they could be landed with crippling debts or, worse still, reported to the Home Office and deported. Some attempted to give birth alone in their asylum housing.

In one horrific case I reported on, a woman from Angola took legal action against the Home Office following the stillbirth of her baby in an asylum hostel.[3] For over three hours she had sat in reception, bleeding profusely. Staff had refused to call an ambulance.

Even when migrant groups tried to access medical care, multiple obstacles stood in their way.

In December 2023, I visited St James' Estate in Doncaster, ranked one of the most poverty-stricken neighbourhoods in Britain.[4] At the foot of a high-rise building, its windows boarded up, a row of trestle tables had been set up, laid with clothes and food parcels. A van was parked nearby with community nurses offering mental and physical health advice. One told me that drug use had spiked in recent years and there was frequent violence, with multiple stabbings among rival gangs living on the estate.[5]

Nearby was another health bus, this one unmarked. It was a mobile clinic run by a retired GP, Dr Fiona Glynn. After more than four decades serving the local community in and around Doncaster, she noticed that asylum seekers were being dispersed to the area in greater numbers with no information about how to register with the health services. There were now more than 600 people in Home Office accommodation spread across Greater Doncaster, a number that was growing fast.

Throughout the pandemic, the softly spoken, indefatigable medic had done the rounds of Home Office housing in the ex-mining villages, helping new arrivals to fill out paperwork to register with local surgeries, get their prescription medications and occasionally bring them to appointments. But then Doncaster started to be used as a 'dumping ground', with new transfers every week, often placed in former pit villages like Stainforth, a half-hour drive from the city centre.

When Dr Glynn heard that the Home Office was dispersing people to deprived areas like this, her heart sank. Many asylum seekers who were brought there told her they had never lived in such a racist place. A couple of years earlier, a Somali family had been 'hounded out' of the village after months of harassment. Stones had been thrown at windows and abuse shouted in the street. It was easy to spot them in an all-white neighbourhood. Most of the locals had never had a non-white family living next door to them.

Just off Stainforth's main road, down the lane towards the entrance to the colliery, is where the picket line had formed in 1984. Remnants of the winding shaft and the pit head could be seen in the distance and the lively Hatfield working men's club, its lights bright, was running a quiz. Beside it, where the vast majority of miners went out on strike, is a bronze statue which reads: 'We stand on the shoulders of giants.'

Dr Glynn's friend had been the pit nurse who tended to miners' wounds and dressed burns during the strikes. Like everybody else in the community, she had found the closure of the colliery gut-wrenching.

Stainforth had never recovered – there was no housing, no opportunities. Its spirit had been depleted over time.

The dispersal programme in the villages had been poorly and inappropriately managed. Some asylum seekers had been moved into former miners' homes overlooking the now-closed pit. The flat-roof terraced houses had once been home to hundreds of mining families, a warm-hearted community where people helped each other out, where children played freely in the streets and doors were always open. Surely the Home Office knew putting them there was like throwing fuel on a fire?

Dr Glynn worried about the tension between the communities. She had started organising informal day trips for asylum seekers to the National Coal Mining Museum near Barnsley, taking them down the pit shaft to familiarise them with some of the local history. Most of those dispersed to Greater Doncaster were families, or they would be starting families there. She felt they needed to understand 'what the pits mean to these communities'.

Perceptions were somewhat different in Westminster when it came to healthcare. The week of my visit, Doncaster MP Nick Fletcher stood up in the Commons to dog-whistle about new arrivals in his constituency upsetting the peace. 'Doncaster is full,' he declared. 'We are turning parts of our community into a ghetto. You have a twelve-hour waiting list at A&E and the reason why the waiting list is so long is because people don't speak English in these places any more.'[6] No figures featured in his four-and-a-half-minute tirade, but it's perhaps useful to consider them here. The Don Valley is 96 per cent white. 94 per cent of the population were born in the UK.[7] Just 0.5 per cent have been in the UK for two years or less.

Despite her best efforts, Dr Glynn – 'a modern-day saint', some called her – had faced backlash from all quarters of the local community. The council had repeatedly refused to endorse their work, meaning Dr Glynn and ten other locals, all retired teachers, medics and a pro-bono solicitor, were propping up the system with little to no funding. She had wanted to move to the Peak District when she retired, to go walking in the mountains, to slow down, read books, but she couldn't leave now. If she stopped, who would help these hundreds of people?

When we dropped off an asylum-seeking man in Askern, another ex-mining village, he told us the boiler had stopped working and there were leaks in the house. Calls to Migrant Help and the local housing provider, Mears, had been redirected to Dr Glynn. It wasn't just new arrivals who relied on her; the authorities did too. 'We can see what needs to be done and there's a need, a growing need, but never enough resources.'

Mental health among the migrant community was a particular concern for her. Most were isolated in the pit villages. It would have been quicker to get to Sheffield than Doncaster for some of them. The cost of going into town just didn't make it worthwhile. Nobody could afford the £4 return journey when they were already living on a pittance.

Instead, what she consistently saw was people arriving 'full of hope then gradually having their dreams crushed'. Invariably they would all, at some point, need to access support.

Over the course of my reporting, trauma had been a recurrent theme. During the research for one of my pieces, I was put in touch with Ann Salter, a psychologist who specialises in support for migrant groups.

Dr Salter worried that patients were often being sent to her too late. Sometimes it might be six months after they arrived – maybe longer – by the time a client was referred to her. Chronic post-traumatic stress disorder gone untreated for too long could be detrimental to their wellbeing. It could mean people didn't go out in case they were triggered by a police siren or a backfiring motorbike. Some limited their friendship groups or self-medicated with alcohol or drugs. Insomnia, nightmares and flashbacks were consistent symptoms at her surgery.

The dispersal process only stymied progress. Dr Salter had managed to secure agreement with the Home Office that if treatment had started, her clients wouldn't be transferred out of the area, but mistakes kept happening. It made it all but impossible to build a life again from scratch if somebody was being moved around. People needed somewhere stable, with access to services and a community, to be able to recover.

I had been sent some new evidence[8] which showed that the failure to meet basic human standards, including access to healthcare, in former military barracks such as Napier was exacerbating depression, anxiety and PTSD.[9] Reports of suicide attempts had emerged, but had been quickly quashed by the Home Office press office, who called me to bat the allegations away, telling me that an official from Migrant Help, a nurse and a duty doctor were present on-site.

I went back to Napier one Sunday afternoon to hear from those in the camp first-hand, arriving in Folkestone West to heavy rain and navigating my way up slippery woodland slopes. The accounts of those placed there were markedly different to the Home Office's confident riposte.

'I have bad nightmares. I need pills for sleeping but the GP said to me, "Go to YouTube, it will tell you how you can sleep." I don't have [a] phone, so how can I see that? I asked for help, but nobody will help me,' one man staying at the camp said.

'We don't have a good nurse here,' said another. 'I needed immediate help – I couldn't eat properly, there was so much pain – but they refuse to do [anything]. They said there is nobody who can help. It will get better on its own.'

On my return home to London, I called the Home Office for a right to reply before filing my article.[10] (Unlike every other government department, it has no general press office email address, forcing journalists to call up, set out the story and then 'stick it in an email' – a process designed to intimidate reporters out of stories from the get-go. Many of these emails were forwarded directly to special advisors.)

Several phone calls back and forth ensued. A *Guardian* lawyer got involved, then a senior lawyer. Readers' editorial, effectively the complaints department, was alerted. A Home Office policy official intervened. This wrangling went on for two days before publication, with demands to see the embargoed report, then the copy I had filed. We refused.

At 11.30 p.m., eight hours before the story was scheduled to run, we received their curt reply. 'We reject these claims,' they said, adding that round-the-clock support was available and that the welfare of all those in Home Office accommodation, including Napier, was treated with the 'utmost importance and sensitivity'.

Shortly afterwards, the charity Doctors of the World provided written evidence to the Home Affairs Select Committee[11] which showed that over two-thirds of those at the barracks had a diagnosed psychological condition requiring medication and 40 per cent reported suicidal ideation or attempts while staying at Napier. The Royal College of Psychiatrists described the healthcare at the site as 'bordering on non-existent'.[12]

Since its inception in the wake of the Second World War, the National Health Service has relied on overseas workers to fill labour shortages. In the early 1960s Enoch Powell, then health minister, made a visit to the Caribbean to invite people to Britain to work as nurses, before later turning the tables on them in his infamous 'rivers of blood' speech in

April 1968. 'As we look ahead, I am filled with foreboding,' he warned, in what has gone down in history as one of the most overtly racist speeches ever made by a British politician. 'Like the Roman, I seem to see "the River Tiber foaming with much blood".'

His speech, as it was designed to do, caused a storm in Westminster. Powell was sacked, but graffiti continued to appear on walls around the country celebrating him: 'Powell for PM'. What he had neglected to mention was that every person he had recruited from the colonies – populations which Britain had violently repressed for centuries – had been given the full rights of a British citizen under the 1948 Nationality Act. Britain did indeed have blood on its hands.

During the pandemic, as we clapped care workers every Thursday evening at 8 p.m., overseas medical staff were inside our hospitals, risking their lives to save our loved ones. A research paper from the British Medical Association found that minority ethnic doctors, nurses, porters and administrators died at seven times the rate of their white colleagues: more than 90 per cent of all medics who lost their lives.[13]

Emerging from the pandemic into post-Brexit Britain, the government finally sat up and took notice of the healthcare sector, which was already on its knees. As it had done years before under Enoch Powell, the Conservative Party began to drum up recruits from overseas, expanding the existing health and social care visa in early 2022 to invite more people from Britain's former colonies to fill the gaps. The warm welcome wasn't to last long.

One dark, drizzly December evening I made my way north-east to Scarborough,[14] arriving on the last train just after midnight and letting myself into a cosy guesthouse, its corridors filled with black and white photos of yesteryear. The lady who cooked me a full English breakfast the next morning showed me some more of their pictures, pointing out children with breeches and women balancing parasols against their shoulders. 'A bygone era,' she said sadly. Scarborough, once a thriving fishing town, was now largely reliant on the McCain's chip factory and pub-tending for employment outside the tourist season.

I wandered along silent streets, arriving at St Cecilia's nursing home just before 7 a.m. for the handover from the night to the day shift. Notes were read out on each patient: one had been 'a bit wandersome' in the night and had had to be cajoled back to bed. Another was 'quite vocal', shouting out in their sleep, while an elderly man had been pinching food from somebody else's plate. An eye needed to be kept on him.

Minutes into the briefing, an emergency buzzer went off, screens flashing red. Registered nurse Evans sprinted up three flights of stairs, two at a time. One of the residents may have fallen out of bed, or choked on their fluids; it happened often. Four members of staff threw back doors, reaching the room to find that it was, thankfully, an accidental push of the red button. There was a collective sigh of relief, nervous laughter and pats on the back. Evans was stood down.

Back at the nurses' station, he began to get medication boxes ready for the morning rounds. Tiny pink pills were placed in paper cups, glucose injections prepared. His colleagues noticed he was particularly subdued. Evans had just heard that one of his favourite residents, someone he had had a 'strong bond' with, had passed away the day before when he was off-shift. Now he would have to take phone calls from the GP to document what end-of-life treatment the patient had been on. 'No matter how many times it happens, it always gets to you. They feel like your granny or your grandfather. But you can't dwell on it; you have to move on.'

Family meant everything to Evans. He had left Ghana a year before but home was never far from his mind. 'I lost my daddy when I was six. Ever since then, I knew I wanted to be a nurse. I never wanted to see anyone else suffer like he did.' It had been a time-intensive and costly process to get his visa arranged and he had had to make significant sacrifices, but Evans knew this was the next step for him. Putting his medical training to use in an 'advanced country' would offer him the professional development and opportunities rarely found in Ghana. He began to search online for jobs in the UK, the US and Canada. Within days he had had an interview with the team in Scarborough, who offered him sponsorship, and the visa process was underway.

Now, though, the door that had opened the year before to workers like Evans and thirty-one of his overseas colleagues had started to close. On 4 December 2023, a few days before my visit, then home secretary James Cleverly unveiled the government's latest plans to cut net migration, which would prevent the spouses and children of care workers from coming to the UK.[15] For the Conservative government it was an obvious place to make cuts: in the year to September 2023, 143,990 people had arrived through this route, bringing 173,896 dependants.

The day the news broke, Evans' colleagues watched the television in the lounge and cried. A carer from India who had arrived six months earlier on a five-year contract had been waiting for a visa appointment for her two children. 'I thought that was it, that it started from that moment, and I wouldn't see them for three or four more years.' If she had known about the changes before she applied to come to the UK, she might have chosen a different country, where the immigration rules allowed families to settle together.

'My friends in Ghana, they keep asking me about it – is it true?' said Evans as we walked between rooms. 'I always tell people the UK welcomes families. Now it seems like "You want my skills, my knowledge, but not my family? OK, let me look at other places."'

Some of his friends who worked in domiciliary care and residential care in London and Manchester had already started to think about a move to the US, Canada and Australia, where there were fewer limitations and higher salaries. In the US, the average salary for a registered nurse was 'double or triple' the UK rates, at around $80,000 a year. Evans received well above minimum wage, but less than he would get in other countries.

Downstairs, next to the kitchens, the care home group director, Mike Padgham, had a sober view of the government's latest move. They had only just relaxed the social care visa route; now, eighteen months later, they were moving the goalposts again. Mike had run out of words to describe how neglected social care in the UK had become. It was 'on a cliff edge', a precipice, at breaking point. Whatever way you wanted to describe it, it surely wasn't strong enough to express what it was really like.

Mike couldn't operate his care homes without overseas workers. As a business owner, he was reluctant to say that there would have to be closures if the route narrowed further, but that was the harsh reality. There would be a significant knock-on effect to the NHS, too. If social care was weak, it would impact the number of hospital beds taken, of staff attending to each patient. Resources were already pared back enough. 'If we fail, the NHS fails.'

Mike had invited MPs to visit his homes, and he had been a regular visitor to Westminster to make them see how bad it was. He was frequently asked why he didn't recruit more British workers to fill vacancies. Like so many other care home providers, he wanted to hire locally, but then he would have to put the prices up in order to pay staff more – it was the only way of attracting applicants. Mike had found it very challenging to recruit from across the UK; young people wanted to work in major hospitals, not in homes for the elderly.

He believed the government needed to be bold. When the NHS was created, it had been difficult, it had taken time and it had been contentious, but now it was a source of national pride. What was required – and what Mike had long advocated for – was a National Care Service to bring health and social care together on an equal footing. The appetite for changes in social care was low, not least when the Home Office got involved, but they were necessary.

Mike's approach to journalists had become more cautious over time. Much of the coverage surrounding social care had been unhelpful to the sector and to the overseas workers scheme specifically. Part of the reason I had been allowed to visit St Cecilia's was because the homes were operating above-board, paying and treating their overseas staff as equal to their British colleagues. Many other care homes weren't.

Mike was aware of that. There were undoubtedly unscrupulous agents who charged thousands of pounds for a visa before carers left their home country then locked them into slavery and servitude, providing no jobs when they arrived.[16] Those who were still unemployed after twenty-eight days had their visas cancelled by the Home Office. Due to the conditions applied to their visa, they were unable to then claim asylum, indefinitely stuck in limbo without documents to work. Though most were too afraid to report it to their employers, allegations of rape and sexual harassment pervaded sections of the social care system.[17]

The problem was, the Home Office wasn't doing the checks. An individual could simply wake up one day and decide to set up as a care home provider with one or two members of staff. The Home Office would then issue thousands of visas to that provider. (In a series of inspections of the social care visa route completed in February 2024, David Neal found that the Home Office had issued 275 visas to a care home that didn't exist. One company, which said it had four staff, was issued with 1,234 visas.[18])

While, of course, this needed to be tackled with the utmost urgency, Mike wanted to be clear that not all social care providers operated in this way. His overseas staff were highly valued and would always be treated with the same respect as British staff.

Back up on the ground floor, Evans was rigging up a karaoke machine next to a Christmas tree. Care staff were massaging hands with cream, tucking cushions behind backs. There were moments of tenderness and love: a wedding photo clutched between paper-thin fingers, yoghurts spooned carefully into smiling mouths. A man who came in to have lunch with his wife every day sat close to her, singing Christmas songs softly in her ear.

After a dinner of pork hotpot and home-made cheese and onion pasties, the residents were ready for bed. There were hoists to prepare, pressure wounds and skin tears to dress, wheelchairs to wheel. Evans would now begin the handover to the night staff, after a long thirteen-hour shift. He would do the same again the next day, and the next.

'People always ask me why I do this work when I am so young,' he said, smiling gently. 'I tell them, even if somebody doesn't remember you, or they don't appreciate you, there are moments of connection. In those moments they feel warm and cared for. That is all that really matters.'

10. Advice Sharks

> *'Most liars are tripped up either because they forget what they have told or because the lie is suddenly faced with an incontrovertible truth.'*
>
> John Steinbeck, *East of Eden*

Gabriela had always considered herself an honest person. That's what made being scammed so difficult to bear.

After three years living undocumented in Britain, she had spotted an advertisement on a Facebook group set up to help migrants in the UK to regularise their status. In the post, Ousmane Hawa, a 'first-class' immigration advisor, promised a smooth process. He appeared to have clout. Comments underneath his post recommended his 'highly professional' service and excellent track record. Each one had hundreds of 'likes' and thumbs-up emojis.[1]

Gabriela searched his name and found an accompanying video interview. In the ten-minute film, Hawa sets out his credentials, stating that he is registered with a regulator and has previously worked as an immigration official for the Home Office. He then issues a word of warning to potential clients: 'You must be very careful and not talk to someone who pretends to be a lawyer . . . It is best to know what they do and whether they are really a lawyer or not.'

Gabriela began asking around the local Colombian community in south London and a couple of people vouched for Hawa. They knew of others who had submitted applications through him and they now had residency in the UK. She went back online and clicked through to his website. There she found a phone number and an address for his office nearby. He must, she rationalised, be a bona fide advisor.

She messaged Hawa on Facebook and, sure enough, less than an hour later he had got back to her to arrange a meeting in a coffee shop. All she had to do was bring an initial down-payment of £500 and he would explain more in person.

Arriving at the cafe, she felt a sense of unease: £500 was a lot of money to her. For the last six months she had been working as a cleaner, cash-in-hand, while trying to support her young daughter. She had often struggled to put food on the table. Now here she was, meeting a stranger to give him the only money she had to keep a roof over their heads. Gabriela tried to stay calm, telling herself that this man had helped many others in her community before, that he would be 'the answer to all my prayers'.

Hawa arrived promptly, with a file of paperwork under his arm, dressed in a suit, tie and smart shoes. In fluent Spanish, he began by telling her that most of his clients were Latin American; he understood the context very well and he would do all that he could to help her. He was charming and persuasive, flattering her with compliments, repeatedly telling Gabriela that she was beautiful.

The best approach, he suggested, would be for her to marry a French man, an EU citizen, he was already in contact with. She wouldn't need to meet him or live with him. In fact, she wouldn't even need to go to France: they would get married by proxy. Once she had a marriage certificate, Gabriela could apply for residency as the spouse of an EU national, securing her status in the UK. This service, which would need to be paid for in cash, would total £5,000.

It sounded straightforward enough. Hawa would arrange everything and, while it was more money than she had anticipated, it would mean Gabriela and her daughter could live in relative peace. They were one document away from a future in Britain.

The idea of being returned to Colombia and all that she had left behind was unimaginable. Five years earlier, Gabriela's husband had been shot dead by members of the Marxist guerrilla group FARC. Despite a peace accord between FARC and the Colombian government, massacres, kidnappings, hijackings and torture had continued, forcing hundreds of thousands of people to flee their homes.[2]

After a period of living in deprivation on the outskirts of the capital, Bogotá, Gabriela had put her life, and that of her young daughter, in the hands of smugglers to reach Europe. While most Colombians wanted to reach Spain, where they could speak the language, Gabriela had connections to Britain. Her cousins had arrived several years earlier during a particularly violent moment in the armed conflict. She could communicate in English and was confident that her language skills would improve in time. Most importantly, they would be welcomed into a warm community where she could find work, where her daughter could learn and grow up in safety.

Two weeks after their meeting, Hawa sent Gabriela a message to say that he had returned from France. They met up at the same cafe, where he told her that he had completed the formalities and presented Gabriela with a marriage certificate. The document, which was sent to me, is full of mistakes. Dates of birth, names, countries of origin: everything was incorrect.[3]

Gabriela asked for the details to be corrected before the paperwork was submitted to the Home Office, but she was told it was too late. Hawa had already sent off the package of documents containing the falsified marriage certificate, including details taken from a stolen identity card.

Gabriela's application was inevitably rejected. Worse still, she was left with an immigration record of deception for submitting fraudulent documents, giving the government grounds to refuse all future visa and residency applications. She remains undocumented and destitute. Hawa, meanwhile, disappeared without a trace.

Hawa might have dropped off Gabriela's radar, but that didn't prevent me from trying to track him down. It wasn't long before I had the address for his new office. I went there one day to see if he would be willing to talk and luck was on my side. I was the third in line for a consultation, after two women – one Ecuadorian, one Colombian – who hoped to extend their tourist visas. Both had arrived in the UK within the last month and were seeking right-to-work papers for the next eighteen months.

As I waited in the adjoining cafe, singer Gilberto Rosa crooned through the speakers. There were hanging baskets of spiky, dried-out plants and a colourful mural in the bar towards the back, with bottles of rum crammed together. Next door was a Venezuelan herbal medicine clinic, a hairdressing salon and a kitchen, where a sturdy lady in a knitted purple beret cooked quinoa and beef soup. It was a quiet day, so when the two ladies in the queue went in together, the larger-than-life owner made me a cappuccino. I sat perched on a high bar stool, chatting to her for over an hour.

Hawa was, she said, a 'very clever man'. He spoke four languages fluently and had helped thousands of people to stay in Britain over the last twenty years. His Christian faith was central to all that he did, which was important to their clients too. Allowing him to use the side office in the cafe was good for her business. There were always people queuing up and they often had a coffee or a snack while they waited to speak to him.

He was 'fair', she thought. The charge for an initial consultation was £50. To go through the paperwork for a visa extension the full charge would be £500, to be paid upfront, she told me. Asylum claims usually cost more but asylum seekers didn't tend to have much money, so Hawa tried to keep the costs low. Everybody in the community recommended his services and, while they were flanked either side by the offices of other immigration advisors, he was the best.

Just as I was getting started on my soup and *arepas de chicharrón*, Hawa came out to see me and invited me into his office.

It was dingy, dripping with plastic gold crucifixes and a portable air conditioner that whirred noisily. Behind his desk was a prayer in Spanish and various certificates. One read: 'Housing Management and Maintenance Officer'.

He began by telling me that business had been slower over recent years. Brexit and the pandemic meant that many people had either returned to their home country or went elsewhere in Europe. Most travelled on to Spain, but they earned far less there than they would in the UK. The EU Settlement Scheme now provided much of his business.[4] Those without settled status before Brexit were lining up outside his office. There had been twenty new clients the day before my visit; some had waited all day for a consultation.

Reputation was crucial to keeping his business alive. Hawa was a sole trader who could converse with clients in multiple languages. He charged less and his success rate was known to be far higher than others who provided the same services. 'Honesty, this is very important to me,' he said, banging his palms down on the desk for emphasis. 'Honesty and a clear conscience.'[5]

He told me that he had worked for the Home Office, first as a caseworker and then as an interpreter. He had, he claimed, also spent time overseas with Amnesty International, 'defending people who have nothing', and ten years studying for a PhD in international law in

Russia. I asked when he had qualified as a solicitor. 'Solicitor is not a qualification,' he stated. 'It is a certification. I have this certification.' At that, he gestured vaguely towards a piece of card on the pinboard behind him which showed that he had supported young prison leavers years earlier.

When I put Gabriela's case to him, he became flustered, denying ever having provided falsified documents. He knew of others that would do such a thing, but he couldn't. 'These things happen,' he said, laughing nervously. 'But I have my Christian faith to preserve.' Sham marriages were less of an issue nowadays, and anyway, it wasn't illegal to get married by proxy in a different country. 'The UK law says that if they get married where it is legal by proxy, it is OK – they will recognise it here,' he asserted. He would never advise people to do that; he would simply explain the law to them. 'In France, this is legal . . . In all European countries, it is legal.' All he wanted was to help people. He fervently believed that marriage was a 'human right'. He would do what he could to help people secure that right.

On the way out, Hawa wanted to know if I planned to vote in the upcoming 2024 general election. Politics was important to him. Every day, he read the *Daily Mirror*, the *Telegraph*, 'all the papers'. He followed the small boats issue closely and regularly consulted asylum seekers who had arrived through that route and tended to need help translating documents from the Home Office. 'These letters, they mean nothing,' he would tell new arrivals. 'All that matters is that you can get through the interview, to convince them that what you are saying is true.'

I had become aware of exploitative immigration advisors years before I met Gabriela, but it was only in spring 2022 that I really understood how intimidating they could be.

At that time, I had been put in touch with a Nigerian woman whose local NHS trust had erroneously operated to remove her fallopian tube while she was pregnant, after a suspected ectopic pregnancy. Within two days, an overseas visitor team began calling her to demand payment of over £4,000, followed by letters from debt collectors. Confused and wanting to 'make the letters go away', the woman contacted an immigration advisor she had found on social media for advice.

Having interviewed the woman and spoken to the NHS trust responsible, I then got in touch with the woman's advisor, asking for a comment before publication. Sitting in the car outside my son's nursery, already running late and racked with guilt, I received a phone call. From the other end of the line came a woman's shrill, raised voice. After hurling abuse at me for speaking to her client without consulting her first, she threatened to take legal action if I proceeded to publish the story. She gave no explanation for her behaviour towards me, which only got worse when I asked who her regulator was.

Returning home, irritated and slightly unnerved, I looked the woman up online to see whether she was licensed. Unsurprisingly, the name I had been given was not on the register of regulated advisors. In fact, it was nowhere to be found. She had used an alias, making her difficult to track or to report. I warned the woman who had been scammed, but she refused to listen. In all likelihood, the advisor is still operating under a different name.

Identifying the crooks was half the battle. Shortly after the incident with the advice shark, I attended an event in east London, sitting tucked between two ebullient migrant women in the front row. On stage was James Conyers, a legal advisor from the charity Refugee Action.[6]

Like many others in the sector, James had come across nefarious actors multiple times and wanted those in the audience to be aware of their rights. One of the slides in his presentation was headlined 'Questions to ask yourself':

Is it suspiciously cheap? It shouldn't be cheap. There are documents to gather, expert reports, interpretation and translation costs to consider.

Have they guaranteed success? They can't and they shouldn't, 'no matter how many times you ask', so that should be a red flag.

Are they behaving as an advisor should? 'Good advisors don't shout, threaten, flirt or hit you.'

What should happen, James said, is that difficult questions had to be asked. It may seem as though the advisor didn't believe their client, but a legitimate legal representative needed to put themselves in the mind of an asylum decision maker. That might involve casting doubt on some aspects of an individual's case to see how they responded.

The case should be kept confidential and a letter with full details, including information about how to complain if things went wrong, should be provided. If trust is broken, a complaint should be made to a regulator. Rogue advisors get away with it, knowing that many people are too afraid to complain.

Gabriela had found herself in exactly this situation, with 'no power to speak'. She refused to complain about Hawa or approach another solicitor or third-sector organisation because she felt she could no longer trust what she was being told. Now she had an immigration record for deception, she doubted anybody would take on her file. She chose instead to live undocumented, in fear of being visited by the police and prosecuted or deported by the Home Office, rather than pursue a complaint.

It wasn't only migrants who had concerns about reporting bad practice to the authorities responsible. There was an overriding sense among legal practitioners I spoke to that not nearly enough was being done by regulators on compliance and enforcement. That had a knock-on effect to clients, who often didn't believe that anything would happen to their advisor if they complained. 'Regulators focus on financial auditing rather than on quality. I feel they don't do much, basically,' one frontline advisor told me.

Prosecution rates were paltry. Regulators were meant to seize the records of individuals and companies who failed to adhere to the standards they had set, disciplining or prosecuting anyone who didn't. But in the year 2022–23 the Office of the Immigration Services Commissioner (OISC) received seventy-five complaints against unregulated advisors, flagging up potential illegal activity – nearly double that of the previous year. Not one of the complaints resulted in a prosecution.[7]

'OISC just don't have the punch that's needed,' one legal director told me. 'Maybe it's that these advisors are good at covering their tracks so they escape detection, but the risks for operating in this way should be high enough that they fear being caught out. That's obviously not the case.'

The problem was, there simply weren't enough qualified, low-cost legal representatives within the sector. Since 2013, when the Tory–Lib Dem coalition scrapped legal aid, solicitors and barristers had warned of a crisis. The system was now at breaking point, with so-called 'legal deserts' springing up around the UK.[8] Demand far outstripped supply.[9]

In 2022, the Immigration Law Practitioners' Association (ILPA) calculated that across England and Wales, 63 per cent of the migrant population had no access to legal representation or advice.[10] In some areas, legal aid had been stripped completely bare. At the end of 2023 there were only four legal aid lawyers working in the whole of the South West region of England.[11]

Some people had even started showing up at tribunal hearings to represent themselves, without the necessary documents or any understanding of how to navigate the legal complexities. Their cases were invariably rejected.

Tribunal courts began calling charities for help. 'I had one client who was in the mental health section in detention – very, very vulnerable – who had no legal rep,' a charity caseworker told me. 'The tribunal could see how badly this person needed help, so they got in touch with us to ask if we could do it. It's really incredible that's the state we're in – that a tribunal can call a charity for this kind of support.'

Many of the charity caseworkers being called by the tribunal courts had no legal training or background, but with more and more people falling through the cracks they needed to step up. Most had started in the sector by running English classes and providing pastoral support, but before long they ended up doing specialist casework. 'The need is so huge, we essentially become legal aid advisors,' one frustrated caseworker told me. 'It's really clear how much we are all propping up the sector. It's all about putting a sticking plaster on it and trying to prevent it from collapsing.'

A consultation took place across the sector, with solicitors, barristers, caseworkers and legal advisors writing to the Ministry of Justice to set out how dire the situation had become.[12] The file of documents was leaked to me.

'There exists a significant disparity in resources and power between the client and their opponent, the home secretary, and his department, the Home Office, a government body which wields substantial power and has access to significant resources,' ILPA said in its submission.[13] 'These deep-rooted battles mean that providers are fire-fighting every day, both to stay afloat and to try to meet a soaring level of demand. Practitioners are overworked and overstretched as a result. All of this has a very real impact on the ability of practitioners to provide high-quality legal services to those who need them. Access to justice is undoubtedly and dangerously compromised.'

Immigration law was changing at such a pace that it was difficult for even the most experienced lawyers to keep up. Not only was it complex; it was the most politicised area of law. The rewards were so few that qualified legal aid lawyers were handing in their notices at a rate nobody had ever witnessed before.

'It's heartbreaking to see so many hanging up their hats and leaving the profession,' one ILPA member wrote on their last day.[14] 'The whole system is at breaking point. It is staggering how bad it is. It seems to be more and more clear over time that the government's plan is to destroy legal aid in asylum law by making it as unsustainable as it could possibly be, getting rid of as many lawyers as they can . . .'

Day in, day out, lawyers were, they said, 'on the frontline in one of the darkest areas of law', speaking to traumatised, highly vulnerable people – victims of trafficking, torture, conflict, persecution – yet there was no provision for mental health support. Barristers and solicitors appealed to the bodies advocating on their behalf to push for changes to legal aid, to make the Home Office see that they were there to help make their work easier, not harder, ensuring that the system functioned more efficiently and effectively. 'Without that, I honestly do not see how much longer it will survive,' one barrister with decades of experience warned.[15]

But, if anything, the politics made it even harder. Immigration and asylum was the area of law which generated the least sympathy from the general public. Recruiting a new generation of qualified social justice lawyers into immigration and asylum was a constant challenge. What's more, a young solicitor or barrister could earn a lot more in a City firm working in corporate law. Newly qualified lawyers could see, too, that solicitors and barristers on the frontline were being targeted by the government.

On the morning of 5 August 2023, the indefatigable human rights solicitor Jacqui McKenzie received a phone call from the *Sunday*

Times, then an email from the *Sunday Express*. The *Sun* and the *Mail on Sunday* also got in touch, all telling her that they had been passed a dossier about her from the Conservative Party's headquarters. She imagined it would be a 'government-inspired hit job'[16] following her work supporting victims of the Windrush scandal, but, to her surprise, there was no mention of Windrush.

The dossier linked Jacqui to the Labour Party, alongside a briefing document entitled: 'Revealed: senior Labour advisor is lefty lawyer blocking Rwanda deportations'.[17] Tory aides had included the file of a client she represented, a man who faced removal to Rwanda and who had sat shackled on the tarmac, the plane in his eyeline.

'Starmer has been keen to distance himself from previous remarks and convince voters that he can be trusted on immigration,' Tory HQ members wrote. 'But his decision to hire lefty lawyer Jacqueline McKenzie is further proof that "Sir Softie" can't be trusted.'[18]

Jacqui had had to take additional security measures after receiving 'ominous' emails. 'The hit job on me was vile and self-serving, and put me and those close to me at considerable risk of physical harm,' she wrote in a *Guardian* opinion piece a few days later.[19] 'This flagrant attack on me and my work, built on misinformation and mischaracterisation and underpinned by racism and misogyny, is a dark day for our political sphere.'

The government had form when it came to attacks on 'lefty lawyers'. On 4 October 2020, then Home Secretary Priti Patel made a loud dog-whistle of a speech she hoped would get the attention she craved. 'For those defending the broken system – the traffickers, the do-gooders, the lefty lawyers, the Labour Party – they are defending the indefensible. And that is something I will never do,' Patel told the baying online members of the virtual Conservative Party Conference.[20] Prime Minister Boris Johnson jumped on the bandwagon, going even further to declare that his party was hellbent on 'stopping the whole criminal justice system from being hamstrung ... by lefty human rights lawyers'.[21]

The language set a dangerous precedent. Around the time Patel and Johnson spewed out their bile, the brave, principled immigration solicitor Toufique Hossain was visited at his law firm by a member of the public.[22] Cavan Medlock, a twenty-eight-year-old man from Harrow, was wearing black gloves reinforced with knuckle pads and carrying a backpack. Inside the bag was a combat knife with a six-inch blade, handcuffs and rolls of gaffer tape. Medlock had also packed a Nazi swastika flag, which he planned to place in the window of the solicitor's office after killing him.

At reception, Medlock demanded to see Toufique. When the receptionist refused, stating he didn't have an appointment, the man reached into the backpack and withdrew the combat knife. When Toufique appeared shortly afterwards, Medlock told him that he planned to kill him, using racist language and telling him he didn't belong in the country because he wasn't 'fucking white'. He added: 'Enoch Powell was right.'

At Kingston Crown Court in March 2024, Medlock said he wanted to murder Toufique because he was bringing 'foreign invaders' into the country.[23] He had been overheard blaming Duncan Lewis, the firm where Toufique worked, for high-profile immigration cases they had taken on, telling staff they had been 'helping these rats come to this country'. Medlock said that he had seen Toufique's name in a *Daily Mail* article that named him as a lawyer who assisted immigrants.

'Clearly I should have finished the job,' Medlock told the court.[24] When asked what job he was referring to, he gestured towards Toufique and replied: 'To kill this fucker.'

Immigration and asylum law hadn't always been at such a critical point. Just over a decade earlier, large, national bodies, part-funded by the government, had helped to provide quality advice, acting as centres of excellence, providing training, guidance and career development for practitioners. These had been the 'halcyon days' for legal aid, one barrister told me. The government had engaged and been willing to fund solicitors' firms to manage the volumes of claims coming through the system. Many of the senior partners now working in Britain's immigration firms know each other because they came up through the ranks at the same place and at the same time.

But after the Tory–Lib Dem coalition government scrapped legal aid, there was no replacement for the advisory centres. Tens of thousands of people were left without legal representation, placing a significant strain on the existing firms and creating a vacuum for criminal elements and negligent advisors to step in.

Application fees – rates set by and paid to the government – exploded. Where once a citizenship application cost £200, it now costs £1,500.[25] A spousal visa application costs £3,000, including the NHS surcharge.[26] And then there were other costs: English tests, a 'life in the UK' test, always more tests, more documents, more legal fees. But while costs mounted, quality dropped. Taxpayers' money was now being doled out to represent vulnerable people without even the most basic standards being met.

Even qualified, regulated legal aid advisors didn't always meet the required standards. Contacts told me that some in their profession took the £430 fixed fee from the government, then left the claim sitting there for months, sometimes years, at a time. Others opened claims they knew had no chance of success, took the money and ran. This wasn't on the criminal end of the spectrum, but it marked a steep decline in levels of integrity and competence, doing a significant disservice to those who acted with professionalism.

Still, awareness of the pressures faced by legal representatives was low among clients. Some caseworkers had started to deliver information sessions in asylum hotels, to let people know the challenges they were facing. They told asylum seekers that they received a fixed fee, which was low – lower than they perhaps realised – and that was why their solicitor may be rushing through meetings and phone calls, or might not reply as promptly as they would like. 'People were taking it personally. It's been really useful for them to understand why,' a third-sector caseworker said.

But however hard qualified representatives tried to keep the system afloat, unregulated advisors continued to pervade the sector, filling the gaps. I put a call-out on Twitter to see whether any of my contacts had stories they wanted to share and inadvertently opened a can of worms.[27] Solicitors, barristers and charity caseworkers filled my inbox within an hour.

In one case, a single mother, a survivor of female genital mutilation, was told to bring £3,000 cash to a car park for her advisor to make a citizenship application on her behalf. A falsified document which had been witnessed at a magistrates' court was handed over with a first-class stamp stuck to it. Had she tried to use it she would have gone to prison for a year. 'I reported it to the police, who threatened to arrest her, so that was nice,' the woman's solicitor messaged.

Intimidation and sexual advances were common. 'The hold these people have is just magnetic,' said a barrister whose client had been offered the opportunity to waive all fees in exchange for 'kisses'.

Once somebody had fallen victim to a rogue advisor, digging them out of it could be extremely time-consuming and complex. The system was notoriously unforgiving. If a client had got into trouble, or factual errors had been made, the Home Office made it difficult to rectify those mistakes. Barristers and solicitors had to go out on a 'fact-finding mission' to gather evidence. Advice sharks typically refused to communicate with them or send the client's file, if they still had it. Sometimes contacting them was 'a red rag to a bull', one solicitor said. Threats and intimidation increased, adding significant stress to an already pressurised situation.

Only one of dozens of legal representatives I spoke to said they felt in any way optimistic about being able to clear up the mess left by advice sharks like Hawa. There were ways round it, they thought, but it was about being 'creative'.

'You have to be upfront with your client about their rights, letting them know what the risks are if they are undocumented,' one contact told me. 'Sometimes it depends on human rights arguments, which aren't always available to people. So how do you pick up the pieces for those clients? Well, sadly, for some, you just can't.'

In August 2023, a press release from the Home Office landed in my inbox.[28] The department would, it said, be cracking down on unscrupulous lawyers, with a dedicated taskforce and tougher sentences for bad actors. The 'Professional Enablers Taskforce' was to be a 'government clampdown on crooked lawyers who coach illegal migrants to lie'.

Interestingly, the language wasn't worlds away from the rhetoric at the earliest stage of the asylum process aimed at people smugglers. The government stated that it would 'disrupt the business models of firms that are enabling abuse of the immigration system', improve intelligence-sharing and increase referrals to law enforcement.

Its tactics weren't dissimilar, either. Six months later, the Home Office began the first in a series of raids on law firms. Three companies were shut down in one day, suspected of being run by Chinese and British nationals out of a garage attached to a residential property converted into an office.[29] The company, which wasn't regulated by either the Solicitors Regulation Authority or OISC, was run by a married couple, alleged to have supplied fake documents for asylum claims, charging £3,000 per client.

Michael Tomlinson, then minister for countering illegal migration, was jubilant. 'This operation shows once again that we are relentless in our pursuit of those we suspect of abusing and gaming our immigration system for profit. Anyone who is found guilty of this will face the full weight of the law.'[30]

The *Daily Mail* hung on his coattails. 'Dramatic moment Home Office officials arrest three in raid', the headline boomed, stuffed with 'extraordinary pictures'.[31] An embedded video showed just how undramatic the moment really was. In it, two people can be seen walking calmly out of a house in silence. The sting had, the paper wrote, been sparked by a 'sensational investigation' the summer before, led by none other than the *Daily Mail* itself.

That 'bombshell exposé' involved an undercover reporter posing as a migrant in need of help.[32] The legal advisor told the reporter that they needed to invent claims of torture, beatings, exploitation and false imprisonment in order to secure refugee status. The article led to the Solicitors Regulation Authority suspending three firms, but while the *Mail* patted itself on the back, what had happened to the clients of those firms?

'They all ended up coming to us,' one charity's legal advisor told me. 'Most of them still haven't been able to get reps for over a year.' None of them had had their money back and their files had been taken.

And so the cycle continued. As the government stepped up its raids, set up taskforces and desperately grabbed tabloid headlines, migrants disappeared. Amid the chaos, many would be made more vulnerable to exploitation, destitution, detention and deportation.

PART FOUR
INTEGRATION

11. Big Brother State

*'You had to live – did live, from habit that became instinct –
in the assumption that every sound you made was overheard,
and, except in darkness, every moment scrutinised.'*

George Orwell, *1984*[1]

Arian was particularly suspicious of drones. He probably knew a little too much about them. For five years, he had studied their design and development at a leading university in Tehran, graduating with a first-class Master's degree in aerospace engineering.

Walking between classes at the university institute, he could see advertisements and leaflets for coveted positions with large aviation manufacturers hanging on the noticeboards. Pressure was being applied to graduates to take up roles within 'the system'. Then a competition was announced to design a drone, pitched as a game to help the regime solve a problem. What that problem was, nobody knew. Studious and razor-sharp, Arian was urged to participate, offered a reduction in military service from two years to one as an incentive. He took on the challenge, revelling in it, and gained first place, an article appearing on the institute's website to announce the news.

Now he had the attention not only of his lecturers but of all those at regime-run universities across the capital too. An academic connected to the Revolutionary Guard approached Arian to ask if he would be interested in working to support their mission, that everybody at his level was 'begging' for a job. The roles were lucrative and he was gifted.

Arian refused, saying he wanted to work in rocket propulsion, not in producing military capabilities – to be free, not to be institutionalised so early in his career. In truth, he couldn't bring himself to work for the regime or anybody connected to it, no matter how much was involved and how much was at stake. 'They are all murderers, these people. It was impossible to work for them.'

Iran had long since built up an arsenal of drones. During the Iran–Iraq War in the 1980s, the death toll on both sides had numbered more than half a million, with heavy losses among those flying crewed aircrafts. Now unmanned drones allowed the Islamic Republic to produce cheaper, more versatile technologies, ensuring no lives were lost, bolstering the state's security and military forces and allowing the regime a degree of plausible deniability following a strike.[2]

By early 2024, Iran was one of the world's leading global exporters, supplying drones across four continents and to several proxy militias in the Middle East: Hamas, Hezbollah, the Houthis in Yemen.[3] Chief among its international clients was Russia, which bought thousands of suicide drones from Iran, flying them into cities and towns across Ukraine and devastating their targets on impact.[4]

In other conflicts, both in the region itself as well as in Europe, Asia and Africa, whenever Iranian assets appeared the sands shifted. In Sudan its drones halted the progress of the paramilitary Rapid Support Forces, allowing the army to gain swathes of territory around the capital, Khartoum.[5] Ethiopia's government, too, prevailed against Tigray's rebels in 2021 due, in part, to Iranian drones.[6]

'A new era has begun,' said Yahya Rahim Safavi, a major-general in the Revolutionary Guard and a close advisor to the Supreme Leader,

Ayatollah Ali Khamenei. 'We are now witnessing great changes in new technology, wealth, power and global order.'[7]

Arian didn't want anything to do with the geopolitical or military side of the technologies. He was only interested in the physics and the creative design behind them. Years before, he had tried to make his own quadcopter drone for recreational use, flying it, 'buzzy like a summer bee', near his home. But as the job offers gave way to intimidation and interrogations, the playing stopped. He quickly understood that 'these were not toys'.

After fleeing Iran, Arian always had one eye on the sky. All along the migration route he saw aircraft overhead. Helicopters, aeroplanes: nothing to worry about. But he knew that drones were never far away.

One day, near the camp in Dunkirk, he stood squinting up at the charcoal-grey sky, a familiar noise overhead. Then he caught a glimpse of it. A drone, skimming, hovering low, almost but not quite camouflaged by the clouds. He became paralysed with fear, his mind spinning. Could the regime back in Iran know where he was, where he was intending to go? Would they coordinate with the British to harm him, to lock him up? And, crucially, what information did the authorities have and how would it be used against him?

By the time Arian reached the UK, hundreds of millions of British taxpayers' pounds had already been funnelled into border surveillance technologies designed to deter migrants from making the crossing.[8]

In December 2021, following the worst mass-drowning in the Channel for more than forty years, both the British and the French governments stepped up their investments. The Home Office committed to spending a further £220 million by the end of 2022, on top of the £100 million already allocated.[9] Frontex, the EU's border and coast-guard agency, was contracted to fly an aeroplane over the Channel, equipped with sensors and radars. Its advanced search capabilities would 'prevent the rising number of sea crossings', it promised.[10]

Land-based radar technologies dotted the landscape too, with cameras around the same size as the CCTV devices used in shops. Some were so tiny you could hold them in your hand. But it was the airspace that the government wanted to control, to detect exactly who was crossing.

Ostensibly, this focus on aerial surveillance was to decipher the numbers of people in the dinghies, determining whether women and children were on board and identifying if there were any casualties or bodies in the water. Optical sensors, infrared cameras and high-visibility zoom lens cameras could tell the coastguard who was making their way over.[11] Any weapons concealed in clothes could also be picked up. Video footage and images would then be beamed down from the drones to the coastguard at Langdon Battery, before being radioed down to Border Force officials on the quayside.

Near Lydd airport on the Kent coast, I met with a recreational drone pilot, begrudging about newly implemented no-fly hours. Simon had been told he couldn't take his four-winged quadcopter up any time between seven and four: 'That's how busy this airspace is now.' His was so small, you couldn't see or hear it. It was battleship-grey, blending right in, and it could fly higher than the eye could see – sometimes three-quarters of a mile up or more, depending on cloud cover.

Simon loaded the Flightradar app on his phone, icons flashing, a conglomeration of AI-powered satellites and manned aircrafts such as helicopters and planes. Over Dover there were at least two drones that looked like gliders, with sleek white arms and conical noses. Others could easily be spotted by the naked eye.

I drove on to Lydd airport in the hope that I might speak to a government-contracted drone operator, fully expecting to be thrown out. I had heard that Tekever, a Portuguese company contracted by the

Home Office, was based there, flying its AR3 and AR5 drones out over the Channel.[12] Each aircraft was assessed to cost around £420,000, its data and images being analysed in the control room at Lydd before being passed to the coastguard.[13]

As I waited in the faded, damp hall overlooking the hangars, sipping a cup of instant coffee, a cheerful receptionist dutifully called up to the control room. A man in military uniform and full-sleeve tattoos came down to speak to me, telling me the contracts were operationally sensitive and referring me to the Home Office. When pressed, he added that Tekever's drones were used to detect 'potentially illegal vessels', to track and identify individuals. That intelligence would then be provided to the authorities.

A nervous-sounding Tekever representative wrote to me shortly afterwards to say that the company carried out these missions for 'humanitarian purposes', adding that they were intended to 'protect and preserve human life'.[14] A statement followed. 'We are pleased to be working with the UK Home Office and we are proud of the partnership we have created to date, where we get to be part of a greater and more meaningful cause that is impacting lives every day.'

Impacting lives they certainly were – but humanitarian purposes? The authorities could use the information gathered from the drones flying over the Channel to prevent people drowning, but they chose not to use the technology in that way. In fact, ministers were at pains to assure the public that their money was being used to criminalise small boat arrivals, not to protect them.

A post from the Home Office Twitter account showed Priti Patel's right-hand man, Dan O'Mahoney, the comically titled Clandestine Channel Threat Commander, boasting about the UK's fleet. 'Drones have been absolutely critical in securing convictions . . . The evidence we get from the drone is so strong that they often plead guilty at a very early stage.'[15] He added a word of warning: 'Every single one of these boats has to be piloted by somebody. If you're that person, you can expect when you arrive in the UK to be arrested and prosecuted and go to jail.'[16] Later, there were photo opportunities of Rishi Sunak standing aboard Border Force boats and pointing gleefully up at the drones from the coastguard's control room.

The lack of transparency about the extent of their use was rarely, if ever, called into question. The Home Office consistently cited national security reasons for not divulging information on who they had awarded procurement contracts to, how much the contracts were worth and what the private-sector companies were required to do.

With the government unwilling to cooperate, I was obliged to contact a Border Force official, who told me exactly what information they gathered. 'The drone takes a picture of the person driving the boat,' they said. 'That's beamed up to the coastguard. Then we'll get radioed. "It's a black guy in a green hoodie driving it." That's how law enforcement knows who to arrest when they come onshore.'

Just before 3 a.m. on 14 December 2022, Navine Singh, the first mate of the *Arcturus* fishing vessel was up on deck, dredging for scallops in the Dover Strait. It was a still night, with a gentle breeze and calm waters around him.

Suddenly, Singh heard shouting in the waters nearby. He couldn't see anybody, but he could hear their cries, insistent, urgent, close and getting closer. Then there were tiny lights glinting in the darkness – torches from phones – and arms and a head in the water. Somebody was swimming towards their boat.

He ran to wake the skipper, Raymond Strachan, warning him that there were bodies in the water nearby. The bleary-eyed captain took a moment to stir. He had settled down to sleep only a couple of hours before. Peering out of the portside window, Strachan could see five people clinging to the side of the trawler, pleading for help. He asked Singh to wake the rest of the crew and made his way quickly to the wheelhouse.

No more than twenty metres away was a dinghy, flooded and foundering. Strachan instructed his crew to drop their ropes, and they helped the five exhausted men to clamber up to the deck.[17]

As the *Arcturus* moved closer to the scene, panicked passengers still on board the sinking dinghy stood up, desperately waving their arms. There was a loud cracking sound as the sodden wooden boards in the base of the boat gave way. The dinghy was, Strachan later said, 'just a rubber tube, folded in half, the floor gone'.[18]

Amid the swell of bodies in the water, the passengers scrambled to reach the trawler's ropes, swimming over each other, pushing and flailing, trying to pull themselves on to the freeboard.[19] One man slipped as he was climbing up and was crushed to death between the dinghy and the fishing vessel. Another was hit on the head by a broken wooden slat as the boat collapsed, knocking him unconscious.[20] He, and at least three others, drowned in the freezing water. Five more passengers were pushed out to sea by a strong current. Their bodies remain missing.

One of those rescued was acting particularly strangely, Strachan later recalled. 'It was as if things hadn't gone his way. He was very mouthy, trying to give the impression he was in charge.'[21] Strachan alleges that the young man asked him for a cigarette, then stamped his foot when he was told there weren't any.

As the *Arcturus* made its way back to Dover, the rescued teenager became distressed. Pointing and shouting, he could see the body of his Guinean friend, eighteen-year-old Allaji Ba, lying face-up in the water. Still attached to the boat was the corpse of another teenage boy in a black T-shirt, a rope tied round his waist, being dragged alongside the trawler.[22]

INTEGRATION

In January 2024, the anguished young man, nineteen-year-old Ibrahima Bah, stood in the dock at Canterbury Crown Court to take an oath before a twelve-person jury, accused of piloting the stricken dinghy. He faced four counts of manslaughter – one for each of those known to have died in the boat incident – and one count of facilitating illegal entry to the UK. It was the second time the teenager had been hauled through the courts, after the jury in summer 2023 had been discharged, unable to reach a verdict on whether he was guilty or not guilty. Videos and images provided the bulk of the evidence, much of which was played and displayed for the jury to deliberate. Some had been taken by Strachan and Border Force at sea level, and some by the British authorities from an 'eye in the sky'.

The timing of the incident had worked perfectly in the Conservative government's favour. In December 2022, as the boat made its way into British waters, the Nationality and Borders Act had just come into force, making it a criminal offence to arrive in the UK without entry clearance (under what is known as Section 24) or to facilitate entry of an asylum seeker (Section 25).[23] The sentence for Section 25 cases, under which Ibrahima was being tried, ranged from fourteen years to life imprisonment.

Ibrahima had already confessed to piloting the dinghy that night. On the promise of a free crossing for him and his friend Allaji, he had told the smugglers in northern France that he knew how to steer a boat. He had learned in a long, low wooden pirogue near his home in Senegal, where he went out with fishermen, earning a pittance as one of their crew.

When he discovered that the inflatable dinghy provided by the smugglers was not wooden, as he was used to, he had refused to drive. Eyewitnesses said the smugglers had threatened Ibrahima with a knife, hitting and kicking him. 'This is human trafficking so you have to follow their instructions and if you don't follow or you fall behind, then they will beat you up,' one of the Afghan survivors testified. Ibrahima said that he had seen the outline of a gun in a holster.

In its opening statement, the prosecution – a well-spoken, bespectacled man acting simply for 'Rex', the King – acknowledged that the 'threat of death or serious violence was the direct cause of his piloting the boat'.[24] But Ibrahima had a 'duty of care' to protect the other passengers, he stated. His failure to do so resulted in a breach amounting to gross negligence manslaughter. Ibrahima had known, he said, of the smugglers' violence – he had, after all, already been beaten and threatened by them – but he had 'voluntarily associated himself' with them anyway.

For three weeks, Ibrahima sat under the strip lighting, listening as his future was decided by strangers in a language he didn't understand. I became accustomed to dialling in, or watching from the well of the courtroom, as Ibrahima was brought up from the cells beneath the court, his head bowed, his mental health in tatters. At the back of the room behind a screen he stared ahead, blank-faced and statue-still, his interpreter talking rapidly beside him.

In cold, hard language, the prosecution asked him to describe – 'perhaps briefly' – how it felt to watch his friend die under the boat. 'I couldn't see him. I was distraught,' Ibrahima told the court. The questioning swiftly moved on.[25]

> Prosecutor: Did you think it was lawful or unlawful to seek asylum in the UK?
> IB: Lawful.
> Prosecutor: How did you come to think [a small boat] was the way to cross?
> IB: It was the only way for me to get here to claim asylum. There was no other way.

> Prosecutor: The passengers knew, as you did, you were entering illegally.
>
> IB: We all wanted the same thing – to come to this country.

Alongside the visual evidence – the images, the video footage from sea and air – were survivors' testimonies. Most had been gathered hours after they arrived in the UK, having narrowly escaped death. I went to meet them one gusty day in September 2023 at the dilapidated guesthouse on the Kent coast where they had been holed up for nearly a year.[26]

Within an hour of arrival in the UK, the group of survivors had been instructed to point out which of the passengers drove the boat, in what they said felt like a 'police line-up'. Ibrahima had been separated from the group shortly afterwards as they, disoriented, traumatised, were interviewed by law enforcement officials. Their phones had been taken, they were held in a police cell and they had no legal representation. Though they didn't know it, the witness statements they gave at the time formed a component of the evidence used in Ibrahima's trial – the man who had, they said, been a friend, 'like a brother', to many on the boat.

'What happened to Ibrahima?' Abdul-Azim, one of the survivors, asked me. Seven other Afghans who had been on board that night huddled around us. I pulled up a news article and they pointed, nodding at the illustrator's courtroom drawing of their friend. I explained that the jury in Ibrahima's initial trial had been discharged but he would remain in prison until his retrial. Shocked mutters rebounded around the group. None of them had been told. 'Ibrahima is not a criminal. None of us are criminals,' Abdul-Azim said. 'We saw our friends under the boat, we saw them die out at sea. Why can the government not see that we are not to blame for this?'[27]

In court, Abdul-Azim described Ibrahima as an 'angel'. Another witness told the judge, the Honourable Mr Justice Jeremy Johnson KC, that they would all be dead if it weren't for Bah. The judge acknowledged that Ibrahima had done all he could to save those on board and noted that his upbringing had been tough: he had been subjected to child labour and had endured great hardship.

Little consideration was given as to why Ibrahima had left West Africa, or why he was making the crossing to begin with. Records released to the court showed that the teenager had harboured dreams of making music and doing sheet-metal work once he reached the UK: dreams now far out of reach.

I was familiar with the circumstances Ibrahima had fled. In February 2016, I made the first of three visits to Senegal in quick succession, with a view to moving to Dakar as a stringer for the BBC. I began to gather stories there, travelling out to the capital's northern suburbs in a rattly yellow tin-can taxi over dusty, potholed roads. There I visited a DJ school which had received a tiny amount of funding from local municipalities to get young people, hampered by generational poverty and a lack of opportunities, off the streets.[28] A poll from the Oxford Migration Observatory had found that three-quarters of Senegalese people aged nineteen to twenty-five said they wanted to leave in the next five years. Here were some of them.

'We have a growing problem of jihad here in the suburbs,' Amadou, the project coordinator, told me, flicking his waist-length dreadlocks over his shoulder and tugging his baseball cap firmly down. 'If we don't occupy the youth, the youth will occupy themselves.'

In a sticky, darkened room, the trainer, DJ GG Bass, showed the group how to mix records as they watched, filming on their phones. At the end of the set one of the participants turned towards me, smiling and shaking his head in disbelief. I took that to mean the maestro's skills were exemplary.

With the thud of the bass reverberating behind us, I spent the rest of the afternoon taking shade from the red-hot sun under an acacia tree

INTEGRATION

and listening as they told me about their training, their aspirations and their lives in Dakar's suburbs. Many of the group's brothers, cousins and friends had already left to begin the journey to Europe and they wanted to follow closely behind. 'I want to go to Europe to work in construction,' said one of the group, Oumar. 'When I have money, I will return home to Senegal and build a house for my family.'

They asked me about the UK: what London looked like, whether it was different to their surroundings and how people found work there. 'We want to play the big clubs,' Ismaila, another participant, said. 'We want a future and that is just not possible in Senegal.'

Ibrahima may have had the same hopes once, but now, whiling away his days behind bars on the Isle of Sheppey in Kent, the dream of Europe had been shattered. At the end of an arduous three-week trial, he received a nine-and-a-half-year sentence.

Outside the courtroom in Canterbury, the midwinter sun shone beatifically. Ibrahima would be brought to the bowels of the court, then on to HMP Elmley, rarely seeing daylight again for months on end.

A jubilant tweet from the Home Office appeared shortly after his conviction: 'JAILED'.[29] Ibrahima's sentencing showed, it suggested, that it was doing what it had always said it would: stopping the boats.

State surveillance, both over the Channel and across Britain, became more opaque. Multi-million-pound contracts were being quietly awarded to private-sector behemoths. I started to notice the same names cropping up – Capita, G4S, Airbus, Telefonica – all being given generous contracts to carry out the monitoring of migrant groups.

One afternoon, I was on a briefing call with campaigning group Privacy International, discussing the various ways in which the Home Office monitored migrant groups. We talked through GPS-enabled ankle tags, which were being used to racially target and sentence young black men. We spoke about phones being seized from new arrivals at the port of Dover, their data downloaded, ostensibly to track down smugglers in northern France. (Less than a handful of leads resulted from more than 400 phones taken.) And we talked through social media monitoring, used to decipher which individuals would be reunited with their loved ones and which relationships were not genuine.

As the call was ending, a member of the team threw in a 'one last thing' nugget of information. 'There's another company that it may be worth looking up,' they said. 'They make facial recognition smartwatches. We have major concerns with those.' I got off the phone and spent the rest of the afternoon doing exactly that, scouring company listings, looking at impact assessments and submitting freedom of information requests.

It emerged that the government had awarded Buddi Limited, a British technology company, more than £6 million to produce the smartwatches, requiring migrant groups – specifically foreign national offenders, subject to deportation orders – to scan their faces up to five times a day.[30] The intention was that photographs taken using the smartwatches would then be cross-checked against biometric facial images on Home Office systems. If the image verification failed, a check would be performed manually, the documents showed. The data, including 24/7 location-tracking, could be stored for up to six years and shared with the Home Office, Ministry of Justice, Metropolitan Police and local authorities. It was truly Orwellian.

Thankfully, the watches never saw the light of day. 'The Home Office's original requirement for facial recognition technology significantly narrowed the available market,' the House of Commons Public Accounts Committee heard.[31] 'Eleven months after [the Prison and Probation Service] decided to pursue [this] solution, the Ministry of Justice's Security Function advised that the device should no longer be pursued as the operating system was not compliant with cyber security standards... The Home Office has now opted to pursue devices which capture fingerprints instead, which has opened up more options in the market.'

The company awarded yet another generous contract to capture those fingerprints was none other than Buddi Limited.[32] Handheld fobs were rolled out, requiring users to scan their fingerprints up to five times a day. Biometric data, including names, dates of birth and nationality, would be recorded, as well as round-the-clock geolocation tracking. Like ankle tags, the devices would provide a deep insight into an individual's life, revealing intimate details including daily activities, social relationships, medical issues, religion, family and sex life.

I wanted to better understand the psychological impact this kind of everyday surveillance could have on a tagged individual. Over the course of six months, I followed a Nigerian man who was subject to a deportation order and had been released on immigration bail. One of the conditions of his bail was to carry a mobile fingerprint scanner.

Ade had five children, all British-born. He had spent most of his life in the UK, had grown up here and laid down roots. 'Respect, this is a big, big thing for me,' he would tell me often. He had been ankle-tagged previously and had found it heavy and cumbersome. 'When I go to the gym, everyone can see it – it's embarrassing. It makes me feel like people are scared of me because of it.' Ade had specific vulnerabilities, including complex mental health needs. Having been assessed as unsuitable for an ankle tag, the device had been replaced by a portable fingerprint scanner.

The fob was, he felt, lighter but even more invasive than the ankle tag. He had to carry it everywhere with him and leave it out of his pocket so he didn't miss alerts. It would vibrate multiple times a day – 'way more than five, more like fifteen' – often going off in the evenings or at night. As soon as it vibrated, Ade had to scan his fingerprint, or it would be considered a breach of his electronic-monitoring bail conditions. Any breach would then be reviewed by the Home Office. Battery depletion could result in a criminal conviction.

'I feel like I can't move without them breathing down my neck,' Ade said by phone one day. 'It's like I'm always being watched, always being followed. I can never relax any more.' He had been leaving me regular voice memos and sending messages, but a few months in he asked if we could speak on the phone. I sensed that the constant state of hypervigilance made him restless and paranoid. 'I don't trust no one no more.'

At the end of 2023, a report found that the Home Office had increased its use of monitoring devices by 56 per cent on the previous year.[33] The devices created social stigma, had a negative impact on mental wellbeing and could be faulty, the report's authors noted. 'This level of surveillance is not only harmful, it is unnecessary,' they wrote. 'The rate of absconding from immigration bail is tiny. In 2021 it was 2.7 per cent and in the first six months of 2022 it was 1.3 per cent.'[34] There was an assumption within the Home Office that non-fitted devices were less intrusive. Their evidence pointed to the contrary.

'We've seen no safeguards in the latest immigration bail policy to protect individuals,' lawyer Lucie Audibert told me. 'We also have no information nor guarantees about the accuracy rates of the technology and hence no guarantees against misidentification. The introduction of non-fitted devices shouldn't be taken as a more humane or proportionate measure; it's smoke and mirrors, trying to divert attention from the core intrusiveness of these devices. It's just another step in building the total surveillance of migrants.'[35]

Regardless of the evidence of widespread negative impacts, the Conservative government was hellbent on expanding the use of GPS tagging. A pilot study explored how best to roll it out to a broader group.[36] 'In particular, but not exclusively, this is aimed at deterring arrivals by small boats,' the government's report optimistically concluded, as if the threat of an ankle tag or a handheld fob would convince desperate migrants in northern France not to get on board a dinghy bound for the UK. It would have been laughable had the implications not been so serious.

By early 2024, the Home Office had been issued with an enforcement notice by the data protection watchdog, which found that the policy of tagging those who arrived by small boat breached data protection law.[37] The department had, it said, failed to address the privacy intrusion of continuously collecting information on somebody's location.

The Home Office was determined to wrest control by any means, no matter how unethical, invasive or unlawful the method.

12. Raided

'There's really no such thing as the "voiceless". There are only the deliberately silenced, or the preferably unheard.'

Arundhati Roy[1]

In January 2024, just a few days after the new year rolled in, a Brazilian woman and her three children were at their cafe in Brixton market when eight immigration enforcement officers paid them a visit. They began by asking some straightforward questions, nothing too intimidating. How long have you been in the UK? What status do you have? Can you show us your right to work papers?

Two blue-and-yellow-striped vans and a police car could be seen at the end of the lane, parked adjacent to the market entrance. Officers wore stab vests and steel-toecap boots and carried batons and handcuffs. Their questions became more probing, their tone more direct.

A few minutes later, from down the market lane, shouting could be heard as the woman was bundled into a van, arrested on charges related to immigration offences.[2] She had no lawyer, or even a number to call for advice.

The Home Office issued a statement shortly afterwards. 'Illegal working causes untold harm to our communities, cheating honest workers out of employment, putting vulnerable people at risk, and defrauding the public purse.' Its visits to workplaces had doubled in 2023 from the previous year, along with arrests, it boasted. 'This is working,' James Cleverly claimed.[3] 'Of course, they're going to try and hide, but we go looking for them and we find them and then we deport them.'

The day after the Brazilian woman was prised away from her children, I attended a rally in nearby Windrush Square, where anti-raids activists had gathered to galvanise supporters.[4] One held a loudspeaker, raising her voice to be heard over the incessant honking of horns and ambulance sirens around us.

'People are being encouraged to snitch on their neighbours, to tip off the Home Office, who come round and break down the doors of their houses,' she said. 'What's at the heart of these raids is fear. Fear based on racism and classism. This is racial and ethnic profiling, targeting ethnically, racially diverse areas. We have to stay vigilant, we have to stop the raids.' The fifty members of the group raised their fists in unison, cheering each other on.

Another activist began by asking if anybody knew how to resist a raid. There were shakes of the head and a few suggestions. Steps to follow were set out.

> *If you see immigration enforcement or police officers, ask them why they are targeting that individual. Film the officers on your phone.*
>
> *Encourage the person being targeted to lock their doors and close their curtains. They don't need to answer any questions and they don't need to let them in. They are free to leave unless they're under arrest.*
>
> *Tell people nearby 'They're here, they're trying to take people away.' Gathering more people could outnumber the authorities and force them to give way.*

The activists, like other groups in London, were part of a network of grassroots movements, set up in response to an increase in the number of raids in their communities. There were students, parents with children on their shoulders, and people who had themselves been targeted.

Some of the anti-raids group members told me about the use of force they had been subjected to or witnessed while resisting raids. One showed me a video on their phone of a police officer repeatedly punching their friend in the head as he tried to prevent their van from leaving with a deportee inside.[5] 'They're brutal – they show absolutely no restraint. If they're going to do that to us in broad daylight, what about the people inside the vans?'

At the end of the rally, the group of activists split off to walk the streets around Windrush Square, handing out leaflets to inform the local community about their rights. 'See a raid? Don't walk by!' the leaflets urged.[6] Another was a Q&A brochure: 'What should I do if I'm arrested?' (Say 'No comment' and seek legal advice). 'Do I have to answer police questions?' (No). 'Do I have the right to protest?' (Yes).

While raids like the one in Brixton had increased in recent months, the tactics deployed by the Home Office were nothing new. For years, immigration enforcement raids had been a key feature of the hostile environment, with vans circulating around areas where people of colour lived. The intention was to either scare them into leaving the country voluntarily, or to detain and forcibly remove them.

Some of those targeted had come over at the invitation of the British government, to rebuild the nation from the rubble left by the Second World War. Most infamously, this included the Windrush generation: pension-age, long-term residents who had moved to the UK as children from Britain's former colonies in the Caribbean.

As the courageous *Guardian* journalist Amelia Gentleman, who exposed the scandal, writes in her book *The Windrush Betrayal*, this was 'the latest chapter in a long, guilty history of colonial occupation and exploitation. The names of many of those affected – Winston, Gladstone, Nelson – speak to their colonial childhoods.'[7]

Those who came forward to tell their stories described their terror and confusion at the sight of Home Office immigration enforcement teams smashing their way into their houses before hauling them away. At least 164 people were wrongly detained and deported.[8] Some later died, or were forced into destitution, living homeless on the streets of a country they had left decades before.[9] Despite being entitled to compensation, most never received any payment. They were, Amelia writes, dismissed by the authorities as 'a group of people who didn't matter, a group who, if nothing else, were sufficiently marginalised that they were unlikely to complain'.[10]

Immigration enforcement practices have long been a blot on Britain's reputation for just and equitable law and order. Their remit is broad. The Home Office states that the objectives of the units are to prevent illegal entry to the UK, limit unlawful access to services and other support, disrupt criminal gangs and perform enforcement visits to businesses and residential properties before removing any of those deemed to be in the UK without permission.[11] In reality, it's a sprawling and unruly body that causes no end of headaches for Home Office officials. I distinctly recall the sound of groans around my bench in the press office whenever a story emerged about another raid gone wrong.

In a scathing report in 2021, the House of Commons Public Accounts Committee found that the Home Office had 'no idea' what impact its £400-million-a-year immigration enforcement unit had achieved, adding that the department relies on a 'disturbingly weak evidence base'.[12] A lack of diversity at the top of the Home Office risked a repeat of the Windrush scandal, the cross-party committee said, warning that, without substantial evidence, immigration enforcement risked making decisions based on 'anecdote, assumption and prejudice'.[13]

Misdirected raids continued to blight the Home Office and waste valuable resources. Questions were raised about how intelligence-led the visits were. The evidence it used was classified as 'low-grade' – usually tip-offs from employers, rival business owners and concerned members of the public – which tended to be inaccurate. Each year, it is estimated that police and immigration enforcement receive around 50,000 tip-offs: about 150 a day.[14] The majority (around 60 per cent) of the alerts turn out to be bogus.

The government stepped up its activities regardless. In April 2024, an embattled Conservative Party began to target reporting centres, with asylum seekers being pulled aside during routine Home Office appointments.[15] Several were told they would be detained and then deported to Rwanda, that they were wanted criminals. 'When I went to sign they told me they want to give me papers,' a Syrian man told Channel 4 News.[16] 'They took me aside and after that there was a police van. They took my phone and put me in a [cell]. I'm very scared.'

Car washers, nail bar technicians, beauty therapists: immigration enforcement was coming after them all. Within a few weeks of Labour sweeping to power in July 2024, over 1,000 staff who had been working on the Rwanda scheme were redeployed to the new government's 'returns and enforcement' programme. A 'summer blitz' was carried out, aimed at removing more people from the country. In just one week alone, over 225 premises – predominantly car washes – were visited and seventy-five workers detained pending deportation.

'We cannot pretend everything is OK,' Yvette Cooper told the *Sun on Sunday*.[17] 'Not when criminal gangs are making millions out of dangerous small boat crossings that undermine our border security and put lives at risk.' Those caught up in the raids would, like so many others, be given no chance to explain or provided with any legal recourse.

*

INTEGRATION

One morning during the holy month of Ramadan, Abdul woke up early to pray alongside his wife and daughter. All was peaceful and calm outside, and a day of fasting and worship at the nearby mosque lay ahead. Their *fajr* recitations said, the family all returned to their beds.

A short while later, at around 7 a.m., there was a sudden commotion outside his home. Parting the curtains, he could see eight officers outside, dressed in navy-blue uniforms with stab vests on, carrying heavy-duty equipment. Who were they here for? he wondered. It couldn't be for him, could it?

Abdul began to panic. He had recently found himself caught in a 'grey zone'. His asylum claim had failed. He had been offered no explanation why. It had taken a few days to gather himself and draw together more evidence to support a fresh claim. He had thought that once he submitted the evidence to his solicitor, the process would be underway again.

It came as a shock to find out that his solicitor had forgotten to file the paperwork, leaving a window of time during which he would be locked out of the system. Abdul knew from the stories of others at his community centre in north-east Glasgow that this was when it could all go very wrong. His case could flag up as red, with immigration enforcement seizing the moment to swoop in and catch their prey. Lying still in the darkness, Abdul felt his chest constrict, afraid to breathe.

The buzzer sounded, making him jump. Abdul's wife stirred. He remained frozen, fixed to the mattress beneath him. A loud knock at the door followed, boots skidding on the flooring in the stairwell. His daughter came into their room, confused: she didn't know anything about her father's problems. They had wanted to protect her from the instability of it all.

Now his name was being shouted through the door, the knocking more insistent. He thought he heard counting – counting down – 3, 2, 1.

Then the door was forced open with a battering ram. The officers moved room to room, looking for him. A man of dignity in his mid-sixties, Abdul hadn't had time to put on clothes. He stood before the immigration enforcement officers in his T-shirt and underwear, feeling small and frail and frightened.

His wife and daughter were pulled away into a separate room. Three officials guarded the door to ensure they couldn't get to him. They tried to push through with all their might, their eyes wide, hands grasping for him, and were forcibly moved back from the doorway.

One of the officials gave Abdul a letter telling him he would be removed from the country. 'You have to come with us,' they said. He asked to call a solicitor and was told he couldn't.

An immigration enforcement officer spotted little packs of pills on the table. He picked them up and waved them in Abdul's direction. 'What do you need these for?' he asked. Abdul was being treated for a heart condition. At that moment, he felt a sudden pain in his chest and collapsed on to the floor.

'I have never before in my life seen eight police – not in Pakistan, not in Libya before I came here, nowhere,' he later told me. 'I came here for protection, for a better life, not for more problems.' Alone in a hospital bed, Abdul was told the immigration enforcement officers would return again soon.

Members of the Scottish Parliament from across the political spectrum took up his case, writing in ever greater numbers to the Home Office. The highly controversial dawn raids were an 'appalling practice', they said.[18] MSPs, who had long argued that immigration should be devolved to the Scottish authorities amid a divisive debate surrounding Scottish independence, were feeling the pressure from their constituents to act. They called upon the UK government to 'urgently clarify' whether the decision to carry out the raid on Abdul's home represented a change in policy.[19]

INTEGRATION

It did. Days later, two Indian Sikh men were bundled out of their homes on Kenmure Street in Glasgow's Southside in another dawn raid, handcuffed and held inside a stuffy, windowless police van.[20] Outside, hundreds of people gathered to block the path of the van, staging a sit-in and chanting, 'Let them go!'. One activist, later dubbed 'Van Man', crawled underneath, remaining there throughout the day-long stand-off. Two hundred riot police armed with batons and shields and more than forty riot vans surrounded the group.

Meanwhile, a tuck shop was set up in a bus shelter, providing food and water. People brought cakes to celebrate Eid al-Fitr, while local cafes and residents in the area opened their doors to allow onlookers and demonstrators to use their toilets. 'I couldn't believe that the Home Office had done this on one of the holiest days in the Muslim calendar,' said Aamer Anwar, a prominent civil rights lawyer resident in Glasgow.[21]

Eight hours later, after fraught negotiations with Police Scotland, Anwar boarded the van to explain in Punjabi to the men that they were free. 'I said, you're free because of these people, the people of Glasgow.' Videos show the two men standing at the open doors of the van, raising their fists over the heads and joining their hands in gratitude as the victorious crowd cheered and chanted.

Watching events unfold on television, Abdul felt overwhelmed by the memory of what had happened to him. 'This was a wonderful moment, to see everybody helping,' he told me in early 2024. 'But it continues. They come for people in the night, in the morning. I still cannot sleep and I wake up, worried they will come for me again.'

The West London town of Southall has been a hub for the burgeoning South Asian community for over seventy years. Known locally as 'Little India', many arrived from the Punjab region in the 1950s, drawn by the promise of work at the town's factories and neighbouring Heathrow airport. Its Broadway is packed with street food carts selling crunchy, golden-brown panipuri and pakora and its vibrant shop windows showcase collections of embroidered pink and turquoise saris. *Bend It Like Beckham* was filmed here, and leaders including David Cameron and Boris Johnson have made visits to meet faith leaders at the largest Sikh gurdwara outside India.[22]

Tailors, money exchange shops, restaurants: once the Punjabi community settled, they established businesses which soon flourished. The first factory to produce Indian ready meals was built in the town, with the owner taking out a loan of £650,000. Noon's Foods went on to turn over £650 million.[23]

Despite the success enjoyed by many in the local community, racial tensions have long been a feature of life in Southall.[24] Riots dated back generations to some of their first days on British soil. In the late 1970s, the National Front took to the streets, stabbing teenager Gurdip Singh Chaggar to death.[25] 'One down, one million to go,' the far-right group's chairman John Kingsley Read threatened.

Five years later, in 1981, more than 200 self-proclaimed 'skinheads' travelled by bus to the town, shouting neo-Nazi slogans, smashing shop windows, throwing bricks and clubbing children in the streets. When a terrified resident called the Metropolitan Police, they were told that if they didn't like it they should leave.[26] The local community gathered together to protect themselves, defiant organisations taking root. One prominent leader said they needed to make the town a 'no-go area for racists'.

In 2013, Southall became a target area for Home Office immigration raids, being one of the six London boroughs where 'Go Home' vans circulated during Theresa May's tenure. 'We can help you return voluntarily without fear of arrest or detention,' read posters plastered on walls around the town. The bizarrely named Operation Vaken ran for just a month in the summer of 2013 and it had limited success.[27] A Home Office report later found that only eleven people had self-deported during that time.

The Home Office had largely left the town's residents alone after that, but it continued to argue that voluntary returns remained the most 'cost-effective and dignified' way to remove migrants from the country.[28]

When I visited Southall in autumn 2023, immigration enforcement vans were still present. It was the first time I had seen the units circulating and it took me by surprise. The reason soon became clear.

Among the Asian confectionary shops and Afghan supermarkets was a large and growing street homeless community of undocumented migrants. A black market had sprung up around them. Each morning, as men emerged from sleeping bags under bridges and in shop doorways, construction companies would drive around, stopping at street corners and offering cash-in-hand work on building sites. Most were promised pay at the end of the week, but they rarely got it. Terrified of the authorities, they couldn't go to the police to ask for help or to local authorities for the correct paperwork to find regulated jobs. Many had been destitute for decades. There was no Citizen's Advice Bureau, no free immigration advice, no information at all.

Amid this climate of fear, with an omnipresent Home Office, places of worship had become sanctuaries for the local community. In that, Southall was bountiful: there are more than forty faith spaces in the town, each with enormous congregations. On every street there is at least one white-marble gurdwara, gold-gilded temple, ornate mosque or elegant church. One of the gurdwaras I visited hosted, on average, 3,000 worshippers a week, with queues out the door.[29] These were trusted spaces which anybody could visit without judgement to get a hot meal in the community kitchen and a place to rest, safe and warm, if needed. They were obvious places for immigration enforcement to pay a visit.

Rather than raiding the places of worship, the Home Office was engaged in a more underhand exercise. It ran what it euphemistically called 'surgeries' inside the faith spaces, ostensibly offering advice to help undocumented people regularise their status.[30]

Shakila Taranum Maan had seen the Home Office in Southall numerous times. They went to a gurdwara or a temple knowing they would find people who 'fit the bill': homeless people who had no money, no papers and were likely working on the black market. 'Low-hanging fruit, basically.'

Day in, day out Shakila came into contact with street homeless members of the community during drop-ins at the charity she ran, Southall Black Sisters. She tried to warn them about the government's intentions. Did they know what the Home Office was really there to do? She wondered whether people knew that when they attended, they were giving their personal details — including information about their immigration status — to a government official.

Worse, faith leaders — trusted by so many — had encouraged members of their congregations to attend the Home Office surgeries. Leaflets could be seen on noticeboards inside the places of worship, in Punjabi, Portuguese (for the large Goan community) and English.[31] Some of the sacred spaces were charitable organisations, set up to help people. She thought that was where their focus should be, not working alongside the government. 'I mean, God knows, there are many people who need help around here.'

A couple of years earlier, Shakila had attended one of the immigration enforcement surgeries at a faith space nearby with the husband of one of her clients, a woman who was critically ill and could no longer walk. She had been known to the Home Office. After several hospital visits, the NHS Trust had contacted the department to inform them that the woman had lapsed status.

As her health deteriorated, the woman's husband began to receive phone calls encouraging him to attend a surgery. Initially he ignored this advice, but then he started to be approached in the street by members of the community, telling him this would be the 'best thing' for his family. Harassed and intimidated, the man reluctantly decided to go along to find out how they could regularise their status so that his now very sick wife could stay in the UK to continue her treatment.

Outside their place of worship, there was a table with three officious-looking people behind it, all wearing lanyards and blue shirts – people who, Shakila said, had a 'magnanimous, powerful aura' about them. Her client's husband appeared frightened and confused by their presence.

Inside the door a promotional video played, which had been filmed in the Punjab region, with 'freshly painted houses' behind smiling children.[32] In a voiceover to the video, which was later sent to me, an official from the Home Office's voluntary returns team tells viewers this is where their future awaits them. Shakila's client was told that he and his wife would be given £3,000 to help them 'reintegrate' into a community they had left decades before. The couple felt they had no choice, so they went.

The bright future depicted in the video was very far from the reality. Shakila knew what awaited people once they returned to the Punjab. Almost every state-run school was closed. It was almost impossible to find work. If they were lucky, they would have somewhere to stay, but many relatives would likely have died, leaving countless voluntary returnees homeless and destitute. They faced 'massive ostracisation, massive stigma' from their communities. Heroin was rampant. 'The Home Office might try to sugar-coat it but we know the truth. There is nothing for them when they go back.'

I began to investigate the Home Office surgeries and the voluntary returns programme to understand how voluntary the scheme really was.³³ One day I got hold of some data, which contained a surprising level of detail. Not only was I sent a spreadsheet with the number of surgeries held per quarter since records began, but also the addresses of each place of worship and how many times they had invited the Home Office on to their premises.

The data showed that there had been 722 non-enforcement visits from the third quarter of 2019 to the fourth quarter of 2023, and at least five enforcement visits.³⁴ The Home Office included a helpful clarification in its cover note: 'The purpose of these [enforcement] visits was to transport individuals to airports to make voluntary departures that had already been arranged.'³⁵ Immigration enforcement was taking people directly from the place of worship, their sanctuary, to an airport for return.

One of the premises which had hosted the highest number of surgeries was the annexe to a place of worship in Old Southall. I drove down there on a day when I had heard that the Home Office would be present.

In the dark hall next to the kitchen, over a hundred people – predominantly Sikh men, wearing saffron-coloured turbans – lined up for warm bowls of dhal and cups of milky tea. Some talked on the phone or huddled around low tables on plastic chairs. Others sat in rows in front of a screen playing a Bollywood film. Well-meaning volunteers were dishing up, washing up and signposting people to the desks surrounding the perimeter of the room.

I explained to the volunteers that I was a journalist interested in how voluntary returns worked and they told me I was in luck. Near the door was a member of the Home Office's returns team, happy to discuss the scheme.

'We've helped get more than forty people repatriated in two years,' the department's representative said. 'They get to know us over many years and we build their trust, so then people come to us and they say,

"Please help us."' Referrals were often made, with members of the street homeless community passing names on to them and occasionally bringing people to the drop-in sessions.

The official explained that the returns process could take a while: eight, sometimes nine months, from start to finish. What they needed to establish first was whether someone still had family in their home country – if they did, that sped up the process. An affidavit confirming that the person had come from that village originally, alongside their mother and father's name and any other documentation, such as a birth certificate, would be gathered. The Home Office official would then 'escort' the individual to a passport centre, secure an emergency travel document and a flight would be booked for them. The £3,000 payment would then be made to help them settle on their return.

For the last few days in the UK, accommodation was booked 'to make sure they return fresh'. Charities provided suitcases and clothes. If somebody changed their mind at the last minute, they were obliged to have a meeting with the Home Office to explain why they no longer wanted to leave. 'This doesn't happen,' the official assured me. 'Indians, they go. It's the Eastern Europeans who go and then come back again – it is sometimes very messy.'

At a table nearby were representatives from St Mungo's and Thames Reach, two charities involved in a controversial operation which had rounded up European rough sleepers – primarily members of the Roma community – then arrested and deported them.[36]

St Mungo's and Thames Reach had been contracted by the Greater London Authority under 'payment for numbers' schemes, with fees increasing depending on the number of rough sleepers they flagged to the Home Office for removal. The joint missions were intended to target 'high-harm' foreign offenders, but were later found to have caught individuals who may have only spent one night rough sleeping. A freedom of information request from Corporate Watch in 2017 revealed that 141 patrols had been organised by the Greater London Authority in twelve boroughs. In under a year, 133 rough sleepers were detained, with 127 people deported from the Westminster area alone.[37]

When the scandal emerged, the two charities' chief executives acknowledged that their outreach missions had been intended to persuade non-UK rough sleepers to leave voluntarily. Internal reviews had been conducted.[38] The chief executives had apologised for collaborating with the Home Office to share information about migrant rough sleepers.[39] Yet here they were at a surgery alongside government officials.

I asked the voluntary returns lead why the charities were present at the drop-in, given historic controversies. 'We invite them here – it's a place where they can meet our clients,' I was told. 'It's where they find the most people.' (St Mungo's later told me it never shares information about its clients with the department unless the client has given 'full and informed consent', while Thames Reach stated that its involvement at the drop-ins was 'purely to connect people with the advice and support they need, not to facilitate enforcement actions'.)

At the end of the session, as chairs were stacked and pots put away, I asked my Home Office contact whether they ever felt any guilt for encouraging people to leave the country. There were stories, I said, of lives ruined once people returned. 'No guilt, no,' the official said, head shaking vigorously. 'I keep in touch with many of them and they tell me they are so happy to be back. Here, they were sleeping on the streets, working cash-in-hand. Now they are back, working in their fields, helping with their father's business. Yes, sometimes it is difficult, but many people, they show me the beautiful house where they are living. It is better for them, I am sure.'

13. When The State Gives Up

> *'In the first place, as the homeless wanderers of the twentieth century prove, the question of nationality no longer necessarily involves the question of allegiance. Allegiance, after all, has to work two ways; and one can grow weary of an allegiance which is not reciprocal.'*
>
> James Baldwin, *Nobody Knows My Name*[1]

At just before 10 a.m. on a bitterly cold January morning, a queue was forming outside an access hub in Glasgow's city centre. Many in line had sleeping bags wrapped round their shoulders, and tattered woolly hats and mittens. One man had spent the night on the streets wearing sliders and socks with holes in the toes. He stamped his feet and blew on his hands to try to thaw out. A young woman in a long-sleeved T-shirt rocked a pram back and forth. Her jumper, an extra blanket, was wrapped round her baby. It was minus five and many had endured the biting winds and frost huddled in parks or walking the streets, with temperatures dropping as low as minus seven.

Among those waiting at the Simon Community's doors were refugees who had recently been granted status as part of Rishi Sunak's drive to clear the legacy backlog. In mid-2023, having realised that the government was nowhere near meeting his target of processing

92,000 asylum claims by the end of the year, the prime minister had got his skates on. The Home Office took 'immediate action', nearly tripling the number of asylum decision makers to rattle through old cases and either grant leave to remain or withdraw claims en masse.[2]

Then, on 1 January 2024, a triumphant press release rolled into my inbox: Sunak had done it! 'LEGACY BACKLOG CLEARED', the headline roared.[3] 'Quite a bit of number-fudging,' a Home Office contact messaged, as reporters across the UK used their New Year's Day napkins to do some rudimentary maths.

A rebuke from the UK Statistics Authority swiftly followed.[4] Sir Robert Chote, economist and chair of the watchdog, said voters had been 'misled' by repeated false claims that the backlog had been cleared when, in fact, nearly 100,000 people were still in limbo. The episode, Chote said, 'may affect public trust' on this and other targets which had not been met.[5]

The embattled prime minister likely had little understanding of the impact his career-saving move had on those at the tail end of it. All the recently granted refugees waiting outside the access hub had found themselves cast out on to the streets and forced into destitution, automatically locked out of their accommodation now that they had leave to remain. While the Home Office had promised a hiatus over the Christmas period, evictions resumed as soon as the festive season was over.

As the charity's doors opened and people filed inside the centre, pinched mouths and narrowed eyes relaxed. Paper cups of coffee were handed around, plates of biscuits laid out. At either side of the room were two stations: one for Scots and another for migrant groups. Over the course of three days, I stood at the advice desk for destitute asylum seekers with Hazem, a Libyan refugee who had arrived to study a Master's in law some years before.[6] On completing his studies, he had quickly found himself in a precarious position, his student visa expired and his status insecure.

It had taken time, but now he and his wife both had leave to remain. With his immaculate English, Hazem had chosen to support people who, like him, had fallen on hard times. Leafing through Home Office letters, photocopying documents and contacting the local council were now his focus. He had precisely the unflappable, assured manner required to navigate the messiness of destitution.

Every day now, Hazem saw at least a dozen people coming in who had just been granted status and who now faced homelessness. They arrived distressed, either fragile or furious. They had waited for this moment; it should have been time to celebrate. Instead, their access to state benefits had been cut off, Aspen card top-ups stopped. They needed to get in touch with the local authority themselves, often with limited English. The job centres were losing patience. Then there was the whole range of housing issues. Too many people were left with no option but to sleep rough.

A teenager from Yemen hovered nervously around the desk, appearing disorientated. He had been evicted from his asylum hotel in the centre of Glasgow two weeks before, after being granted leave to remain. For four nights he had gone to a mosque to get a couple of hours' rest, but when it closed at midnight he had been forced back out on to the streets. 'I was walking, just walking, all night, trying not to be so cold.'[7]

Hazem rifled through the paperwork then sat him down privately to discuss the best course of action, speaking calmly to him in Arabic. He noticed that talking to people in their own language helped them to know he was on their side.

While he didn't have exact numbers, Hazem had been on the front desk long enough to detect a spike in newly granted refugees requiring emergency accommodation. The Scottish Refugee Council said that the number of referrals they received for this specific group increased by 91 per cent between July and October 2023.[8] That figure didn't surprise Hazem. What he couldn't get his head around was how little had been done to prepare for this eventuality. Everybody across the country had warned the Home Office that this was an inevitable consequence of its policies, but their words had fallen on deaf ears.

The timing of the jump in referrals was no coincidence. In the summer of 2023, the Home Office had introduced another policy which had undermined the possibility of newly granted refugees settling and progressing. They had quietly slashed the so-called 'move-on time' – the period between being granted leave to remain and being evicted from Home Office accommodation – from twenty-eight days to, in some cases, as little as seven days.[9] The refugees – who had all been considered in genuine need of protection by the department's own caseworkers – were given only a few days to find somewhere else to live.

Tents sheltering newly granted refugees began popping up in inner-city areas. Outreach teams in Glasgow spotted young migrant men in parks in greater numbers. One member of the Simon Community street team said his primary concern was those who remained unknown to them, who had gone underground, either through choice or out of necessity. 'The tendency of refugees is to try and be invisible, probably because of their experience of violence and racism, and not knowing if streets are safe,' he told me.[10]

By September 2023, a report from the Refugee Council found that there had been a 239 per cent jump in refugees requiring homelessness support in London alone.[11] Two in every five people were street homeless. After an outcry from campaigners and charities, the department was forced to reverse its policy, bringing the move-on time back up to twenty-eight days. But for many caught up in the maelstrom it was already too late.

Shortly after I got back from Glasgow, an Afghan family – one of the first to cross by small boat following the Taliban takeover in August 2021 – contacted me one Sunday morning. Abdullah was frantic, explaining that they had been granted refugee status and promptly issued with an eviction notice. He had three young children and a three-month-old baby. Both he and his wife had been diagnosed with PTSD and claustrophobia after months spent in hiding in Kabul.

The only offer of accommodation was a flat on the eighth floor of a high-rise tenement block, far outside Newcastle. When he went to visit he had found mould in the bathroom, no shower and cracked windows. Abdullah worried about his family's security. 'One of my children could fall. It is inappropriate for six people, and it is unsafe.' He had refused to leave the hotel, telling me staff had threatened to call the police if they had not moved on by 1 p.m.

After hours stuck on phone lines – Migrant Help, Gateshead Council, a once-helpful caseworker, their local MP, charities – I was the only one who responded to his calls. I put out a post on Twitter asking for support. A short while later, the council got in touch with them, but they had already fled further south. I asked Gateshead Council whether they knew that the family had been forced to leave the area to find secure accommodation. 'Aware they've moved on,' came the terse reply.[12]

It had become difficult to ignore the way in which Afghans, in particular, were being consistently disrespected and disregarded. The same summer, the Home Office had announced that it was closing all 'bridging' accommodation and moving the 8,000 Afghans staying there to permanent housing.[13] At the time of the announcement, around half of those in temporary hotels and flats were children. If they refused the first location offered, they would be made destitute and risked losing access to all support. Within a couple of weeks, the Local Government

INTEGRATION

Association said that 20 per cent of all those presenting as homeless across the UK were Afghans.[14]

Instead of pledging support for those facing homelessness, Defence Minister Johnny Mercer surreptitiously recorded a video statement informing those in bridging accommodation that, while their work alongside the British forces was appreciated, it was time to go. A contact leaked the video to me.[15]

In it, a suited-and-booted Mercer speaks directly to Afghan people, with Dari subtitles underneath and a Union Jack flag beside him. He tells Afghans that ensuring their safe relocation to the UK had been a 'matter close to [his] heart', but that something had to change. Hotel accommodation wasn't a viable long-term option. Within three months, they needed to be out. 'I want to make it really clear that the government will stop paying for your hotels . . . There is no reason why anyone should not have somewhere to live by this time.'[16]

A find-your-own accommodation scheme was set up with funding allocated to local authorities to support Afghans to move into private rental accommodation. Local authorities would, Mercer said, help Afghans to budget their allowances, looking at how much they could spend on rent each month.

'You must look in affordable parts of the UK,' Mercer instructed, like some kind of imperial viceroy, condescending and patronising his loyal subjects. There was enough housing, he claimed – despite all evidence to the contrary – but Afghans needed to 'manage their expectations' about where they could live. Never mind whether they had laid down roots, found jobs, arranged school places or integrated in their communities. 'These are not good enough reasons to say you cannot move to another part of the country,' Mercer warned. 'It is what all other people in the UK have to do.'

The minister finished his rallying cry by telling Afghans, many of whom had been more senior in the military than he ever was, that they were unlikely to be offered a council house and shouldn't wait. 'I need you to take responsibility for your future.'

With an acute shortage of housing stock nationwide, a surge in the number of people living in temporary accommodation and strained local authority budgets, many bewildered refugees decided it was better not to hang around and wait for a leaky roof over their heads. Like Abdullah and his family, many chose to pack their bags and try their luck elsewhere.

For local authorities, the problems created by central government had an immediate financial impact. Across the country families were already struggling to keep pace with the cost-of-living crisis. The issue of evicting refugees and fobbing them off to councils only added to already constrained budgets. Now they were being forced to shell out £1.74 billion a year on hotels, BnBs and other temporary housing to keep people off the streets.

In October 2023, more than a hundred local authority leaders met at an emergency summit amid fears that record high temporary accommodation bills would push more councils into bankruptcy.[17] Together, they pleaded with Chancellor Jeremy Hunt for a funding package to tackle the climbing homelessness levels. They needed an 'urgent intervention', they said. Without it they would have 'no option' but to scale back the essential safety net relied upon by some of the most vulnerable people in society.[18] Historic underfunding and unprecedented pressure to find savings was, by that time, leading many councils to insolvency. Additional pressures from refugees reporting as homeless – in particular those from Afghanistan and Ukraine – had become unsustainable.

Councils received no response from Jeremy Hunt's Treasury. The Home Office rowed in, though, saying it would 'continue to demand that local authorities deliver on their mandated commitments to their regional dispersal plans'.[19]

But councils were already doing all they could to manage allocations of dispersal accommodation. There simply wasn't enough. The country was, after all, in the midst of a housing crisis. The social housing stock had largely been sold off and none had been built to replace it. The saturated and precarious private rental market profited nobody except landlords, who hoarded their wealth while Generation Rent added to their pension pots. There were no protections in place. Putting down a deposit to buy a house was, for most, implausible. Even if they could afford it, mortgages, particularly for first-time buyers, were harder to come by. Sofa surfing, rough sleeping and temporary accommodation were at an all-time high. Meanwhile, properties lay empty, with no meaningful discussion from the government about bringing them back into use.

As central government abandoned local authorities to their fate, morale dipped lower. Contacts across the country told me of unmanageable workloads, the impossibility of helping those who urgently needed help. The Home Office, meanwhile, ramped up the rhetoric. A couple of weeks after councils sounded the alarm, Suella Braverman took to Twitter to demonise rough sleepers, describing homelessness as a 'lifestyle choice'.[20] Unless she acted, British cities would turn into places like San Francisco and Los Angeles, she posted, 'where weak policies have led to an explosion of crime, drug-taking and squalor'.

But Suella wasn't weak. Oh no. She had a novel way of tackling the issue, vowing to make it a civil offence for charities to give out tents to rough sleepers in urban areas. Anybody found to have supported them would be fined. Just in case there was any doubt about her intentions, she took to social media to stipulate that the measure was intended to target migrant groups, tweeting that rough sleepers are primarily 'from abroad'.[21]

The Home Office started a nationwide consultation with local authorities to set an annual cap on the number of refugees who would be settled in the UK each year.[22] The consultation would involve meetings with councils to understand how many people could be accommodated in each area. The Local Government Association responded with its concerns. How were councils to know how many new arrivals there might be over the coming months? What were they to tell local communities who were struggling? And, crucially, where was the money going to come from?

Hot on the heels of the cap came another proposal badged 'British homes for British workers', in which UK families would be given higher priority and faster access to social housing.[23] The slogan was straight out of the Reform UK playbook, insinuating that migrants simply arrived in the country and took homes from under the noses of Brits on waiting lists. Changes proposed included banning specific nationalities from social housing, which would likely be unlawful under equalities law, and barring those with refugee status from accessing social housing, which was also controversial, given that their status permitted them access to benefits.

What it failed to highlight was that 90 per cent of social housing went to UK nationals anyway;[24] 81 per cent of new housing went to white British citizens. Most migrants in the UK were excluded; the so-called 'no recourse to public funds' community (who have certain conditions attached to their visas and limited access to homelessness assistance and most other benefits) were not allowed to claim for social housing.

'It is unnecessary, unenforceable and unjust,' said Shelter's chief executive Polly Neate. 'It blames a group of people for a housing emergency that they did not create.'[25]

*

INTEGRATION

With toothless suggestions from central government and local authorities facing bankruptcy, charities were forced to try to find their own solutions.

In Glasgow a new model was trialled, set up through a charity called Safe in Scotland. They had once run a night shelter for destitute asylum seekers, which I visited in 2016. There were beds, a kitchen providing hot meals and cups of tea and a warm TV room. I met Algerians, Nigerians, Poles, a mixture of languages floating through the slightly stagnant air. It was an inclusive place, though not without its challenges. Fights regularly broke out, and there was competition for resources, but it had provided a roof over many heads. Then Covid hit, and the shelter was shut.

When I returned to Glasgow seven years after that first visit, I went to their new site, where asylum seekers were now housed in supported accommodation in the community. As part of the pilot project, a couple of dozen people had been provided with an en-suite room, a caseworker and cash support. There were asylum seekers, appeal-rights-exhausted migrants, those with no recourse to public funds and European Economic Area (EEA) nationals without settled status after Brexit. Securing funding was an ongoing issue, but it worked. They were able to do a lot with very little.

Over copious cups of black coffee laced with sugar, Bilal, a refused asylum seeker from Bangladesh who had been on Section 4 support for over a decade, described the relief of finding a stable roof over his head. 'It's like a family, we can sit together, eating together. We're not isolated. At last, we have a safe space.'

While Safe in Scotland had managed to make it through the pandemic, others had struggled. Some had even been forced to close their doors, their staff furloughed and volunteers asked to stay at home.

Two days before the first national lockdown hit, I went to a food distribution point on the Strand, where rough sleepers were being given a warm bowl of dhal and rice.[26] Though Boris Johnson carried on shaking hands and refuting it, the writing was on the wall: Covid was coming to Britain. The streets were already falling silent. Aeroplanes overhead were fewer, buses passed less frequently. Talk of self-isolation was starting, a two-metre rule. As I walked over Waterloo Bridge, I noticed people rushing suspiciously past each other, almost hugging the kerbs. Masks were flying off the shelves and there was a 200 per cent mark-up on tiny bottles of sanitiser gel. Many had started to stockpile tins of food and toilet paper. Those huddled round the trestle tables wouldn't ever get any.

Seeing my dictaphone and notepad, a man called Sabah approached me to ask what I wanted to know. He had been rough sleeping for over a decade. Sometimes he found a bed in a shelter, or on someone's sofa, but more often than not, he would be found in a doorway somewhere around central London. At eighty-one, and with myriad health complications, Sabah greeted each day as a celebration. He felt lucky to still be alive.

A failed asylum seeker from Pakistan, he had become stuck in Britain and locked out of the system. When he first arrived, he had hoped to find work and secure status before bringing his wife and children to join him. After multiple failed claims, Sabah knew that his options were limited. He could either remain homeless in the UK or return voluntarily to Pakistan, with not a penny to his name. He felt he couldn't live with the shame and the stigma if he did that. He would wait out the rest of his days here, 'in God's land', still more free than he would be if he went back.[27]

Having finished his dinner, Sabah prepared to bed down for the night. It was around 9.30 and temperatures had dropped. He tucked himself into the doorway of a closed stationery shop, pulling a sleeping bag over his knees. I sat down beside him next to two large blue-and-red-chequered storage bags, mainly full of clothes.

INTEGRATION

Things were starting to change now. Everybody was talking about a virus, an ominous note lingering in the air. Sabah worried that the first place it would hit would be the streets around him. 'When it reaches us, it will spread like wildfire,' he said.

He usually found safety in numbers, moving as a group with a few others – 'the good thing for us is we're mobile!' – but they were all over sixty-five and more likely to become seriously unwell if they got Covid. The police would be circulating soon, he had heard, detaining anyone who tested positive. That could spell trouble for him and his friends, who were all undocumented.

A Polish man with a wispy beard in a Cossack hat approached Sabah's stoop to ask if they would be quarantined. He had arrived only a few weeks before and there were a lot of mixed messages from the government. Like Sabah, he didn't have a smartphone with internet access to find up-to-date information. He had been going to the library to use the computer there, but almost all public spaces had closed now. Sabah told the newcomer he didn't know what the plans were, but he feared that they would be the last to find out.

A £3.2 million funding package had been announced by Robert Jenrick, then housing minister, to reimburse local authorities for the cost of accommodation and services so that those on the streets could self-isolate to prevent the virus spreading.[28] Then, a week later, the government announced a new scheme known as 'Everyone In', which would house anyone, regardless of their status. During the first national lockdown in spring 2020, councils accommodated more than 37,000 people who were already rough sleeping, or at risk of it.[29] 'Everyone In' showed there was enough space, if the government was willing to fund it.

But by September 2020, the pot of money had run out. In a reckless move, both for the health of migrants and that of the wider public, the Home Office restarted evictions. Those with no recourse to public funds were swiftly turfed out of accommodation and on to the streets.³⁰

Through a grassroots charity in Brighton I was put in touch with Tinashe, a Zimbabwean man with diabetes and poor eyesight. The housing manager had removed the clothes from his room and put them in storage. When he tried to return to pick up the rest of his belongings, he found that the locks had been changed. With limited vision, he spent the nights walking around the streets, and the daytime in the park on a bench.

'At night, it's really bad,' he told me. 'I can see if somebody is there, but not who it is . . . It's a very scary thing being on the streets, but now there's also the virus, and I could get it any time, any place.'³¹

Mercy, a Nigerian woman whose claim had been refused and was pending an appeal, had also received an eviction letter in the middle of the pandemic. Less than three weeks later, the financial top-ups on her Aspen card had stopped. When she came home one day, a man was there changing the locks. 'He said if I don't go, the police will come for me and remove me back to my country.'

The only choice that remained was for her to leave. Within a year, once flights had resumed, Mercy had returned to Nigeria through the voluntary returns scheme, where she found herself destitute once again.

In February 2024, the government released a raft of reports on the same day in a bid to bury the news. The immigration statistics were published alongside figures on prisons, the collapse of local government budgets and twelve reports from the 'excessively critical' former immigration watchdog David Neal, who had just been sacked for speaking to the media.³²

The homelessness statistics ran too, and they were particularly dire. Rough sleeping was up 27 per cent nationwide, and up 34 per cent in

INTEGRATION

London. Children in BnBs: up 65.4 per cent. Temporary accommodation: up 10.3 per cent.[33]

The morning the slew of statistics was released, I was at a shelter for young people aged sixteen to twenty-four. The New Horizons centre was round the corner from King's Cross station, occupying the ground floor of a Grade II-listed building, with two floors of social housing above. There was an on-site nurse providing sexual health support, help with medications and existing injuries. There was a therapist, a group of cooks, and six staff to advise on housing. And there was a team of outreach workers, one of the only teams in the country to focus specifically on young homeless people, both British and not.

When I arrived, a crowd had already formed outside the centre's doors. All but two were asylum seekers and refugees who had been sheltering from the driving rain in the British Library nearby, waiting for the day centre to open. At the door were staff with clipboards, 'triaging' new arrivals and assessing their needs. It reminded me of an A&E department at a hospital, with a hatch near the door and the hustle and bustle of names being called out and young people shuffling in.

New Horizons staff had seen a 168 per cent increase in newly granted refugees accessing its services since August 2023, when the move-on period was reduced to seven days.[34] There had been no let-up since then, and no break over Christmas, despite the government's promises. Many of the young people at the centre had been issued with eviction notices shortly before the Christmas break. They too had found their belongings in a bag at the reception of their hostels and were sent out on to the streets.

Throughout the morning, young people – some as young as thirteen or fourteen – turned up with letters in English telling them they had days to leave their housing. Most were already sleeping rough in parks, Tube stations, public bathrooms, night buses, twenty-four-hour takeaway places – anywhere hidden from the police where they may be able to blend in.

Frontline staff had done their best, but their funding for emergency accommodation had run out. They had received £50,000 the year before, but that had gone by the end of August. It had been doubled, but depleted again by December. 'We've had to pay out of our pockets to house them,' said Polly Stephens, one of the regular staff. 'Then hotels chuck them out anyway, just saying, "We don't like your kind" and claiming they're causing problems.'

For Polly, the situation had never been so bad. She went to regular meetings with local London councils, but there was little anyone could do without adequate funding from central government. Sometimes, charities and local authorities looked at each other and acknowledged regretfully that it was only going to get worse.

Her team had started going into asylum hotels to tell young people that once they were granted status, they would be evicted. 'We just say, "This is what you need to do, go here, go there."' Though it was difficult to explain, and hard to tell young people, they never wanted to hide the truth. She and her colleagues felt it was important to be realistic. They would, in all likelihood, end up sleeping rough.

'Now it's literally at a point where they come to us and we have to just send them back out on to the streets with a sleeping bag,' she said. 'Can you imagine how traumatising that is? It's absolutely fucking awful to have to do that, but sometimes we have no choice.'

PART FIVE
DEPARTURE

14. Locked Up

'It is said that no one truly knows a nation until one has been inside its jails. A nation should not be judged by how it treats its highest citizens, but its lowest ones.'

Nelson Mandela

What I remember most are the sounds. The heavy metallic clunk of cell doors locking. Keychains clinking. Boots clanging up and down the stairs. Shrill orders bellowed along corridors. For much of the day, I watched events unfold with goosebumps on my arms and a shiver down the back of my neck. It was loud, and it was cold, and there was a distinct sense of trepidation that put me on edge.

It was 2014 and I had been sent on what was called a 'familiarisation visit' to Harmondsworth immigration removal centre, the biggest facility of its kind in Europe. There were no ministers present; it was considered part of my training as a new Home Office recruit to speak to those at the coalface about the challenges they faced. Not those held there, of course, but the detainee custody officers, whose role it was to manage the 600 incarcerated men.

Over the course of the day we were shown inside cells, recreation areas and the yard where the detainees could get some fresh air. There we found groups gathered around the perimeter of a small basketball court, the weight of their gaze on me and my colleagues. We must have looked strange – incongruous to the surroundings – in our smart shoes, lanyards tucked under neat shirt collars.

I can still vividly recall the face of a man from the Democratic Republic of Congo who I exchanged brief words with while my colleagues were distracted. He was confused, perhaps suspicious, about why we were there. Were we going to help them or were we voyeurs to their suffering? I was swiftly moved on when officers overheard me asking him about the conditions at the facility.

At lunchtime we went to the canteen to have a sloppy lunch on brown plastic trays. It reminded me of a petrol station cafe, with tables nailed to the floors and bright, surgical surroundings, all bare walls and laminate flooring. It was quieter than I thought it would be. Nobody stopped there for long; they seemed to want to get in and out as quickly as they could.

As I tentatively ladled spoonfuls of slop into my mouth, I saw the man from the DRC towards the back of the canteen. I felt a strong inclination to continue my conversation with him, rather than the officers we were sitting with, but I couldn't and I regret it still, often wondering whether he was released or removed from the country.

While there are some convicted criminals in immigration removal centres (or IRCs, as they're commonly known), the Home Office doesn't detain people because they have committed a criminal offence. Detention is for administrative purposes only: it is not a criminal procedure. An asylum seeker or migrant may be detained to establish their identity or to facilitate their claim. The decision to detain is made by an individual Home Office immigration officer rather than a judge, and is not subject to review at any stage of the process. In many cases, the Home Office is never required to justify why it has detained somebody or set a timeframe for their release or removal.

Little is known about what is happening inside. Detainees are not allowed smartphones, making it difficult for them to search for, or send documents to, a lawyer for a bail application. Access to healthcare is limited to cut costs and food is notoriously poor-quality. Immigration removal centres are high-security, category-B facilities. They are, to all intents and purposes, prisons.

During the first Covid lockdown, I remembered that brief encounter with the man from the DRC and the day spent at Harmondsworth, and I wondered what it was like for those incarcerated during a pandemic. Surely social distancing was impossible? And what about quarantine for those infected with the virus; where would they go?

Through a campaigning organisation, I was put in touch with Hadi, an asthmatic man who should have been on the IRC's list of those medically vulnerable to Covid.[1] (There was no list, so he wasn't.) By phone, he described nightmares where he couldn't breathe and felt a hand wrapped tightly round his neck. He woke suddenly, clutching through the darkness to find his inhaler. 'My chest always feels tight, but now I am having an attack once or twice every time I wake up,' he told me by phone. 'We live thirty of us close together. I don't know these people. Maybe they got it but they don't know it. Thinking about all this, the virus . . . I feel down now . . . really down, to be honest.'[2]

Hadi's mental health was at its lowest ebb. He had been seeing a psychiatrist once every three weeks following episodes of psychosis, but now medics worried that he was showing signs of attempting to end his life.

Within a matter of weeks, Covid had ripped through the detention centre and the isolation wards were full. A doctor at the facility contacted me to say that some detainees were being put in isolation without being tested. Those who had Covid would likely be mixing with those who didn't. A psychiatrist working at the facility described asylum-like conditions, saying that it was almost impossible to support all those experiencing mental breakdowns. Psychologically, almost everyone left worse than they came in.

A legal challenge followed, as the charity Detention Action argued that the Home Office had failed to protect detainees from outbreaks and had neglected to identify particularly vulnerable people such as Hadi. Under pressure, the department was forced to release more than a quarter of the men locked up.[3] Those who remained protested against their incarceration.

I couldn't shake off Harmondsworth. Almost a decade on from my visit there, I was put in touch with detainees who had occupied the courtyard inside the IRC to demand access to healthcare, which they said had been denied to them, even in instances of self-harm.[4] Sitting in my parents' kitchen one Sunday afternoon as my family played football outside, I frantically scrawled down notes as a group of distressed detainees shouted down the line. In the background were cries of 'Freedom' and banging on gates.

'There's no windows – we can't breathe here,' a man from Iraq said. 'It's the same as a prison, with two people in a two-by-two [metre] cell. I have proof it's not suitable for my mental health to be kept here.'[5]

An Albanian man who had arrived only three months before by small boat was audibly panicked. 'It's a really dangerous situation . . . It's very aggressive here. Everyone is breaking glasses and keeping small pieces in their hands and saying they want to hurt themselves.'

Some detainees had broken down doors and ransacked the kitchen for food and water, which they said they had been refused. Later that day I heard that, as punishment for taking part in the protests, over forty people were allegedly held in solitary confinement, in cells with no mattresses or blankets. Others were put on suicide watch. Some were said to have been stripped so they didn't strangle themselves with their clothes.

'The wellbeing of those in immigration removal centres is taken extremely seriously,' the Home Office said when I asked for a comment on the latest incident at Harmondsworth. 'All IRCs have dedicated health facilities run by doctors and nurses ... First-aid kits are fully stocked to help avoid any unnecessary calls to ambulance services.'[6]

If there was any doubt about how seriously the Home Office took the wellbeing of detainees, it was laid to rest by the Brook House Inquiry.

In September 2017, an undercover investigation for BBC's *Panorama* found that custody officers working at Brook House, an immigration removal centre near Gatwick airport, had used strangulation, hand-binding and humiliation rituals against detainees.[7] One officer working for the security contractor G4S was filmed boasting about banging a man's head against a table and holding him face-down. The best way of dealing with those on his wing was, he said, to 'turn away and hope he's swinging'.

Another guard is seen digging his fingers so deep into a suicidal detainee's throat that he nearly passes out and is left gasping for breath on the floor of his cell. 'Don't move, you fucking piece of shit,' the custody officer tells the man as he throttles him. 'I'm going to put you to fucking sleep.'[8]

In another incident, the secret filming shows a restraint team responsible for deporting a Romanian man who had previously suffered three heart attacks. When the team discuss how to remove him, a guard is recorded on-camera as saying: 'If he dies, he dies.'

Of the 450 men detained at Brook House at the time of filming, more than half were asylum seekers and those who had overstayed their visas. The remaining detainees were foreign national offenders, who were transferred to the removal centre having served prison sentences. All of them were locked up together, as the Home Office didn't insist on segregation. 'The hardline criminals swarm around the asylum seekers and migrants like sharks around small fish,' undercover detainee officer-turned-whistleblower Callum Tulley says in his voiceover. 'They can get eaten alive, just snapped up, just like that.'

Within Brook House there was said to be a drug epidemic, with weed and spice – a psychoactive synthetic cannabis – snuck in during visits while custody officers turned a blind eye. In some cases, G4S staff were found to have brought the 'zombie drug' into the centre themselves, whether to make extra money or to pacify distressed detainees.

The rules governing IRCs say that the Home Office must provide 'secure, humane accommodation in a relaxed and safe environment'. Callum Tulley's film exploded that notion. The Home Office was forced to apologise for 'failures in the contract', before going on to award G4S another two-year contract straight after the *Panorama* film aired.

In 2021, the first public inquiry into abuses at an immigration removal centre ever to take place in Britain got underway. I watched the proceedings by video link.[9] In it, Tulley and other former detainee custody officers set out incident after incident in which staff at Brook House abused highly vulnerable people in their care. Tulley had, he said, no confidence that informing senior management of the incidents would change anything. Company posters which encouraged people to report mistreatment were scribbled over with words like 'snitches', 'don't be a rat' and 'grass'.

At the end of the inquiry, in November 2023, the chair, Kate Eves, set out her findings.[10] There was, Eves said, a 'toxic culture' among staff working for the Home Office contractor G4S, which included the use of racist language. There had been at least nineteen instances where there was 'credible evidence . . . capable of amounting to a breach of Article 3' of the European Convention on Human Rights.

Recommendations were made to report back on all seven immigration removal centres across the UK. Most notably, the inquiry recommended that a maximum detention time limit of twenty-eight days should be set across the estate.

The Home Office had long said that immigration detention was 'used sparingly and for the shortest period necessary'. In reality, there was no time limit for how long somebody could be held. While some were detained for twenty-eight days, many – most – were held for a year or more. Remaining incarcerated, with no option to remain in or leave the UK, can, on occasion, be indefinite.

With private-sector companies competing for contracts to run the facilities, profit tends to trump humanity. In 2020, the G4S contract to run Brook House and Tinsley House, also near Gatwick, was passed over to Serco. Just the week before the £200 million contract was awarded, a Nigerian rape survivor told a court she had been thrown to the floor 'like a bag of cement' in an incident involving eleven Serco guards.[11] The contract was signed regardless.

'Serco has a great deal of experience of caring for people in the immigration system both in the UK and internationally, and we understand the sensitivity and complexity of this role,' Rupert Soames, Serco Group's chief executive, said.

By mid-2023, Serco was thought to hold around £10 billion worth of UK government contracts. Its anticipated revenue had risen to £4.8 billion, and its profits to £245 million.[12]

The Home Office might have publicly committed to ensuring that mistreatment never happened again, but in practice that didn't appear to be the case. In November 2023, only a fortnight after the conclusion of the Brook House inquiry, two Albanian men attempted suicide at the facility. One of the men later died in hospital while the other was deported and immediately returned to the UK after his deportation order was revoked. A psychologist had urged the Home Office to assess the man's wellbeing prior to removal, but their advice had been ignored.

Medics gathered clinical evidence to show that little had changed. The charity Medical Justice found that 74 per cent of its clients had self-harmed or attempted suicide in detention between June 2022 and October 2023.[13] Seven people (out of sixty-six clients interviewed) had been subjected to force or restraints in detention; three of them sustained injuries requiring medical treatment. Fourteen people had been put into 'segregation' and had experienced increased suicidal thoughts and self-harming episodes in response.

'The [Brook House] inquiry cannot be another one for the bookshelves,' the charity said.[14] 'Action could not be more urgent as the government plans to significantly expand detention and implement the provisions of the Illegal Migration Act, knowing the harm that is still being caused.'

David Neal was frustrated that his reviews into safeguards in detention went largely ignored too. 'The Home Office's responses to my reports have been characterised by defensiveness and excuses,' he wrote in an eviscerating *Guardian* opinion piece on the day the final Brook House inquiry report was published.[15] 'Rather than maintaining a sharp, clear-eyed focus on protecting the vulnerable, the department has been fixated on a narrative of abuse of the system by detainees and their legal advisors.'

Despite receiving warnings about a lack of safeguards for those deemed to be 'adults at risk', Suella Braverman – then home secretary – ordered that annual inspections of immigration detention centres should be halted.

In 2023, nearly 16,000 people entered immigration detention across the UK's seven facilities, at a cost of around £107 per day per person.[16]

The Home Office wanted to increase that number in order to effect swifter deportations. The success of its Illegal Migration Act, Safety of Rwanda Act and its migration and economic partnership with Rwanda was contingent on it. It needed to remove people. It just didn't have anywhere to put them before they were removed.

Some slight logistical complications wouldn't stop the Home Office. In mid-2024, protesters gathered outside Lunar House in Croydon where two men – one from Sudan and one from Afghanistan – were being held.[17] Both had attended routine reporting appointments and had been taken aside and arrested. Officials told the men they would be removed to Rwanda. Later that day they were brought to an undisclosed detention centre. But after the twenty-eight-day limit pending removal, no flights had been arranged: the Home Office couldn't find an airline to work with. All those needlessly detained were released.[18]

Word quickly spread around hotels and friendship groups, advising each other to avoid contact with the authorities rather than dutifully attend their fortnightly appointments with the department. Inevitably, many chose to go underground, where they faced heightened risk of exploitation, re-trafficking and destitution. It was a vicious circle over which the government had lost all control.

It wasn't only at-risk adults who were being detained in greater numbers. Unaccompanied children were being criminalised under new powers, too. Among them was Mohammed, a seventeen-year-old boy from Sudan.

A few hours after arriving by small boat, Mo was told by immigration officials that they believed him to be twenty-two. He was taken to Manston holding facility in Kent where, three days later, he was arrested for arriving in the UK without valid entry clearance. The first thought that ran through his mind was whether he was on the list for deportation to Rwanda. Everybody had been talking about it at Manston. 'It didn't matter that I was under eighteen. They thought I was an adult, so I could be next.'

Like Mo, hundreds of others had been charged with the same offence. Between June 2022, when the Nationality and Borders Act came into force, and October 2023, at least 253 people were convicted and jailed for arriving in small boats to claim asylum.[19] Nearly fifty of those cases were charges for 'facilitating entry', having allegedly been found to have their 'hand on the tiller', as in the case of the convicted Senegalese teenager Ibrahima Bah. Victims of torture and trafficking, as well as children with ongoing age disputes like Mo, were among those unlawfully detained and hauled through the criminal justice system.

At his hearing, Mo couldn't stop his legs from shaking. His advisor sat alongside him, while his barrister set out the age dispute issue. Then it was Mo's turn. He was asked to confirm his date of birth. He said that the date attributed to him by the Home Office immigration officer in Dover was wrong. He was not twenty-two; he was seventeen. The judge disregarded the dispute, stating that the Home Office had decided he was an adult. That had been presented as fact; there was no argument to uphold.

Mo was then detained in an adult prison, where he shared a room with a thirty-year-old man. He says he was subjected to repeated violence and discrimination during his three-month stay at HMP Elmley, an adult prison for hardline convicted criminals.

'Not knowing why you are there, knowing you are not guilty, this has had a big effect on me,' he later said. 'To be discriminated against because you are not a British national, a white prisoner, this is very hard.'

Mo's case was not an isolated incident. According to one report, at least fifteen children were wrongly age-assessed and criminalised between June 2022 and June 2023.[20] Fourteen young people spent periods of up to seven months in adult prisons. Those figures were likely to be a significant underestimate. Many had gone to ground.

One charity worker found that young people were starting to 'pop up' in adult hotels, having recently been released on bail. Sometimes referrals were made to them by friends or following a volunteer's visit to a prison where migrants were being held. Solicitors occasionally got in touch to let charities know that they believed their client to be a child. None of this was foolproof. Many children were still falling through the cracks, incarcerated with nobody knowing their whereabouts for months on end.

When he was eventually found and released, Mo had a criminal record. He maintained he was seventeen, but he had been advised by a community care solicitor to plead guilty to illegal arrival in order to reduce his sentence. There was, after all, no route to appeal. The only way to overturn his conviction was a reassessment, but that required the local authority to spend time and money they didn't have. A year later, the criminal record still stood against him, putting him at increased risk of deportation.

Like Mo, many former detainees struggled to clear their names and move on with their lives. Some would spend years, even decades, trying.

One blustery autumnal day, I attended a talk in East London for those who had been through immigration detention. Over a lunch of crunchy spiced falafel and creamy hummus, I got talking to an easy-going, affable Sudanese man in his mid-forties named Omar.

Though he had been released from immigration detention nearly three years earlier, Omar could still vividly recall the sound of the keys, the gates slamming, the anguished screams in the darkness. The memories often reoccurred to him in his dreams, sleeping 'like a dog with your ears up', never able to switch off. He worried, he said, that that sense of hypervigilance, of always being on alert, would never disappear.

That afternoon, Omar came to a side event I ran on speaking to the media. There were around two dozen ex-detainees around the table, evenly split, half men, half women. 'Why do the media think we are all the same, like we're criminals?' a young woman from Guinea began by asking me. I said that different publications tackled these issues in different ways and they were playing to their audiences. Most media outlets were politically aligned and partisan. It wasn't fair, but that was often the way public opinion was shaped. Telling their story to a trusted journalist was one way of taking back agency.

What I didn't say was that I, too, was acutely aware of the way in which migrant groups – and particularly former detainees – were perceived by large sections of the British media. The government's rhetoric – 'illegal immigrants, gaming the system' – was, of course, highly problematic, but I found it even more troubling when editors latched on to it too. Once, a senior news editor at a national broadcaster asked me to look into why migrants 'often turned to crime'. It was clearly a discussion which played out among audiences, they said, and one we couldn't ignore in our reporting. I refused and the project went uncommissioned. (In fact, it turned into this book.)

The following summer, on a humid but glorious day, I boarded a train to Burgess Hill in Sussex with my feet squashed into a friend's walking shoes. In the car park outside a church hall, a group of around a hundred former detainees and volunteers formed a circle, swivelling their hips and doing star jumps to warm up. We were about to embark on a fifteen-kilometre walk through cornfields, climbing up rolling hills, over stiles and through woodland before venturing back down the valley to the seafront in Brighton.

There were teachers and foster carers, doctors and barristers, all volunteers who visited or wrote letters to detainees in removal centres in their free time. Some were local, while others had travelled from across the country. Omar was there too, alongside around forty other former immigration detainees, walking and talking in a bid to overcome the negative impact incarceration had had on their mental health.

Omar and I immediately fell into step and, as we ambled along, seeking out shade, he described a day during his detention at Tinsley House which he would never forget. That morning, a guard told him somebody was coming to visit him. They didn't know who, but they did say that she was an elderly lady who lived near the IRC close to Gatwick airport.

At around midday, Omar was called to the visitors' area. Sitting upright in front of him was Ann, an eighty-three-year-old retired teacher with a silver-grey perm, fizzing with energy. Rather than taking a break after her retirement two decades earlier, Ann had continued volunteering for a range of causes. Support visits like this were just one of many commitments she had each week. She would sometimes bring books, or puzzles, or just sit in silence, her hands outstretched. Omar felt safe for the first time in several years. 'Until my last breath, I will never forget that woman's name,' he told me as we walked together. 'That woman is this light here, this sunlight. She saved me.'

Omar had been at war and lost many people he loved. He had crossed the desert, the Mediterranean Sea, the Channel. But never had he felt more despair than when he was detained. Ann's first visit gave him hope. She told Omar that she couldn't get him out of detention, but she could try to ease him out of his mental turmoil. She kept her word. Every Wednesday for seven months, Omar woke and waited to be told she had arrived. He would bound down the stairs to the visitors' room. He felt like she was his mother, that she listened. 'I don't know why, but I had nobody and she wanted to help me.'

This retired teacher really was a ray of light. During one of her visits she told Omar she had located his mother in Sudan and would help him to reconnect with her, to let her know that he was alive. She found a solicitor for him, acted as a guarantor and helped him to secure bail. Then, one day, 'because of her, they opened the door, they just said: "Go."'

On his release, Omar was given a piece of paper to convert into a train ticket. He had only £10 to his name, which Ann had given him. He made it to Cardiff, where he had a couple of friends he could stay with. At a local centre, he helped other asylum seekers with translation and interpretation, sometimes acting as a caseworker, chasing up phone calls and filling in endless documents. Finally, two years and several solicitors later, he was granted leave to remain.

That evening, at an event run by the charity Refugee Tales (based on Chaucer's *Canterbury Tales*), I listened in a church hall as former detainees told their stories through poetry, prose and song. Some broke down in tears while others were angry, with only a faceless edifice in Marsham Street to direct their anger towards. They had, they felt, been through some of the darkest days of their lives and, while they were here now, those memories would always remain with them.

'You never know how it feels to be free until it is taken away,' Omar told the 200-strong audience. 'This is a feeling it is impossible to describe. We have it now, and we never want to let it go again.'

15. Say Goodbye

'We are here because you were there.'

Ambalavaner Sivanandan

The rain was hammering down as I ran towards the tribunal court, skirting round puddles, my tights already soaked through. Inside the atrium, a queue snaked its way towards the security gates. Latecomers tutted as umbrellas and wedding rings set off the incessant bleep. The guards seemed in no rush, patting people down and issuing brusque instructions to swig water from bottles.

I wasn't the last to arrive that morning: the Home Office presenting officer was late to the hearing too. Waiting anxiously outside the courtroom for the official to arrive, I found Winston, a Jamaican man in his early forties, sitting hunched between his barrister and solicitor, staring at a point on the scuffed carpet in front of him. Winston was distressed, tears rolling down his cheeks, puffy with the pills he took each morning. He worried that he would lose his composure and break down in front of the judge, shaking uncontrollably as often happened when he felt overwhelmed. At times, he didn't know what was happening. He just felt 'strange in the head', unable to cope, his mind suddenly overtaking his body.

DEPARTURE

Winston was fixated on a TikTok video on his phone shared earlier that morning by a friend. 'I watched it maybe thirty times,' he told me, his brow furrowed, his feet shuffling. He wanted me to watch it on loop as well. The video showed a woman, a 'street person', who had been deported from the UK back to Jamaica.[1] She had, he said, committed no crime, but she had 'gone crazy' sleeping rough, triggering a steep deterioration in her mental state. I suggested that watching the video on repeat might be adding to his distress, but Winston insisted that everybody should know how those with severe mental health conditions were treated in Jamaica.

Panicked, he had started to imagine what life might be like if he was sent back there, a country he hadn't been to for over twenty years. He had heard that it was very different now to when he was young, 'guns everywhere, even more corruption'.

Winston's mother had died when he was a teenager and he had never known his father, who left the family before he was born. To support his siblings, Winston had found work climbing evergreen trees barefoot to gather ackee, the fragrant lychee-like fruit ubiquitous across the island. On a good day he made thirty cents – around fifty British pence at the time – selling a dozen of them on the side of the road. Once he was even given a dinner of saltfish and ackee, digging hungrily into his plate, mixing handfuls of spongy, sweet yellow flesh with the chewy fresh white fish.

Friends had sent him other videos of life in Jamaica, showing children selling ackee at traffic lights, as he had. They were being groomed by criminal gangs, he was told. Winston had managed to escape the men who had violently abused and trafficked him to Britain, but he had had to live for more than two decades on the run, sleeping on sofas, sometimes sleeping rough. A cascade of catastrophic problems had followed, landing him in detention, convicted of drug offences.

During the pandemic, he had been handcuffed and brought on to the tarmac at Gatwick airport. Outside the window, beyond the fence, he could see the plane that was to take him to Jamaica. Then, at the eleventh hour, his solicitor applied for a judicial review, challenging the Home Office's decision and buying just enough time for Winston to be taken back to Colnbrook detention centre, from where he was later released on bail. He was, he felt, like 'a cat with nine lives'.

Now, though, those nine lives were almost up. He had attended a fortnightly reporting visit and been detained. Winston found himself facing deportation orders once again. This time, with a different judge, a different government official and a different legal defence team, he might not be so lucky.

Deportations are one of the most complex areas of the immigration system to administer. Those who are about to be forcibly removed require emergency travel documents from embassies and a host of other documentation that is usually difficult, time-consuming and costly to acquire. In the vast majority of cases, deportees appeal the decision to send them back and, until the last moment, protest their removal.

Airlines willing to carry out the deportations stand to make significant profits. In 2022, the government spent £3.6 billion on chartering deportation flights in one three-month period alone.[2] Two airlines pocketed the bulk of the profits: Privilege Style and Stansted airport-based Titan Airways, which between them were responsible for 87 per cent of deportation flights that year.[3] Privilege Airlines had become known as the Home Office's 'airline of last resort', attempting to fly asylum seekers to Rwanda on the infamous grounded flight.[4] Both Privilege and Titan eventually pulled out of the scheme following sustained pressure from campaigning organisations.[5]

The deportation of Jamaicans is notoriously controversial, given that some people have lived in the UK since they were children and others are second-generation Windrush descendants. Removal targets for members of the Windrush generation were, after all, what brought Amber Rudd down in April 2018.

After initially denying the existence of removal targets at a Home Affairs Select Committee hearing, saying this was 'not how we operate',[6] the embattled former home secretary was summoned to the House of Commons to admit that her immigration enforcement officials did, in fact, set targets.[7] Not only that: her department incentivised them to go after 'low-hanging fruit', offering considerable bonuses to officials who met the removal targets. A fraught twenty-four hours ensued before Rudd heeded calls to resign, acknowledging that she had 'inadvertently misled' MPs over the targets she had once described as 'ambitious but deliverable'.[8]

This wasn't the only reason Rudd needed to step down. In saying that she didn't know 'what shape' removals were in,[9] she had shown a failure to grasp the inner workings of her own department. The shape was very clear. There are three parts to it. The first is deportation, which applies to those like Winston who have been convicted of a criminal offence. Then there are administrative removals for those who have no right to remain in the UK. The third part is voluntary return for those whose enforced removal has already been initiated. They are three different instruments with the same outcome.

David Cameron had once sought to increase the number of Jamaican deportees, announcing during a visit in 2015 that Britain would spend £25 million of its aid budget to build a super-max prison for the UK's unwanted to serve the rest of their sentences there.[10] Ahead of the visit, Jamaicans had wondered whether Cameron might formally apologise for Britain's colonial past and offer reparations for the bloodshed of slavery, but no: a brand-new prison to replace the two facilities built by Britain's imperialists was all that was on offer.

At the height of the Windrush scandal, with Sajid Javid keeping the seat warm, it emerged that at least 160 people could have been wrongly detained and deported from the UK.[11] Then, in 2020, the Home Office struck a deal with Jamaica's high commissioner not to deport those who had arrived in the UK before the age of twelve. At that time, the department had arrangements in place to charter flights specifically for Jamaican deportees, averaging a cost of £200,000 per flight.[12]

By the end of 2021, figures for removals had dropped so low that only four people were found on a plane bound for the island's capital, Kingston, despite its 350-seat capacity. After it emerged that the government was spending £50,000 of taxpayers' money per head there was public outcry.[13] Charter flights were abruptly stopped. Now the department had only one route for removals: placing Jamaicans on commercial flights.

In November 2023, passengers on board a flight to Kingston overheard a man calling out for help towards the back of the plane.[14] Escorts had restrained twenty-seven-year-old Lawrence Morgan, convicted for gun- and drug-related crimes, dragging him aboard the plane and holding him in place so firmly that he sustained multiple injuries.[15] On hearing Morgan's pleas passengers staged a protest, refusing to sit down as the plane taxied towards the runway. The pilot was forced to abandon take-off. Morgan thanked the demonstrators as he was led off the plane.

James Cleverly, however, was incensed. 'We must be able to remove offenders from our country without interference from misguided and ill-informed do-gooders,' he told the *Mail on Sunday*.[16] The then home secretary added that he and his officials were looking at 'new ways to handle this issue', to ensure that passengers could no longer frustrate removals. Priti Patel rowed in too, telling the protesters that 'they should face consequences' for their 'ill-advised' actions.

The Home Office might have been well-advised to consider the risks on their return to Jamaica. The only facility for deportees was a shelter in Kingston funded by the UK government. Open Arms was considered a lifeline for some, but for others it kept them isolated and trapped in penury.[17] Many wanted to work, but their British or American accents marked them out as different. They were stigmatised for having wasted a 'golden opportunity' and often denied the chance for a fresh start.

Violence, including murders in broad daylight on the streets, was pervasive. At least five men deported to Jamaica in 2019 are known to have been killed on their return.[18] Even outside the gates of Open Arms men wielding weapons attempted to trespass, threatening recent returnees with guns. Still, the shelter was the sole proof that the UK government was meeting its obligations under international human rights law: that those it sent back to Jamaica would at least be able to survive.

In its country guidance for Home Office staff, the government acknowledges that Jamaica has the world's highest murder rate, with homicides rising 10 per cent between 2020 and 2021.[19] The Home Office noted that there were around 250 organised crime groups and that 'gang clashes often result in gun battles', with residents 'in danger of being caught in the crossfire'.

Much of the country guidance was predicated on a deportee being able to obtain access to secure housing and public services, which many were unable to do. 'It relies on a well person being able to operate in an environment like that,' Winston's counsel said in the waiting area.

Winston was not a well person. A decade before, he had been diagnosed with acute schizophrenia and had suffered multiple episodes of psychosis. Access to medication back in Jamaica, and the ability to take prescription drugs independently, was an area of considerable concern.

'If I go back there, I will die,' Winston worried moments before being called before the judge. 'I will be living on the streets, I won't have my medicines. I will have nobody to help me, nobody to support me. I will have nothing.'

The air inside the courtroom was thick with tension. It was also stiflingly hot, with air vents pumping heating into the room at such a rate that the rail on the window blind banged repeatedly against the wall. Reams of paperwork flapped in the artificial breeze. I took several sips of water from a paper cup, my mouth dry with anticipation.

The judge sat on a raised platform with four computer screens facing him, checking he had what he needed: previous rulings, medical reports, Home Office submissions. Winston's feet curled round the edges of his chair, his hands balled up in his lap. He appeared nervous to make eye contact, the judge repeatedly telling him to speak up, to bend the microphone towards him to ensure he was heard.

The nub of his appeal against deportation rested on his mental health. Winston was, the judge acknowledged, a recognised victim of trafficking – he had a conclusive grounds decision from the National Referral Mechanism stating as much – and the risk of suicide had increased to 'high' since his last court hearing. There was clear evidence of likely self-harm and destitution on return. I relaxed in my chair a little more, scribbling in my notebook.

'Evidence shows he would become acutely unwell very rapidly, suffering auditory and visual hallucinations,' Winston's barrister stated.[20] There was a high probability of complications accessing healthcare. While there was some free care and subsidised drugs in Jamaica, there were limitations. An income was still needed to pay for the medication.

'If his mental health deteriorated on return, he may be left without any assistance at all for a long period,' his counsel asserted. 'Existing NGOs would be unable to provide support and he would not have family to support him either.'

The Home Office presenting officer turned to Winston to cross-examine him, his notes laid out in front of him. If he returned to Jamaica – 'and that's an "if"; I'm not saying that you will' – could he support himself?

Winston had been sleeping on his cousin's sofa in a one-bedroom council flat for three years. His cousin worked as a bin man; he couldn't afford to feed them both. Winston had been reliant on food banks and charities for several years. He would have nothing in Jamaica: no house and no family members to take him in. 'I will be just walking around, I will be on the streets,' he told the judge. 'People there will think I am stupid. They will think, "You get an opportunity to change your life [in the UK] and you messed it up."'

But could he not just live elsewhere on the island, outside Kingston? With so few belongings, he could move to find housing in another area, the presenting officer pressed. 'If you stopped me in the street and asked me how to get to Montego Bay, I wouldn't know how to get there,' Winston protested. 'I have never been to that part. I would be lost.'

Surely his cousin, who was also a Jamaican national, could go with him and help him to adapt to life, to start again? Winston must accept that he still knew about and had links to Jamaican culture, the official said. It had changed over the last two decades, yes, but he would settle eventually.

The Home Office official turned to the judge. While the Secretary of State accepted that Winston had serious mental health issues, 'that doesn't mean he is not capable of deception,' he said. He may well relapse in the UK, not only in Jamaica, and, crucially, there was a suicide prevention programme there. The home secretary took issue with the two medical expert reports, which the presenting officer said were 'not sourced at all'. Neither of the medics had a specialism. 'There is a fine line between expert evidence and informed advice.'

Who, I wondered, was he to judge the credentials of the two expert medics: psychiatrists who specialise in global health and modern slavery, who had extensively footnoted and sourced their reports? A presenting officer is not a lawyer. The Home Office provided a twelve-week training course to build a 'solid base of knowledge' of immigration law, but it wasn't the several-year-long qualification of an immigration barrister.

'You will decide how to pursue cases and develop your own style and approach,' a Home Office job ad promised.[21] Presenting officers needed to be organised, to work flexibly and to build strong working relationships with decision-making colleagues and others within the department. They must stay updated on changes to immigration law, developing the skills to persuade a judge that somebody should be removed from the country. The salary on offer started from £36,000.

On a student forum, graduates applying for jobs as presenting officers discussed their backgrounds, 'lol'-ing at their threadbare understanding of this area of law.[22] Others were already working within the civil service, while a few were attempting a mid-career shift. 'Once training is completed you will be able to work from home,' one user said, reassuring an anxious applicant that they would have a decent work–life balance.

Nowhere did anyone state the magnitude of the decisions made about each individual they presented against. This wasn't simply a case of removing somebody who was not 'conducive to the public good'; there were critical implications for Winston's ability to function and to survive in Jamaica alone. In all likelihood, the individual's circumstances would never have occurred to the official until they entered the courtroom and sat face to face with the person they were trying to deport.

At the bottom of the presenting officer recruitment ad was a slogan for all those interested in applying: 'It matters more here'.[23]

The trouble for the Home Office was that the number of enforced returns was consistently low, and it was dropping lower year on year. Of all those who arrived by small boat between 2018 and June 2023, when the Illegal Migration Act came into force, only 1.3 per cent were removed from the UK.[24]

Deportation numbers had steadily dropped over the previous two decades. In 2004 the Home Office deported 21,425 people. By 2022 that number had plummeted to just 1,566, flown to nine countries.[25]

If deportations were to act as a deterrent, as the Conservative government hoped they would, the Home Office needed to make sure it could get people on the planes and into the air. The two Rwanda Acts railroaded through Parliament relied on it. While the government liked to blame 'do-gooders' and 'lefty lawyers' for frustrating these deportations, the fact was that Brexit had removed the UK's one mechanism to make returns.

The Dublin 3 Regulation, which allows member states to return asylum seekers to EU nations, had been far from perfect, but it was better than nothing. Through the European Union, Britain had been able to send some people elsewhere without considering their asylum claims. In 2019 and 2020, the majority of those who arrived by small boat and were later removed were sent to France and Germany. (In 2019, 120 people were returned to EU member states, as opposed to just three people to their countries of origin.[26]) Once the UK had withdrawn from the EU, the number of returns fell sharply.

In March 2023, Rishi Sunak travelled to Paris to meet French President Emmanuel Macron in the hope he could secure a bilateral returns deal. It was the first UK–France summit in over five years – a high-stakes visit intended to mark a 'new chapter . . . our Entente Cordiale renewed',[27] an attempt to paper over the cracks left during the calamitous tenure of Liz Truss, who had said she didn't know whether Macron was a 'friend or foe'.[28]

'There won't be anything on returns – this has an EU dimension,' a French diplomat friend messaged doubtfully. He was right: Sunak got nothing on returns. 'A returns agreement would not be an agreement between the UK and France but an agreement between the UK and the EU,' Macron announced.

Brussels responded too.[29] They were not willing to negotiate a returns deal to replace the Dublin Regulation. To secure deals with safe countries – on which the success of the government's promise to stop the boats now depended – Britain would need to look elsewhere.

James Cleverly refused to be bowed. The UK had, he said, 'secured close cooperation on migration' with India and Vietnam and signed returns agreements with Serbia and Georgia. But the *pièce de resistance*, the success he liked to talk up the most, was the UK's deal with Albania.

The fast-track removal of Albanians had, indisputably, been viewed as a success for the government, but it was the only such route. The deal had been struck to crack down on the embarrassingly high number of Albanians who were crossing the Channel by small boat (2,165 Albanians were recorded as arriving between January and June 2022, compared with just twenty-three in the same period the previous year[30]). The Home Office wanted to see that number fall immediately, fast-tracking them right out of the country. Albanian police officers would be brought to the Kent coast to observe new arrivals, the department announced.

'It is shameful and absurd that so many Albanian nationals are entering the UK via small boats when their home country, Albania, is a safe country,' Priti Patel told reporters, alongside her grinning opposite number.[31] Figures released that week showed that half of all Albanians seeking asylum were granted refugee status. It was, by the Home Office's own standards, not a safe country.

The day after the deal was struck, I was on a bus on the way to meet some friends when a call came through from a frantic Albanian woman, the daughter of a man who was about to be deported.[32] The day before, as Patel made her announcement, immigration enforcement officers raided a restaurant where her father was working, hauling him into custody and serving removal paperwork.

I got off the bus at the next stop, hovering in the doorway of a shop opposite Brixton station, tapping notes into a Google doc on my phone as we spoke. Her father had, she said, no criminal record. He had never absconded and had always complied with the requirements, reporting fortnightly to the Home Office. Both she and her brother were born in the UK. She couldn't fathom why her father had been picked up now. Though I didn't say it, I understood why: he would be one of the first fast-track removals under the new scheme.

When I reached her father, he was sitting on the edge of a bed with starchy, tightly pulled sheets in a darkened cell in Harmondsworth immigration removal centre. He appeared disorientated but resigned. 'The whole of this place is full of Albanians,' he told me.[33] 'It looks like they're rounding us up to put us on a charter [flight] out of here. The guy I'm sharing a cell with . . . over half the wing . . . they are Albanians.'

Many others in his wing had been detained the same day. They couldn't understand why they were being targeted. None of them had arrived by small boat; they had all been in the UK for many years.

'It's like I have a knee in my neck, like they are suffocating me,' the man said. 'It went through my mind that this is [a] revenge against us. It looks like the government are finding loopholes to take us out.'

He had no lawyer and his family couldn't afford to pay the fees for a solicitor. I told him I couldn't help directly, but I could try to get him some legal representation. It needed to be quick.

A Twitter post, a few WhatsApp messages and a phone call later, Jamie Bell, a tireless solicitor from the law firm Duncan Lewis, had filed a judicial review, halting his imminent removal. The man was released on bail, still reeling when I spoke to him a few days later.

'We have no faith this will not happen again,' he said ominously but, I thought, correctly. 'They can come for us at any time.'

Winston was not to be as fortunate.

At the end of the hearing, spirits had been raised by arguments persuasively put and by the responses from the judge, who had seemed sympathetic to his plight. Winston would have to wait another couple of weeks for the reserved judgement, but he could be confident that it had all gone to plan.

'Sometimes these things seem like a last-ditch attempt to frustrate removal, but actually, in his case, it was the first time anyone had looked at his file for years,' his barrister told me as we walked out of the tribunal court and back into the rain. 'He's been fortunate to get a good solicitor. Many people would just fall through the cracks.'

A fortnight later, the news arrived as I was at my desk, trying to meet a deadline. Winston's appeal hadn't been successful. He would soon be deported.

As he prepared to return to a country he had left twenty years before, where he had no family connections or friends, and only painful memories to recollect, Winston agonised over his future. There were no

DEPARTURE

more protests, no more court appearances and no more documents to submit. It was time for him to say goodbye to the nation he had called home for nearly half his lifetime.

On the phone, as he waited to be brought to the police van and forced on to a plane, I wondered, as I do every time, who I might call; if there was anything more I could do to help. He assured me there wasn't.

'There is nothing left now,' he said. 'Nothing to do and no place left for me. There is nowhere I can call home.'

Afterword: Home

In the Prologue, I wrote that this was not a book about politics; that it was about people. Early into the research, it became clear to me that it would not be possible to disentangle policy from those at the sharp end of it. The two are inextricably linked.

Every time I spoke to an asylum seeker, a member of search and rescue, a barrister, a caseworker, a medic, a social worker – anyone on the frontline of the system – they said the same thing: they didn't want to talk about politics. It already had too much of a hold over their lives, it took too much away. What would it change anyway? They were just cogs in a wheel, pawns in the government's game, shunted around by those who kept a firm grip on power.

The asylum system is a messy, murky place to find yourself for any length of time. Policy gets made on the hoof, sometimes announced in a press release then either quietly ditched or railroaded through Parliament and then ditched. It moves at such a pace, it can be difficult to keep up. It's also needlessly complex, so I've tried, where possible, to boil the process down to the bare bones, to show the ways in which the system is meant to work and the ways in which it doesn't.

Of course, there was much I couldn't include. The focus of the book is on the small boats issue, from 2018, when the first dinghies crossed, to now. It explores the asylum process through the eyes of those who arrived through that route, and while I touch on other migrant groups and aspects of the immigration system, I couldn't cover everything. That is in itself problematic: this is, after all, a book about who is included and who is excluded from society, who is listened to and who isn't.

In truth, even when I focused my energies on a specific group of new arrivals, it was a challenge to garner interest in the subject. One editor at a publishing house asked me how I planned to 'get people to care'. Not an unfair question, but a cynical one. There were suggestions from publishers and literary agents that I focus on one family in a town or village, or take a historical look at the crisis, or lean on my background at the Home Office to tell the story from a whistleblower's perspective. None of those approaches felt right to me. I wanted to bring to life the people caught up in this strange world – a world I have inhabited throughout much of my career and care about deeply.

The first time I saw a small boat being tugged in, it gave me a jolt. Here in front of me was the black rubber dinghy that had, moments earlier, carried fifty people across the freezing Channel. On the deck of the Border Force boat the new arrivals sat, each curled up in a ball, shivering under foil blankets. It might sound obvious, but seeing it first-hand was an entirely different experience to reading an article or watching a television news report. There is much to be gained from ministers and members of the public bearing witness to these scenes, too. When you see the stark reality, when you look somebody in the eye and listen – really listen – to what they tell you, it can sharpen minds, maybe even change attitudes.

I wrote this book because I want people to understand the reality behind the rhetoric, to imagine what these people see, and hear, and

AFTERWORD: HOME

think, and feel. I hope I have never judged; I would be mortified if I had. It is not my place, or my job, to judge anyone.

If the Home Office is considered a poisoned chalice for an incumbent home secretary, it is for a journalist who writes about it too. There will be some who think I have not been balanced enough, that I have written too much about one aspect of the system and not enough about another. My impartiality and my personal politics will likely be called into question. On an issue as divisive as this, it will never be possible to satisfy everyone. That is not necessarily negative. I want to be challenged, to move beyond the echo chamber of those who agree with me, to understand different perspectives on an issue now so central to our society. In my daily work as a reporter I rarely find this opportunity.

Journalism can feel like an extractive process. You spend time plumbing the depths of someone's darkest moments, selecting the best quotes and getting the piece out before it is scooped by another outlet. I hope that I always do this ethically and sensitively, protecting my sources and treating them with dignity and respect; but the competition for exclusives, for exposés, for breaking news means time isn't always on our side. We are, none of us, as considered as we should be under pressure.

One editor at a national newspaper told me a commission hinged on whether I could follow an unaccompanied child who had been exploited into a criminal gang – maybe someone working in a cannabis factory, maybe an Albanian. Safeguarding and consent weren't mentioned in the scrabble to get the story first. I refused and didn't write for that outlet again.

Another senior editor working for a major broadcaster said I would need to answer the question viewers would be asking, which was why asylum seekers were being housed before locals. Again, there was no nuance or subtlety, not to mention accuracy. The issue was to be covered as a polemic, casting an entire group into the role of the fortunate recipient or, worse, the scrounger.

Editors admit they are fatigued by the small boat crossings. They see the audience's attention slipping away and they are businesses: they need the figures. The focus has already started to shift towards Westminster and away from the realities on the ground. The BBC has scrapped the vital specialist role of home affairs correspondent: a short-sighted move which will only serve the government of the day, transferring the attention away from its failings and back to the often senseless noise in the House of Commons.

The only way in which I have consistently been able to follow this brief and report on the ground is by remaining freelance. Following people on the move requires moving yourself. While I have always known that there are a number of reporters who cover this beat, I also knew that I had something slightly different: I had seen the Home Office from the inside. That has been both a help and a hindrance. Some former colleagues see me as a traitor. When I contacted a friend still working there, they messaged to tell me that they would love to talk but that their loyalty would always be to the department. 'Once a press officer, always a press officer,' they said with a winking face.

Others tell me they want to leave but they can't. Maybe they hope to reform the Home Office from the inside, or enjoy walking the corridors of power, or perhaps that is where they built their careers and they fail to see a future beyond Marsham Street's four walls. My fear while I worked in the civil service was becoming institutionalised. Leaving and moving into journalism was one of the best decisions I have ever made.

What few people on the outside discuss is the exhausting nature of plugging away at intransigent issues and nothing really changing. Many people have chosen to leave the sector – not only journalists, but lawyers, charity workers, grassroots activists and countless others

AFTERWORD: HOME

propping up the system. They have been ground down, drowned out by the noise largely coming from Westminster. It is all too easy for the government and its private-sector behemoths to discredit those working on human rights. Lefty lawyers frustrating removals. The 'blob' of civil servants. *Guardian*-reading, tofu-eating wokerati.[1] We've heard it all before and we won't be singing to their tune.

As the anti-migrant rhetoric has ramped up, so have the targeted attacks. Those on the frontline have been forced to take additional measures to protect themselves, both online and offline. Over the course of the last five years I have faced legal threats, attacks from the far right and worse. I have at times been too quick to dismiss red flags. This has made me more cautious when writing this book, to ensure that sources are protected, that they cannot be identified and have adequate support around them. All reporters have a duty of care to those we speak to before, during and, crucially, after interview.

When sources consent to speak to a journalist, they often say they want to tell their own stories, to regain agency. I am a white Westerner, fortunate to have grown up in a stable, secure environment in one of the richest countries in the world. I have never been forced to flee my home. I am all too aware that it should not be me telling their stories. These are their stories to tell. To my mind, I am just a vehicle for their words. In time, many of them – hopefully all of them – will get their stories out in a way that is appropriate for them.

While there has been a tidal wave of support for new arrivals, there have also been powerful populist forces to contend with. In the summer of 2024, hard-right parties across Europe rose to prominence like never before. In France, President Macron announced a snap election following a crushing defeat by the far-right National Rally in the European Parliamentary elections, which resulted in a hung parliament and political gridlock. In Germany, too, the ultra-nationalist Alternative for Germany party surged in the polls, and in Austria the right-wing Freedom Party seized victory, vowing to carry the momentum into a national parliamentary vote. One poll found that immigration was the top concern for EU citizens at the ballot box.[2]

Anti-immigration attitudes are, of course, nothing new for the United Kingdom. I first started to report on immigration and asylum issues soon after I left the civil service, at a time when populist forces were gaining prominence. Nigel Farage's UK Independence Party was on the rise and Tory Eurosceptics were nipping at the heels of Conservative Prime Minister David Cameron. He responded by adopting a more hardline stance on immigration, declaring that there was 'a swarm' of migrants in Calais wanting to 'break into Britain without permission'.

When, in May 2015, the Tories made sweeping gains to secure a majority in the House of Commons, Cameron vowed to fulfil a key manifesto pledge: to deliver an in/out referendum on EU membership. At the heart of the Leave campaign was the pledge to 'take back control of our borders'. A fractious national debate surrounding immigration and identity ensued, dividing regions, communities, even families, pitting patriots against traitors. By the time of the Brexit vote in June 2016, 48 per cent of the public cited immigration as a major issue affecting their lives, compared to just 3 per cent when New Labour came to power in 1997.[3]

To me, Brussels wasn't an impersonal bureaucracy of grey-suit-wearing paper-pushers; it was the place where I had cut my teeth as a starry-eyed civil servant in my early twenties. My parents, both Irish, had met there. My mum had worked as a *fonctionnaire* for the European Commission and my older brother was born there. During frequent visits to Ireland, my dad pointed out the smooth, newly paved roads and the bustling city centre in Dublin, with its packed restaurants and bars. Newspaper headlines and stories celebrated Ireland's links to Brussels. This, clearly, was a country that was doing well, a country which had greatly benefited from EU funding.

From my desk on the eighth floor of the UK's Permanent Representation to the EU – the multilateral embassy which acted as a mini No. 10 – I could see the Berlaymont, the dome of the European Parliament and the hotel where senior *fonctionnaires* and MEPs would take their mistresses for an off-diary lunchtime meeting, with rooms rented out by the hour. For nearly three years, from 2010 to 2013, I made friends with the press corps based there, known as the Britpack, travelling around the continent with them to EU meetings, nervously leading press conferences with ambassadors and officials and spending many hazy evenings sipping potent Belgian beer and munching on triple-cooked chips.

When my boss, Helen, left her posting to move to No. 10 as David Cameron's foreign policy spokesperson, there was a gap of nearly ten months. I stepped in to cover the foreign policy brief in the interim period, advising then foreign secretary William Hague at Foreign Affairs Council meetings in the European Council. With my knees knocking together, I gathered questions from reporters huddled outside the building, then called his private secretary to brief Hague by phone ahead of his 'doorstep' on arrival. It was a high-stakes, high-pressure environment and it was an education, a crash course in diplomacy and world affairs.

Within a few months of Helen's departure, the Arab Spring had swept through the Middle East and North Africa. My focus shifted from the minutiae of sanctions policy and the fallout from the Fukushima nuclear disaster in Japan to the NATO-led military intervention in Libya, the uprisings erupting in Egypt and the outbreak and rapid escalation of the civil war in Syria. The so-called European migration crisis was underway.

As the turbulence in the region was at its height, I was brought over to No. 10's press office to work on the foreign policy desk. On one of my first days there, I was tasked with preparing lines ahead of a bilateral meeting between David Cameron and President Hollande of France, which was to focus on Syria. After photographers had snapped handshakes and fixed smiles, I stood outside the room with my 'opposite number', the French spokesperson I had worked alongside in Brussels, and discussed what likely lay ahead. We feared that internal displacement, the mass-dispersal of those caught up in the conflict and a humanitarian crisis on Europe's borders would lead to a rise in far-right sentiment and calls to close borders. And so it came to pass.

We are only just beginning to see the fallout from Brexit – repercussions which will be felt for generations to come – but the toxic rhetoric surrounding immigration has remained. In the meantime, having laid a path of destruction, Cameron slipped temporarily away from frontline politics, leaving migrants, the ultimate scapegoats, to take the hit.

So what is next? This is not an issue which is going away. A change of the vanguard will still have the same old problems to tackle, the same fires to fight.

While I have been researching and writing this book, the Labour Party has taken office, promising to reduce net migration, smash the people-smuggling gangs, increase enforced returns, and maintain Conservative policies such as cuts to visas for health and social care workers. The focus on law enforcement, immigration raids and militarisation of the Channel marks no clear departure from the Tories. Little looks likely to change.

Meanwhile, violence in northern France has sharply increased, as have the number of deaths at our border, with at least seventy deaths making 2024 the deadliest year yet. Labour says it is committed to closing all hotel accommodation, with no clear idea of where people will stay while they wait for their claims to be decided. The backlog of undecided claims remains high. Some progress has been made – the Rwanda plan has been scrapped – but not nearly enough.

Rather than more knee-jerk, dog-whistle politics, what is required is a bold, radical rethink which will amount to an overhaul of the system. The solution isn't short-term tactics but long-term strategic thinking. While self-serving ministers might not score political points quickly, the answers are more straightforward than they seem. Many are already within reach.

At the point of departure, we must improve intelligence-sharing and cross-border prosecutions, working closely with French law enforcement. Following Brexit, the UK lost access to many systems – the Eurodac fingerprint database, the Schengen Information System – which allowed us to see whether individuals had criminal convictions or had applied for asylum elsewhere. Regaining access to systems like these would shift the dial, should the EU and the French authorities allow it. That would need to involve much deeper shared working across jurisdictions than currently happens.

Yet, for all the rhetoric of cross-border cooperation to break the business model of the people smugglers, the gangs have continued to proliferate. We need to remove obstacles, to create safe routes, to secure pathways to a dignified life. The Ukraine schemes show that resettlement can be expedited. Within less than a year of Russia's invasion, the UK had offered safe passage to tens of thousands of vulnerable people. In sharp contrast, the double standards afforded to Afghans are clear. In 2023, Afghans were the top nationality to make the crossing by small boat. It followed that those dying in the Channel were also predominantly Afghans.

Extending humanitarian visas and rapid mobilisation as conflicts emerge using the full machinery of government – most notably the

FCDO network – is crucial. There is hope that a pathway will be set up for Palestinians fleeing Gaza, but nothing has materialised yet. I am frequently contacted by desperate families in the UK who are separated from their loved ones due to the Home Office's draconian rules. Visa routes for family reunion and rebuilding resettlement schemes should be a priority.

Search and rescue in the Channel is in urgent need of resources. Some experts suggest that the creation of a single organisation, merging Border Force and HM Coastguard, could ensure better coordination and save money. Border Force vessels should be taken out of use and replaced with permanently crewed RNLI lifeboats with an emergency response vessel stationed on standby in the search and rescue zone to bring small boat arrivals to safety. That would be a cost-effective way of ensuring that more lives are saved in our waters.

Swift assessment of claims is crucial to get a grip on the backlog. Under New Labour in 2006, the backlog of undecided claims stood at 400,000.[4] Through calm, considered leadership, the Home Office was able to claw back some control. Resourcing the system with decision makers who are recruited from within the Home Office, rather than high-street agencies, and ensuring that they are properly trained and recompensed so they stay in the job is essential. Their roles were downgraded a decade ago; they are now minimum-wage positions. This should be immediately changed. With skills and experience, fewer mistakes will be made, and less time and money will be wasted fighting appeal cases in the courts.

The cost of hotel accommodation, which currently stands at £8 million per day, is, after the optics of the small boats themselves, the most contentious issue the Labour government has to grapple with. The Home Office should be careful about housing asylum seekers in cheaper parts of the country, where there is already a severe lack of opportunities and a sickening sense, as one man in Skegness told me, that 'tomorrow won't be any better than today'. It may cut costs in the short term, but it will only stoke tensions in the long term. Housing asylum seekers in the homes of former mining families in pit communities overlooking collieries, as I saw in Doncaster, has inevitably fanned the flames of racial tension. Dispersal to these areas will only lead to more attacks from far-right and anti-migrant protesters, as we saw during the riots of summer 2024. Tackling misinformation online and ensuring surge policing for major incidents should also be of prime importance.

The government must provide a significant cash injection for local authorities, many of which currently face bankruptcy, to house people in communities where they can integrate rather than remain isolated on the margins. The pilot programme I visited in Glasgow showed how far this went to relieve pressures on local councils and frontline services. The 'Everyone In' scheme rolled out during the pandemic revealed that there is shelter for all those who need it, including in empty properties and other disused accommodation, should authorities choose to invest there.

By allowing asylum seekers to volunteer and use the skills they have – and loosening, or ideally lifting, the ban on the right to work – research shows that the government could save £1 billion over a ten-year period.[5] Germany and France allow asylum seekers to work after six months; Sweden after just one day. The US, too, gives people permission to work while their claims are being processed. We could do the same. There is a net benefit to the economy from immigration.

Lawyers should be adequately paid, and legal aid should be brought back so vulnerable people aren't reliant on advice and representation from underqualified, sometimes fraudulent advisors. Asylum law must be simplified so people aren't cut out by the complexities. With support and advice from well-informed, well-intentioned advisors, it will be more straightforward for them to navigate the system.

The Conservatives' Home Office was fixated on expanding the immigration detention estate. Labour, too, has announced plans for a 'large surge in enforcement and return flights', saying it will open new facilities at Campsfield and Haslar. We need to find an alternative to costly and damaging indefinite detention – or end it entirely, as many campaigners suggest. It is in nobody's interest.

At the final stage of the asylum process, the UK urgently needs returns deals to replace the Dublin Regulation we lost following Brexit. An agreement with the EU is the Starmer government's priority and work is underway to collaborate with European partners through the Calais Group and the establishment of a new Joint International Irregular Migration Unit. However, the Labour party's interest in the Italian model, and its efforts to learn lessons from Greece, has been highly criticised. The government could instead look to schemes such as the sponsorship programme Joe Biden's administration rolled out to hundreds of thousands of people from Central and South American nations, marking a sharp decrease in irregular migration. Tackling the rising death toll in the Channel will require much diplomatic negotiation and ministers will have to go out on the charm offensive. Immigration is not solely a home affairs issue; it is a foreign policy matter too.

Some suggest that much greater changes are needed from within the Home Office itself. The department's remit is mind-bogglingly broad. National security, policing, crime, immigration: these are some of the most complex, divisive issues in society, issues which 'come at you fast', as Amber Rudd found. Among ministers there is a constant sense of jeopardy, that something is always going wrong, because it often is. Rarely does a week go by without another scandal emerging. In 1942, the Labour home secretary Herbert Morrison described the Home Office as having 'corridors paved with dynamite', so often do crises emerge from within the department. That is partly down to political sensitivities, but it's also about the way in which the Home Office is run.

The Windrush scandal laid the department's shortcomings excruciatingly bare, with a major lessons learned review finding that the department had a 'culture of disbelief' and was 'institutionally racist'.[6] There was, Enver Solomon, the head of the Refugee Council, said, a presumption that all migrants were 'guilty until proven innocent', rather than the other way round.[7] There is no sense yet of the long-promised root-and-branch reform of the department's culture which is so badly needed.

A paper from the Institute of Government, to which I contributed, found that the department failed to work collaboratively with other Whitehall departments and external organisations in handling the asylum system.[8] No surprise there. As we've seen, Home Office officials are being inserted into overseas missions and the FCDO budget is being stripped away, with a third of the aid budget allocated to asylum accommodation. The Department for Health and Social Care managed to get more overseas care workers in to bolster the NHS, but the immigration rules swiftly changed to put a stop to that. The Department for Work and Pensions, which deals with benefit claims, has faced constant interventions from the Home Office. The Treasury, too, has had a battle on its hands balancing the economic benefits of immigration against work visa restrictions and the ban on the right to work. And the Department for Education has found itself largely cut out of managing the cases of unaccompanied refugee children, some of whom the Home Office has subsequently locked up.

The department's stated objectives of 'compassion, respect, courage and collaboration' should be brought back into focus. It is absolutely possible to act in accordance with these values as, say, the NHS does in the face of constrained resources and considerable political pressure.

Perhaps even more radical reform within government is required. Should there, as some have suggested, be a dedicated department which focuses solely on immigration, borders and citizenship?[9] Experts argue that it would be viable, ensuring that the asylum system could function more efficiently and effectively. The creation of a new department may also help to stabilise and shore up the workforce, allowing staff to develop a specialism and get on top of the issues rather than continuing to lurch from crisis to crisis.[10] It could make better use of other immigration functions – Border Force, visa and passport centres and so on – alongside local government. Crucially, it would signal a break from the old guard, ridding itself of the burdensome baggage of previous scandals and creating space for a new, more compassionate approach.

For those I've met and written about in this book, and countless others whose stories are not on these pages, the experience of navigating the UK's needlessly hostile, complex asylum system has meant being kept in limbo, waiting, never sure what tomorrow will bring. It is intended to create fear and to prevent people from wanting to come here and remain here. But many do, and I have seen that communities up and down the country are all the more open and tolerant for them.

Arian, the Iranian-Kurdish aerospace engineer, has been granted leave to remain. He was homeless for a month, sleeping on sofas or wherever he could find shelter. During that period he often sent me concerning messages about harassment he had faced, attacks narrowly avoided. He now has a room in a shared house and is looking for work in his field. One day, he tells me, he will create a 'humane drone'.

Shadi, the charismatic Sudanese man, has also been given leave to remain after a near-three-year process. He has completed his studies in telecommunications engineering and is searching for jobs and a more permanent housing arrangement. For a recent birthday, Shadi gave me a ballpoint pen and an accompanying message which read: 'You have the heart of a warrior. Keep writing and keep fighting.' He plans to do the same.

For others, their stories are still being written. The Qadir family await a decision following their substantive interview. In the meantime, their children are learning fast at school, while Parwen's English improves through language apps and voice memos to me. They speak daily to friends and family in Iraq.

Jamal, the charming teenager from Afghanistan, is still in Home Office accommodation, relying on the meagre subsistence payments of around £8.50 a week. He has joined a football team at a nearby college and hopes he will soon be able to take his GCSE English exams.

And Kewser, the bright medical student from Ethiopia, is still waiting for her substantive interview. She lost contact for a time. I worried, as I always do, that she was struggling. When she resumed contact, she confided that she had been through a difficult period. She hadn't expected to feel so isolated and lonely when she reached the UK. The dream of studying medicine remains out of reach but she has found informal work which keeps her mind occupied. As soon as she gets her paperwork, she will book a flight to see her father.

Writing this book has been an education in many, many ways. I have met people I never would otherwise have crossed paths with and been to places I never would have visited had it not been for this project. I have found myself living and breathing the system, hungry to find out more, to gather more, to do more. Sometimes I wondered when it might all slow down. Often I lay awake, wondering if there was more I could do than write. It rarely feels like enough. Meanwhile, the situation for those I've met has largely remained stagnant.

It is a credit to my sources, after all they have endured to get here, let alone what they have faced since they arrived, that they trusted me and welcomed me into their lives, some keeping in contact for several years. They have shown unimaginable courage when their status was insecure, their futures unknown. All I can hope is that, in return, I did their stories justice. This book is for them.

A Note on Sources

This book is based on more than 200 interviews conducted over five years of reporting. Sources included current and former Home Office officials, search and rescue staff, social workers, lawyers, campaigners, medics, teachers and, of course, asylum seekers who have navigated or are still navigating the system.

I offered anonymity to every person I spoke to. Some decided to waive it and go on-the-record while others chose to have their identities concealed, largely through fear of an adverse reaction if they spoke out publicly. In those cases I adhered to requests that I change their names and, at times, dates, locations and other identifying features. Where I have not mentioned the city or town to which somebody was dispersed it was because they asked me not to.

All of the events and conversations detailed here occurred as I have written them. I have recounted incidents told to me as faithfully as I could. Where a thought or comment is written but not in quotation marks, the source expressed these to me directly, usually in person and sometimes on the phone.

For court trials I either attended in person or via videolink, and was in contact with legal teams – barristers, solicitors and clerks – spending days listening to and watching the proceedings. Some courts did not make transcripts publicly available and did not wish to share

A NOTE ON SOURCES

their records after the trial. In these instances I have relied on extensive note-taking and fact-checking with others present.

Sometimes events moved so quickly in Westminster that I and my sources struggled to keep up. When a scene had already been written, I contacted the source again to update the text with their views, as was the case with the change in government following the 2024 general election. I interviewed most people a number of times. All, or the majority, of what they recounted was then corroborated with at least one other source. On some occasions, where a person was missing or presumed dead, I spoke to relatives and friends about their lives. That has been made clear in the text.

While my government sources have provided unparalleled levels of access to documents, transcripts, screengrabs from internal meetings and other evidence, the Home Office press team have repeatedly attempted to restrict access. Any cooperation they did provide came in the form of a bland spokesperson statement. At times, they acknowledged that the allegations were serious and that the reporting had been both thorough and detailed, but not once did they grant a request for a background briefing, even when the relevant official had agreed to an interview.

On more than one occasion, I have been reprimanded by the communications team simply for reporting the facts. At other times they have attempted to kill the story before publication, weighing in to discredit the work or the legitimacy of my sources. These interactions typically involve numerous others – lawyers, editors and so on – and are an exercise in intimidation and time-wasting. A huge amount could be gained by a more collaborative approach with all journalists, not only those from more friendly media outlets.

Out of necessity, I was forced to seek out former and current members of Home Office staff myself. Some were colleagues during my time there, or those I had known from other departments across Whitehall.

A NOTE ON SOURCES

They have all checked what I have written for any mistakes or omissions. Errors are, of course, mine and mine alone.

While the vast majority of the reporting for this book is original, some of it comes from articles I have researched and written either before or during the drafting of the manuscript. These pieces have been referenced in the endnotes, alongside other journalistic articles, reports, academic papers and legal documents I have drawn on.

Lastly, I am eternally grateful to all those who have carried out painstaking work on the frontline, who are the true experts in this field. It would have been impossible to write a book as heavily reported as this without the work you had already done over many years. For that, thank you.

Acknowledgements

I had been waiting years to write this book and, thankfully, the experience exceeded my expectations. It has rarely been anything other than a joy. That is largely down to the people I have met over the course of the research. There are so many of you making the asylum system work – unsung heroes, striving to do better.

Immigration and asylum is a wonderfully communal, kindhearted world to find yourself in and I have always been made to feel very at home. Toufique Hossain, Maria Thomas, Jamie Bell, Rob McNeil, Hannah Lewis, Lucy Mayblin, Lou Calvey, Daniel Sohege, Zoe Gardner, Colin Yeo, Luke Piper, Annika Joy, Alison Phipps, Julia Rampen, Jenni Regan: thanks for answering my questions, often late at night, chatting and making me laugh over a glass of wine, putting me up during trips and championing my work.

Being freelance often means being a lone wolf but I am lucky to have made many friends along the way. Sally Hayden, Daniel Trilling, Jack Shenker, Oli Franklin-Wells – all brilliant reporters and authors – have helped me to make the leap from journalism to publishing, offering advice and support when I needed it most. Thank you for buoying me up. I am also grateful to May Bulman and all at Lighthouse Reports, Amelia Gentleman, Steve Bloomfield, Rosie Swash, Frances Perraudin, Caroline Gammell, Dave Taylor, Sara Wilbourne and all at

ACKNOWLEDGEMENTS

Article 19, along with so many other editors and correspondents who have supported my reporting. Sam Heller for fact-checking the sections on Syria and Iraq, Beccy Allen on Western Sahara and Luke Piper on legal aid: thank you. Thanks also to Sam Berkman for permission to reproduce the Saharawi poem.

In Glasgow, thanks to Pinar at Maryhill Integration Network, Annika at the Simon Community and Munir for driving me around. I always love my visits to Glasgow. Savan has been so generous, translating voice notes from shopping centre precincts and spending hours on long, emotionally taxing calls. It must be difficult to hear what your fellow Kurdish people are going through. Thank you for taking the time.

To those in Doncaster, who asked to remain anonymous, you are doing such valuable work. Thanks for having me along. Asylum Link Merseyside and Ewan's wonderful choir in Liverpool were a total delight. I sang songs in Swahili, French, Kurdish and so many other languages and I still hum them to myself. In Scarborough, Evans and Mike Padgham were so measured and thoughtful. I was incredibly moved by my visit to St Cecilia's, as Evans knows. I think about it often. The British Red Cross team were helpful during a visit to Preston, and Friends of Napier, Samphire and KRAN during multiple trips to the Kent coast. Those in Witney would prefer not to be mentioned, but you have been so kind and so helpful in many ways. Care4Calais, too, have always provided updates and access, for which I am very grateful. Grassroots organisations in northern France have accommodated my last-minute requests and eased the reporting, in particular Utopia 56. I always come back from Calais and Dunkirk feeling energised; that is largely down to all of you and the incredible camaraderie you have. Charities, campaigners and courageous whistleblowers have added a great deal to the book.

When I started this project, I had just returned from maternity leave and wasn't sure how to make the finances stack up long-term.

ACKNOWLEDGEMENTS

Grants from the International Women's Media Foundation and later a cross-border grant from the European Journalism Fund gave me the boost I needed. I am hugely indebted to the Society of Authors for their generosity too. Organisations like these help so many reporters and writers to do vital work.

I am grateful to have found an agent extraordinaire in Sophie Lambert, who has always shared the same vision for what this book could be. I've learned a huge amount and had so much fun spending time together. Sarah Rigby, my clear-eyed, intuitive editor, has helped to steer this book along the right course, providing great insight and support throughout the writing. Thanks to you, Amy, Katie, Pippa and all at Elliott & Thompson, and to Rhian and Jess, for helping me get this book out there.

My friends have always felt like family to me. Laughter really is the best medicine, and it has sustained and grounded me over the last five years while working on this book and long before it too. You know who you are. Thank you for the love, which means so much.

Mum, Dad, Robin: my overriding childhood memories are of laughter and of well-told anecdotes. I'm so lucky we're all such good friends, as well as family. I don't know what I'd do without you. Thank you for everything you do and have always done for me. And to Sam, Charlie, Milo, John, Mandy, Tom and Amelia: thank you for all your support.

Ross, my number one, you never lost faith in me or in this project, even when my confidence dipped. You have kept the show on the road and helped me carve out the hours needed to do this work. You've offered incisive, constructive criticism, endured long discussions about structure and taught me not to give up. You are the best husband and the best dad to our little guy. I'm so lucky to have you.

Our newest addition has been with me throughout much of the heavy lifting for this book. It has been an unexpected delight to spend

ACKNOWLEDGEMENTS

days, months of solitude and silence, wrapped up in words and preparing for your arrival, tiny one. We can't wait to welcome you.

Lastly, to Robbie, my little ray of sunshine. I had no idea how much my life would change when you came along. Being your mummy is the best job I've ever had. I hope I have made you proud.

Notes

Prologue: No Entry

1. Aubrey Allegretti, 'Home Secretary Sajid Javid cuts holiday short to deal with Channel migrants', Sky News, 29 December 2018.
   https://news.sky.com/story/english-channel-migrant-crossings-a-major-incident-sajid-javid-11593555

2. 'Responding to irregular migration: A diplomatic route', House of Commons Foreign Affairs Committee, 4 November 2019.
   https://publications.parliament.uk/pa/cm201919/cmselect/cmfaff/107/10705.htm#_idTextAnchor004

   See also: *https://committees.parliament.uk/publications/2141/documents/19918/default/*

3. Home Office statistics, 'How many people do we grant protection to?', gov.uk, updated 7 December 2023.
   https://www.gov.uk/government/statistics/immigration-system-statistics-year-ending-september-2023/how-many-people-do-we-grant-protection-to#:~:text=Three%2Dquarters%20(75%25)%20of,or%20alternative%20forms%20of%20leave

4. World Values Survey, 'UK attitudes to immigration among most positive internationally', The Policy Institute at King's College London, 23 February 2022.
   https://www.uk-values.org/news-comment/uk-attitudes-to-immigration-among-most-positive-internationally-1018742/pub01-115

NOTES

1. White Cliffs

1. Elif Shafak, *The Island of Missing Trees* (Penguin Random House UK, 2021), p. 55.

2. Damian Grammaticas and Kate Whannel, 'Sunak and Macron summit: UK to give £500m to help France curb small boat crossings', BBC News, 10 March 2023.
   https://www.bbc.co.uk/news/uk-politics-64916446

3. Human Rights Observers, videos showed to the author in Calais, France.
   https://humanrightsobservers.org/monthly-observations/

4. European Council on Refugees and Exiles, 2023 figures from French Interior Ministry.
   https://asylumineurope.org/reports/country/france/statistics/#:~:text=In%20 2023%2C%20167%2C432%20persons%20were,applicants%20(19%2C049 %20in%202022)

5. Nicola Kelly, X post, 8 May 2023.
   https://twitter.com/NicolaKelly/status/1655471618401923074

6. Amnesty International, 'Iran: Human Rights Abuses Against The Kurdish Minority'.
   https://www.amnesty.org/en/wp-content/uploads/2021/05/MDE130882008 ENGLISH.pdf

7. Ibid.

8. Unrepresented Nations and Peoples Organization (UNPO), 24 December 2018.
   https://www.unpo.org/members/7882

9. Human Rights Watch, 'Iran: Brutal repression in Kurdistan capital', 21 December 2022.
   https://www.hrw.org/news/2022/12/21/iran-brutal-repression-kurdistan-capital

2. SOS

1. Nigel Farage Facebook page, recording of beach landing, 1 May 2021.
   https://www.facebook.com/share/v/PN8a72H7kRqUYc3r/

2. Patrick Cockburn, 'Choke point', *London Review of Books*, 7 November 2019.
   https://www.lrb.co.uk/the-paper/v41/n21/patrick-cockburn/choke-point

NOTES

3. Jamie Rose, 'Western Heights: Dover's so-called seediest spot and why its reputation might be out of date', Kent Live News, 20 July 2021. https://www.kentlive.news/news/news-opinion/western-heights-dovers-called-seediest-5673799

4. Charles Hymas, 'Channel migrants held on double-decker bus as Border Force overwhelmed by record arrivals', Telegraph, 8 October 2021. https://www.telegraph.co.uk/news/2021/10/08/channel-migrants-held-double-decker-bus-border-force-overwhelmed/

   See also: Matt Dathan, 'Officials register Channel migrants in Dover car park', The Times, 28 July 2021. https://www.thetimes.com/uk/politics/article/immigration-service-forced-to-register-channel-migrants-in-car-park-xxzhl5kgv

5. Rajeev Syal, Angelique Chrisafis and Diane Taylor, 'Tragedy at sea claims dozens of lives in deadliest day of Channel crisis', Guardian, 25 November 2021. https://www.theguardian.com/world/2021/nov/24/several-people-dead-migrant-boat-capsizes-channel

6. Aaron Walawalkar, Eleanor Rose and Mark Townsend, 'Horror beyond words: Inside the UK coastguard in the weeks before the Channel disaster', Liberty Investigates and Observer, 29 April 2023. https://libertyinvestigates.org.uk/articles/horror-beyond-words-inside-the-uk-coastguard-in-the-weeks-before-the-channel-disaster/

7. Nicola Kelly, '"We will demand justice": The vigil for those who died in the Channel tragedy', Guardian, 24 November 2022. https://www.theguardian.com/uk-news/2022/nov/24/relatives-of-those-who-died-in-channel-tragedy-a-year-ago-call-for-justice-at-vigil

8. Nicola Kelly, 'Horror in the Channel: Cruel mystery of the missing small boats migrants', Independent, 9 July 2023. https://www.independent.co.uk/independentpremium/uk-news/small-boats-drown-migrants-missing-b2366667.html

9. Marine Accident Investigation Branch, 'Report on the investigation into the flooding and partial sinking of an inflatable migrant boat resulting in the loss of at least 27 lives in the Dover Strait on 24 November 2021', final report published 8 November 2023. https://assets.publishing.service.gov.uk/media/654b77e8e70413000dfc49f0/2023-07-MigrantBoatReport.pdf

10. Nicola Kelly, 'Report reveals mistakes that led to 27 people drowning in Channel horror crossing', Independent, 9 November 2023. https://www.independent.co.uk/news/uk/home-news/migrants-drown-channel-crossing-coastguard-b2444082.html

NOTES

11. Marine Accident Investigation Branch, 'Report on the investigation into the flooding and partial sinking of an inflatable migrant boat resulting in the loss of at least 27 lives in the Dover Strait on 24 November 2021', final report published 8 November 2023.
https://assets.publishing.service.gov.uk/media/654b77e8e70413000dfc49f0/2023-07-MigrantBoatReport.pdf

12. Nicola Kelly, 'UK coastguard to receive legal training for inquest into Channel deaths', *Guardian*, 3 December 2022.
https://www.theguardian.com/uk-news/2022/dec/03/uk-coastguard-legal-training-inquest-channel-deaths

13. Rajeev Syal, 'Priti Patel to send boats carrying migrants to UK back across Channel', *Guardian*, 9 September 2021.
https://www.theguardian.com/uk-news/2021/sep/09/priti-patel-to-send-boats-carrying-migrants-to-uk-back-across-channel

14. International Convention on Maritime Search and Rescue.
https://www.imo.org/en/About/Conventions/Pages/International-Convention-on-Maritime-Search-and-Rescue-(SAR).aspx

15. House of Commons Defence Committee report, 'Operation Isotrope: The use of the military to counter migrant crossings', published 11 March 2022.
https://publications.parliament.uk/pa/cm5802/cmselect/cmdfence/1069/report.html#

16. Nicola Kelly, May Bulman, Tomas Statitus, Bashar Deeb and Fahim Abed, 'Revealed: UK-funded French forces putting migrants' lives at risk with small-boat tactics', *Observer*, 23 March 2024.
https://www.theguardian.com/uk-news/2024/mar/23/uk-funding-french-migrants-small-boat-border-forces

17. Nicola Kelly, 'Yvette Cooper's plan to "smash the small boat gangs" is doomed to fail, warn border force whistleblowers', *Byline Times*, 20 September 2024.
https://bylinetimes.com/2024/09/20/yvette-coopers-plan-to-smash-the-small-boat-gangs-is-doomed-to-fail-warn-border-force-whistleblowers/

18. Ibid.

3. Fortress Britain

1. Giles Worsley, 'An artistic bargain at £311 million', *Telegraph*, 7 February 2005.
https://www.telegraph.co.uk/culture/art/3636603/An-artistic-bargain-at-311-million.html

NOTES

2. Staff and agencies, 'Clarke refuses to quit over deportation failures', *Guardian*, 25 April 2006.
   https://www.theguardian.com/society/2006/apr/25/prisonsandprobation.uk

3. 'Ken Clarke: "Theresa's a bloody difficult woman"', Sky News, 5 July 2016.
   https://www.youtube.com/watch?v=ipW1D2EyDbA

4. 'Full text: Theresa May's conference speech', published in the *Guardian*, 7 October 2002.
   https://www.theguardian.com/politics/2002/oct/07/conservatives2002.conservatives1

5. 'Yes there will be cuts', *The Andrew Marr Show*, BBC News, 10 January 2010.
   https://news.bbc.co.uk/2/hi/programmes/andrew_marr_show/8450542.stm

6. James Kirkup and Robert Winnett, 'Theresa May interview: "We're going to give illegal migrants a really hostile reception"', *Telegraph*, 25 May 2012.
   https://www.telegraph.co.uk/news/0/theresa-may-interview-going-give-illegal-migrants-really-hostile/

7. Vikram Dodd, 'Anjem Choudary released on bail after counter-terrorism investigation arrests', *Guardian*, 26 September 2014.
   https://www.theguardian.com/uk-news/2014/sep/26/anjem-choudary-released-on-bail

8. Nicola Kelly and Jack Shenker, 'Hostile environment: Inside the Home Office', Tortoise Media, Slow Newscast published 15 August 2022. Edited by Dave Taylor.
   https://legacy.tortoisemedia.com/audio/hostile-environment-inside-the-home-office/

9. 'Home Office boss quits over "campaign against him"', BBC News, 29 February 2020.
   https://www.bbc.co.uk/news/uk-politics-51687287

10. Rajeev Syal, 'Priti Patel's alleged bullying: What the case is about', *Guardian*, 6 December 2021.
    https://www.theguardian.com/politics/2021/dec/06/priti-patels-alleged-bullying-what-the-case-is-about

11. Daniel Trilling, '"Incoherence and inconsistency": The inside story of the Rwanda deportation plan', *Guardian* Long Read, 5 October 2023.
    https://www.theguardian.com/world/2023/oct/05/incoherence-and-inconsistency-the-inside-story-of-the-rwanda-deportation-plan

NOTES

12. Nicola Kelly, '"I will die here, I can't go back to Africa": Migrants respond to Rwanda removal', *Guardian*, 15 April 2022.
https://www.theguardian.com/world/2022/apr/15/i-will-die-here-i-cant-go-back-to-africa-migrants-respond-to-rwanda-removal

13. David Barrett, '"The preparation for the next flight begins NOW": Defiant but "disappointed" Priti Patel vows to press on with her Rwanda deportation plan despite meddling European Court of Human Rights judge grounding the first plane 20 minutes before take-off', *Daily Mail*, 15 June 2022.
https://www.dailymail.co.uk/news/article-10917627/Priti-Patel-vows-fighting-Rwanda-plan-European-court-blocks-UKs-flight.html

14. Nicola Kelly and Jack Shenker, 'Hostile environment: Inside the Home Office', Tortoise Media, 15 August 2022.
https://legacy.tortoisemedia.com/audio/hostile-environment-inside-the-home-office/

    See also: https://x.com/NicolaKelly/status/1559495360443289602

15. Steph Spyro, 'First Rwanda flights this summer', *Sunday Express* splash, 19 March 2023.
https://www.magzter.com/stories/newspaper/Sunday-Express/FIRST-RWANDA-ASYLUM-FLIGHTS-THIS-SUMMER

16. Home Affairs Select Committee, 'Oral evidence: One-off session with the former Inspector of Borders and Immigration', 27 February 2024.
https://committees.parliament.uk/oralevidence/14348/html/

17. YouGov politics tracker, figures correct in June 2024.
https://yougov.co.uk/topics/politics/trackers/how-the-government-is-handling-the-issue-of-immigration-in-the-uk

18. 'How many people cross the Channel in small boats and how many claim asylum in the UK?' BBC News analysis, 24 June 2024.
https://www.bbc.co.uk/news/uk-53699511

19. Sandra Smith, 'What they said about immigration', *Guardian*, 20 August 2003.
https://www.theguardian.com/politics/2003/aug/20/immigration.immigrationpolicy

20. 'Gordon Brown calls Labour supporter a "bigoted woman"', Sky News, 2010.
https://www.youtube.com/watch?v=yEReCN9gO14

21. Stephen Bush, 'Labour's anti-immigrant mug: the worst part is, it isn't a gaffe', *New Statesman*, 28 March 2015.
https://www.newstatesman.com/politics/2015/03/labours-anti-immigrant-mug-worst-part-it-isnt-gaffe

NOTES

22. Lizzie Dearden, 'UK government urged to offer "safe and legal" route for asylum seekers as poll shows support', *Observer*, 14 July 2024.
https://www.theguardian.com/uk-news/article/2024/jul/14/uk-government-urged-to-offer-safe-and-legal-route-for-asylum-seekers-as-poll-shows-support

4. On Solid Ground

1. Anonymous, 'Welcome to London: Instructions for new arrivals', *'The Other Side of Hope' anthology*, autumn 23 edition, p. 99.

2. David Neal, ICIBI report, 'An inspection of the initial processing of migrants arriving via small boats at Tug Haven and Western Jet Foil', published July 2022.
https://assets.publishing.service.gov.uk/media/62d7d12bd3bf7f2861b893f4/E02726679_ICIBI_Tug_Haven_and_Western_Jet_Foil_Web_Accessible.pdf

3. Independent Monitoring Board report, 'Cross Channel migrants, some very vulnerable still held in poor conditions – new report says', 16 December 2021.
https://imb.org.uk/news/cross-channel-migrants-held-in-poor-conditions/

4. David Neal, ICIBI report, 'An inspection of the initial processing of migrants arriving via small boats at Tug Haven and Western Jet Foil', published July 2022.
https://assets.publishing.service.gov.uk/media/62d7d12bd3bf7f2861b893f4/E02726679_ICIBI_Tug_Haven_and_Western_Jet_Foil_Web_Accessible.pdf

5. Matthew Weaver, 'Petrol bombs thrown at immigration centre in Dover', *Guardian*, 30 October 2022.
https://www.theguardian.com/uk-news/2022/oct/30/dover-petrol-bomb-immigration-centre-border-force

   See also: 'Man who firebombed Dover immigration centre died from asphyxiation, inquest hears', Sky News, 8 November 2022.
https://news.sky.com/story/man-who-firebombed-dover-immigration-centre-died-from-asphyxiation-inquest-hears-12741516

6. 'Migrant crisis an "invasion", Suella Braverman says', Sky News, 31 October 2022.
https://news.sky.com/video/migrant-crisis-an-invasion-suella-braverman-says-12735371

7. United Nations International Court of Justice press release, 'UN inspectors found no evidence of prohibited weapons programmes as of 18 March withdrawal, Hans Blix tells Security Council', 5 June 2003.
https://press.un.org/en/2003/sc7777.doc.htm

NOTES

8. House of Commons debate on the use of chemical weapons in Syria, delivered 29 August 2013.
   https://hansard.parliament.uk/commons/2013-08-29/debates/1308298000001/SyriaAndTheUseOfChemicalWeapons

9. 'Remarks by the President to the White House Press Corps', 20 August 2012.
   https://obamawhitehouse.archives.gov/the-press-office/2012/08/20/remarks-president-white-house-press-corps#:~:text=We%20have%20been%20very%20clear,somehow%20under%20%2D%2D%20it's%20safe%3F

10. Nick Thompson, 'Iraq's Yazidis trapped, hiding from ISIS in the mountains', CNN, 8 August 2014.
    https://edition.cnn.com/2014/08/08/world/meast/iraq-yazidi-people/index.html

11. UN Human Rights Council report, '"They came to destroy": ISIS Crimes Against the Yazidis', published 15 June 2016.
    https://www.ohchr.org/sites/default/files/Documents/HRBodies/HRCouncil/CoISyria/A_HRC_32_CRP.2_en.pdf

12. Diane Taylor, 'Robert Jenrick has cartoon murals painted over at children's asylum centre', Guardian, 7 July 2023.
    https://www.theguardian.com/uk-news/2023/jul/07/robert-jenrick-has-cartoon-murals-painted-over-at-childrens-asylum-centre

13. Immigration rule change, which came into force on 10 January 2024.
    https://www.legislation.gov.uk/uksi/2024/19/made

14. Nicola Kelly, 'Hundreds of child refugees wrongly sent to adult detention centres by Home Office', Independent, 23 January 2024.
    https://www.independent.co.uk/news/uk/home-news/refugees-children-adults-detention-identified-age-b2482828.html

15. Amelia Gentleman, '"You walked in and your heart sank": The shocking inside story of Manston detention centre', Guardian, 25 March 2023.
    https://www.theguardian.com/uk-news/2023/mar/25/inside-story-of-manston-detention-centre

16. Diane Taylor, 'Man who died after being held at Manston asylum centre named', Guardian, 3 December 2022.
    https://www.theguardian.com/uk-news/2022/dec/03/man-who-died-after-being-held-at-manston-asylum-centre-named

17. Holly Bancroft, 'Woman suffered miscarriage "after stress" of conditions at Manston migrant detention centre', Independent, 6 December 2023.
    https://www.independent.co.uk/news/uk/home-news/manston-detention-centre-migrant-home-office-b2458940.html

18. Diane Taylor, 'Home Office contractors removed for trying to sell drugs at Manston asylum centre', *Guardian*, 4 November 2022. https://www.theguardian.com/uk-news/2022/nov/04/home-office-contractors-disciplined-trying-to-sell-drugs-manston-asylum-centre

19. Joe Duggan, 'Manston migrants abandoned at London Victoria station for hours by Home Office', *inews*, 2 November 2022. https://inews.co.uk/news/migrants-manston-asylum-centre-london-train-station-without-assistance-1949120

20. Libby Wiener, 'Home Secretary Suella Braverman denies responsibility for crisis at Manston', ITV News, 23 November 2022. https://www.itv.com/news/2022-11-23/home-secretary-suella-braverman-denies-responsibility-for-crisis-at-manston

5. No Safe Passage

1. Leaflet seen by the author in Calais.

2. Amelia Gentleman, 'Essex lorry deaths: 39 Vietnamese migrants suffocated in container, court hears', *Guardian*, 7 October 2020. https://www.theguardian.com/uk-news/2020/oct/07/essex-lorry-deaths-39-vietnamese-migrants-suffocated-in-container-court-hears

3. 'Former landlady of Hewa Rahimpur says she is in "shock" over people smuggling allegations', Sky News, 7 September 2023. https://news.sky.com/video/former-landlady-of-hewa-rahimpur-says-she-is-in-shock-over-people-smuggling-allegations-12956583

4. Amy-Claire Martin, 'Kiosk owner who sold sweets unmasked as kingpin who smuggled 10,000 migrants to Britain in small boats', *Independent*, 18 October 2023. https://www.independent.co.uk/news/uk/crime/hewa-rahimpur-people-smuggling-channel-small-boats-b2431296.html

5. National Crime Agency press release, 'Prolific small boats people smuggling network dismantled as part of international operation', 6 July 2022. https://www.nationalcrimeagency.gov.uk/news/prolific-small-boats-people-smuggling-network-dismantled-as-part-of-international-operation

6. 'Suella Braverman appears unsure about how an asylum seeker can apply to enter the UK', *Guardian* video clip, 23 November 2022. https://www.youtube.com/watch?v=UpZAS0yqkJM

NOTES

7. Nicola Kelly, 'British nationals fear permanent separation from Ukrainian family', *Guardian*, 25 February 2022.
https://www.theguardian.com/world/2022/feb/25/british-nationals-fear-permanent-separation-from-ukraine-family-russia

8. Maria Tsvetkova, 'Guards fire shots as Ukrainians try to cram onto evacuation trains', Reuters, 25 February 2022.
https://www.reuters.com/world/europe/guards-fire-shots-ukrainians-try-cram-onto-evacuation-trains-2022-02-25/

9. Nicola Kelly, thread of messages on X, 25 February 2022.
https://twitter.com/NicolaKelly/status/1497208153297010716

10. Rajeev Syal, Jessica Elgot and Nicola Slawson, 'Priti Patel refuses to waive all visa rules for Ukraine refugees', *Guardian*, 28 February 2022.
https://www.theguardian.com/uk-news/2022/feb/28/boris-johnson-urged-by-tory-mps-to-do-more-for-ukraine-refugees

11. 'Afghan President Ghani flees country as Taliban enters Kabul', Al-Jazeera, 15 August 2021.
https://www.aljazeera.com/news/2021/8/15/afghan-president-ghani-flees-country-as-taliban-surrounds-kabul#:~:text=Media%20later%20reported%20that%20Ghani,their%20countrymen%2C%E2%80%9D%20-he%20said

12. 'Photos: Taliban takes control of Afghan presidential palace', Al-Jazeera, 15 August 2021.
https://www.aljazeera.com/gallery/2021/8/15/in-pictures-taliban-fighters-enter-afghan-presidential-palace

13. Sune Engel Rasmussen, 'Afghanistan's economic meltdown leaves ordinary citizens scrambling to survive', *Wall Street Journal*, 18 September 2021.
https://www.wsj.com/articles/afghanistans-economic-meltdown-leaves-ordinary-citizens-scrambling-to-survive-11631969485

14. Nicola Kelly and May Bulman, 'Revealed: UK has failed to resettle Afghans facing torture and death despite promise', *Observer*, 3 December 2022.
https://www.theguardian.com/world/2022/dec/03/revealed-uk-has-failed-to-resettle-afghans-facing-torture-and-death-despite-promise

15. Ibid.

16. Follow-up to Afghanistan inquiry – oral evidence, 17 October 2023.
https://committees.parliament.uk/event/19434/formal-meeting-oral-evidence-session/

Full transcript: *https://committees.parliament.uk/oralevidence/13680/pdf/*

NOTES

17. '"We are at war," Netanyahu says, after Hamas launches devastating surprise attack', *Times of Israel*, 7 October 2023.
    https://www.timesofisrael.com/we-are-at-war-netanyahu-says-after-hamas-launches-devastating-surprise-attack/#:~:text=%E2%80%9CIn%20
    parallel%2C%20I%20am%20initiating,unprecedented%20price%2C%E2
    %80%9D%20Netanyahu%20said.

18. Caroline Davies, 'Afghans in UK visa limbo as Pakistan vows to expel migrants', BBC News, 13 October 2023.
    https://www.bbc.co.uk/news/world-asia-67020994

19. James Gant, 'Minister for Afghanistan Lord Ahmad "was on HOLIDAY" when Kabul fell – as Dominic Raab faces mounting pressure to quit over Crete holiday', *Daily Mail*, 21 August 2021.
    https://www.dailymail.co.uk/news/article-9914599/Minister-Afghanistan-Lord-Ahmad-HOLIDAY-Kabul-fell.html

20. Follow-up to Afghanistan inquiry – oral evidence, 17 October 2023.
    https://committees.parliament.uk/event/19434/formal-meeting-oral-evidence-session/

    Full transcript: https://committees.parliament.uk/oralevidence/13680/pdf/

21. Nicola Kelly, 'UK provided £3m to Turkish border forces to stop migrants, FOI reveals', *Guardian*, 7 June 2023.
    https://www.theguardian.com/politics/2023/jun/07/uk-provided-3m-to-turkish-border-forces-to-stop-migrants-foi-reveals

22. Turkish news article, turkidare.net, 28 June 2022.
    https://turkidare.net/van-iran-siniri-guvenligi-icin-arac-takviyesi/

6. Backlogged

1. 'Settled Wanderers', translated by Sam Berkson and Mohamed Suleiman.

   Sam Berkson, 'Voices of a lost homeland: The poetry of Western Sahara', Middle East Eye, 23 September 2020.
   https://www.middleeasteye.net/discover/western-sahara-algeria-badi-poetry-exile

2. 'Community questions around Napier barracks use', Folkestone and Hythe District Council.
   https://www.folkestone-hythe.gov.uk/community/questions-napier-barracks

3. Nigel Farage Facebook page video, posted 17 September 2020.
   https://www.facebook.com/watch/?v=354859652313947

NOTES

4. Jamie Grierson, 'Covid cases among asylum seekers at Napier barracks higher than thought', *Guardian*, 24 February 2021.
https://www.theguardian.com/uk-news/2021/feb/24/covid-cases-among-asylum-seekers-at-napier-barracks-higher-than-thought

5. Jamie Grierson and Diane Taylor, 'Asylum seekers tell of dire conditions at Kent barracks after fire', *Guardian*, 31 January 2021.
https://www.theguardian.com/uk-news/2021/jan/31/asylum-seekers-dire-conditions-kent-napier-barracks-fire

6. 'Illegal Immigration' debate, *Hansard*, 13 December 2022.
https://hansard.parliament.uk/commons/2022-12-13/debates/DB61C374-16B5-411C-9A29-CC3DCA119EB3/IllegalImmigration

7. Amelia Gentleman, 'UK government "hackathon" to search for ways to use AI to cut asylum backlog', *Guardian*, 29 April 2023.
https://www.theguardian.com/uk-news/2023/apr/29/government-hackathon-to-search-for-ways-to-use-ai-to-cut-asylum-backlog

8. Home Office 'Streamlined asylum processing', first published 23 February 2023.
https://assets.publishing.service.gov.uk/media/66326585352d85a16c3016ed/Streamlined+asylum+processing.pdf

9. Nicola Kelly, 'Revealed: Supermarket staff recruited to make "life and death" asylum decisions', *Guardian*, 5 November 2022.
https://www.theguardian.com/world/2022/nov/05/revealed-novice-staff-making-life-and-death-asylum-decisions

10. The Student Room forum messaging board.
https://www.thestudentroom.co.uk/showthread.php?t=7046942

11. Nicola Kelly, 'Revealed: Supermarket staff recruited to make "life and death" asylum decisions', *Guardian*, 5 November 2022.
https://www.theguardian.com/world/2022/nov/05/revealed-novice-staff-making-life-and-death-asylum-decisions

12. Presented by Nicola Kelly and produced by Simon Mayblin, 'Western Sahara's champion athlete', BBC World Service, first broadcast 26 April 2018.
https://www.bbc.co.uk/programmes/p065bttc

See also: Nicola Kelly, 'I run for the family I'm not allowed to see', BBC News online, 26 April 2018.
https://www.bbc.co.uk/news/stories-43869290

13. United Nations special meeting on decolonization, press release published 13 June 2023.
https://press.un.org/en/2023/gacol3370.doc.htm#:~:text=Recalling%20that%20it%20was%20built,mined%20areas%20in%20the%20world.

NOTES

14. United Nations Mission for the Referendum in Western Sahara (UN MINURSO) mandate.
https://minurso.unmissions.org/mandate

15. Presented by Nicola Kelly and produced by Simon Mayblin, 'Western Sahara's champion athlete', BBC World Service, first broadcast 26 April 2018.
https://www.bbc.co.uk/programmes/p065bttc

16. Nicola Kelly, X thread, posted 20 July 2020.
https://twitter.com/nicolakelly/status/1285156843933900805

17. Nicola Kelly, '"Forgotten" Syrian interpreter attempts suicide after UK asylum delays', *Guardian*, 13 May 2022.
https://www.theguardian.com/global-development/2022/may/13/forgotten-syrian-interpreter-attempts-suicide-after-uk-asylum-delays

18. Ibid.

19. UNHCR, 'As Sudan war drags on, millions still languish in displacement camps', 24 June 2024.
https://www.unhcr.org/uk/news/stories/sudan-war-drags-millions-still-languish-displacement-camps#:~:text=More%20than%20a%20year%20since,Chad%2C%20Egypt%20and%20South%20Sudan.

20. John Vassiliou, 'What is the difference between refugee status and humanitarian protection?', Free Movement, 26 September 2023.
https://freemovement.org.uk/what-is-the-difference-between-refugee-status-and-humanitarian-protection/

21. Emma Thomson with photos by Nichole Sobecki, 'These mighty pyramids were built by one of Africa's earliest civilizations', *National Geographic*, 28 December 2022.
https://www.nationalgeographic.com/history/article/sudan-archaeology-pyramdis-kush-nubia

22. Nicola Kelly, 'Egypt's Nubians call for their right to return home', Al-Jazeera, 8 July 2017.
https://www.aljazeera.com/features/2017/7/8/egypts-nubians-call-for-their-right-to-return-home

23. Nicola Kelly, 'Nubia's musicians', *Newshour*, BBC World Service, 2017.
https://soundcloud.com/nicola-kelly-13313347/bbc-world-service-newshour-nubias-musicians

24. Migration Observatory briefing, 'The UK's asylum backlog', 3 May 2024.
https://migrationobservatory.ox.ac.uk/resources/briefings/the-uks-asylum-backlog/

NOTES

7. No Room

1. Trussell Trust latest statistics, April 2023–March 2024.
   https://www.trusselltrust.org/news-and-blog/latest-stats/

2. Messages seen by the author.

3. Catherine Murphy and Abigail Nicholson, 'Shocking images of police Matrix van on fire in disgraceful scenes near hotel', *Liverpool Echo*, 10 February 2023.
   https://www.liverpoolecho.co.uk/news/liverpool-news/shocking-images-police-matrix-van-26213566

4. 'Video: Asylum seekers film far right rioting outside lodgings', *Metro*, 10 February 2023.
   https://metro.co.uk/video/asylum-seekers-film-far-right-rioting-outside-lodgings-2881683/?ito=vjs-link

5. 'Boy, 13, among five charged over riot outside asylum seeker hotel in Knowsley', ITV News, 14 July 2023.
   https://www.itv.com/news/granada/2023-07-13/boy-13-among-five-charged-over-riot-outside-asylum-seeker-hotel

6. 'Serco, Mears win 2.9 bln stg UK housing contracts for asylum seekers', Reuters, 8 January 2019.
   https://www.reuters.com/article/idUSL8N1Z834B/

7. Nicola Kelly, 'Asylum seekers "abused and intimidated by staff in Home Office hotels"', *Observer*, 20 May 2023.
   https://www.theguardian.com/uk-news/2023/may/20/asylum-seekers-abused-and-intimidated-by-staff-in-home-office-hotels

8. Email exchange between the author and Serco press office.

9. Nicola Kelly, X post, 27 May 2023.
   https://twitter.com/NicolaKelly/status/1662372018526867457

10. Lizzie Dearden, '"Punched, chased and abused in the street": Asylum seekers living in terror at riot-hit hotel', *Independent*, 29 April 2023.
    https://www.independent.co.uk/news/uk/home-news/migrant-hotels-riot-knowsley-attacks-b2328888.html

11. Adam Laver, 'What happened as 200 people protested in Skegness over asylum seekers in hotels', Lincolnshire Live, 25 February 2023.
    https://www.lincolnshirelive.co.uk/news/local-news/people-protest-skegness-over-asylum-8188524

12. Marianna Spring, 'Did social media fan the flames of riot in Southport?', BBC News, 31 July 2024.

NOTES

https://www.bbc.co.uk/news/articles/cd1e8d7llg9o

13. George Wright, 'Seven sought by police after Aldershot migrant hotel protest', BBC News, 1 August 2024.
https://www.bbc.co.uk/news/articles/cmm2mnq9jq8o

14. Mark Townsend, 'Asylum seekers: Home Office accused of "catastrophic child protection failure"', Observer, 22 October 2022.
https://www.theguardian.com/uk-news/2022/oct/22/uk-asylum-seekers-home-office-accused-of-catastrophic-child-protection-failure

15. Mark Townsend, 'Revealed: Scores of child asylum seekers kidnapped from Home Office hotel', Observer, 21 January 2023.
https://www.theguardian.com/uk-news/2023/jan/21/revealed-scores-of-child-asylum-seekers-kidnapped-from-home-office-hotel

16. 'ECPAT UK wins legal challenge on the unlawful accommodation of unaccompanied children', press release published 27 July 2023.
https://www.ecpat.org.uk/news/ecpat-uk-wins-legal-challenge

17. Diane Taylor, 'Home Office defies high court by placing 100 asylum-seeker children in hotels', Guardian, 1 September 2023.
https://www.theguardian.com/uk-news/2023/sep/01/home-office-defies-high-court-by-placing-100-asylum-seeker-children-in-hotels

18. Nicola Kelly, 'Hundreds of child refugees wrongly sent to adult detention centres by Home Office', Independent, 23 January 2024.
https://www.independent.co.uk/news/uk/home-news/refugees-children-adults-detention-identified-age-b2482828.html

Full report: 'Forced adulthood: The Home Office's incorrect determination of age and how this leaves child refugees at risk', Refugee Council, Helen Bamber Foundation and Humans for Rights Network, published 23 January 2024.
https://www.refugeecouncil.org.uk/information/resources/forced-adulthood-the-home-offices-incorrect-determination-of-age-and-how-this-leaves-child-refugees-at-risk/

19. Rajeev Syal, 'Child asylum seekers in UK made to play game about who gets foster care places', Guardian, 29 February 2024.
https://www.theguardian.com/uk-news/2024/feb/29/child-asylum-seekers-in-uk-made-to-play-game-about-who-gets-foster-care-places

20. Ibid.

21. Anna Gross and William Wallis, 'UK has "no strategy" for housing asylum seekers, says borders' chief inspector', Financial Times, 16 February 2024.
https://www.ft.com/content/ddb96596-a164-4633-b1a5-b029ace81708

NOTES

22. House of Commons Library, 'Asylum accommodation: hotels, vessels and large-scale sites', published 7 July 2023.
https://commonslibrary.parliament.uk/research-briefings/cbp-9831/#:~:text= The%20Home%20Office%20spent%20around,in%20the%20last%20 financial%20year

23. United Nations report, 'Addressing poverty'.
https://www.un.org/en/academic-impact/addressing-poverty#:~:text= Nearly%20half%20of%20the%20world%27s,than%20US%20%241.25%20 a%20day

24. International Development Committee hearing, 'Aid spending in the UK', 8 February 2023.
https://committees.parliament.uk/work/7068/aid-spending-in-the-uk/

25. Diane Taylor, 'Profits of Home Office asylum housing provider rise to £90m a year', *Guardian*, 3 November 2024.
https://www.theguardian.com/uk-news/2024/nov/03/profits-of-home-office-asylum-housing-provider-rise-to-90m-a-year

26. Giles Gwinett, 'Mears Group lifts earnings expectations for 2024', *The Business Magazine*, 12 January 2024.
https://thebusinessmagazine.co.uk/companies/mears-group-lifts-its-earnings-expectations-for-2024/

27. Ben Lucas, 'Serco shares nudge higher after raising profit guidance', *City AM*, 27 June 2024.
https://www.cityam.com/serco-shares-nudge-higher-after-raising-profit-guidance/

28. Charles Dickens, *Hard Times* (first published 1854, published in Penguin Classics 1995), p. 115.

29. Ibid., p. 28.

30. House of Commons Early Day Motion, tabled 4 December 1990. 'British aerospace – closure at Preston'.
https://edm.parliament.uk/early-day-motion/3516/british-aerospace-closure-at-preston

31. Diane Taylor, 'Deadliest legionella strain found onboard *Bibby Stockholm*', *Guardian*, 8 September 2023.
https://www.theguardian.com/uk-news/2023/sep/08/legionella-found-onboard-the-bibby-stockholm-is-most-deadly-strain

32. Tom Lawrence, 'Fire Service responds to Portland barge fire safety concerns', *Dorset Echo*, 31 July 2023.

https://www.dorsetecho.co.uk/news/23690218.fire-service-responds-portland-barge-fire-safety-concerns/

33. Ethan Gudge, '*Bibby Stockholm*: Dorset Council powerless to block migrant barge, court told', BBC News, 27 February 2023.
https://www.bbc.co.uk/news/uk-england-dorset-68414195

34. Holly Bancroft, '*Bibby Stockholm* migrant barge "to cost more per head than hotels" despite Home Office pledge to cut bill', *Independent*, 7 November 2023.
https://www.independent.co.uk/news/uk/home-news/bibby-stockholm-migrant-barge-home-office-b2443169.html

35. Facebook Live meeting attended by the author.
https://www.facebook.com/groups/notothebarge/

36. Shari Miller, 'Police separate far-right demonstrators and counter-protesters in row over plan to house 2,000 asylum seekers at RAF base that was home to the Dambusters', *Daily Mail* online, 3 May 2023.
https://www.dailymail.co.uk/news/article-12002449/Far-right-counter-protesters-clash-plan-house-2-000-asylum-seekers-Dambusters-base.html

37. Diane Taylor, 'Deadly experiment? UK asylum sites criticised for "horrific" level of despair', *Guardian*, 28 February 2024.
https://www.theguardian.com/uk-news/2024/feb/28/deadly-experiment-uk-asylum-sites-criticised-for-horrific-level-of-despair

38. Médecins sans Frontières press release, 10 January 2024.
https://msf.org.uk/article/msf-launches-uk-operations-treat-people-seeking-asylum

39. National Audit Office, 'Investigation into asylum accommodation', published 20 March 2024.
https://www.nao.org.uk/wp-content/uploads/2024/03/investigation-into-asylum-accommodation.pdf

8. The Black Market

1. Gaia Vince, *Nomad Century* (Allen Lane, 2022), p. 121.

2. Human Rights Watch report, 'We will erase you from this land', published 6 April 2022.
https://www.hrw.org/report/2022/04/06/we-will-erase-you-land/crimes-against-humanity-and-ethnic-cleansing-ethiopias

NOTES

3. Nicola Kelly, 'Ethiopia drought: Crisis coming', *New Internationalist*, 19 April 2016.
   https://eewiki.newint.org/index.php?title=Ethiopia_drought:_crisis_coming
   See also: https://medium.com/@Nicola_Kelly/drought-in-ethiopia-30-years-later-ba85db7aba14

4. Nicola Kelly, 'Ethiopia's futurologists', *From Our Own Correspondent*, BBC Radio 4, April 2016.
   https://podcasts.apple.com/us/podcast/bbc-radio-4-from-our-own-correspondent-ethiopias-futurologists/id1091741291?i=1000376286603
   See also: https://medium.com/@Nicola_Kelly/ethiopia-s-future-reading-the-stars-ec0d351f2a42

5. Nicola Kelly, 'Ethiopia drought: Crisis coming', *New Internationalist*, 19 April 2016.
   https://eewiki.newint.org/index.php?title=Ethiopia_drought:_crisis_coming

6. International Organisation for Migration, 'Strengthening global cooperation vital in addressing climate-induced migration: IOM', 26 February 2022.
   https://www.iom.int/news/strengthening-global-cooperation-vital-addressing-climate-induced-migration-iom

7. Jonathan Portes, *What Do We Know And What Should We Do About . . . ? Immigration* (SAGE Publications, 2019), pp. 29 and 31.

8. Nicola Kelly, 'Dodging death and immigration officers: 12 hours as a London fast-food rider – and all for £40', *Guardian*, 14 September 2023.
   https://www.theguardian.com/global-development/2023/sep/14/dodging-death-and-immigration-officers-12-hours-as-a-london-fast-food-rider-and-all-for-40

9. Jess Warren, 'Deliveroo driver killed in hit and run', BBC News online, 16 May 2023.
   https://www.bbc.co.uk/news/articles/cjr1098wgq1o#:~:text=A%20Deliveroo%20driver%20who%20was,%2C%20Streatham%2C%20on%2011%20May

10. Robert Booth, 'Men who escaped fire in crowded London flat face homelessness', *Guardian*, 23 April 2023.
    https://www.theguardian.com/society/2023/apr/23/men-who-escaped-fire-in-crowded-london-flat-face-homelessness

11. Ibid.

12. 'The UK's agricultural Seasonal Worker visa – challenges and opportunities'. Written evidence from charity FLEX at hearing into seasonal workers scheme.
    https://committees.parliament.uk/writtenevidence/119986/html

NOTES

13. Home Office statistics, correct in July 2024.
https://www.gov.uk/government/statistics/immigration-system-statistics-year-ending-june-2023/why-do-people-come-to-the-uk-to-work#:~:text=The%20Seasonal%20Worker%20route%20was,(Creative%20and%20Sporting)%20visa

14. Tim Harford, 'Shortage nation: Why the UK is braced for a grim Christmas', *Financial Times*, 14 October 2021. Christmas
https://www.ft.com/content/ff650169-34bc-4ac9-9dc9-dcc429c580ec

15. Alan Beattie, 'The immigration dilemma Labour hopes will go away', *Financial Times*, 11 July 2024.
https://www.ft.com/content/a0e9fe66-5ca1-4fbc-af7a-6cbbe4f1da1d?desktop=true&segmentId=7c8f09b9-9b61-4fbb-9430-9208a9e233c8#myft:notification:daily-email:content

16. *Hansard*, 'Asylum seeker employment and the cost of living', debate on 14 December 2022.
https://hansard.parliament.uk/commons/2022-12-14/debates/783AA4D4-5D03-4D11-BC77-28DBFB2FCBD9/AsylumSeekerEmploymentAndTheCostOfLiving

17. YouGov Refugee Action Survey results, published 9 March 2022.
https://docs.cdn.yougov.com/ihe1pmjsxm/YouGov%20Refugee%20Action%20-%20Working%20during%20asylum%20claim.pdf

    Full report, Refugee Action: https://www.refugee-action.org.uk/lift-the-ban/

18. World Values Survey, King's College London, 'UK attitudes to immigration among most positive internationally', 23 February 2023.
https://www.kcl.ac.uk/news/uk-attitudes-to-immigration-among-most-positive-internationally-1018742-pub01-115#:~:text=The%20UK%20(21%25)%20is,immigrants%20fill%20important%20job%20vacancies.

19. Comments made at an Asylum Action event.

    See also: Charles Hymas, 'Stop "vilifying" asylum seekers and let them work, says former refugees minister', *Telegraph*, 22 December 2022.
https://www.telegraph.co.uk/news/2022/12/23/stop-vilifying-asylum-seekers-let-work-says-former-refugees/

20. 'International students boost UK economy by £41.9 billion', Universities UK, 16 May 2023.
https://www.universitiesuk.ac.uk/latest/news/international-students-boost-uk-economy

21. Home Office statistics to the year ending September 2023.
https://www.gov.uk/government/statistics/immigration-system-statistics-year-ending-september-2023/why-do-people-come-to-the-uk-to-study#:~:text=In%20the%20year%20ending%20September%202023%2C%20there%20were%20just%20under,the%20year%20ending%20September%202019.

NOTES

22. Patrick Jack, 'V-cs "disappointed" by Braverman's overseas students comments', *Times Higher Education*, 3 October 2022.
https://www.timeshighereducation.com/news/v-cs-disappointed-bravermans-overseas-students-comments

23. Richard Adams, 'Sunak's student visas clampdown continues boom-and-bust pattern', *Guardian*, 31 March 2024.
https://www.theguardian.com/education/2024/mar/31/sunak-student-visas-clampdown-boom-and-bust?mc_cid=4723e516b6&mc_eid=38f8370009

24. Patrick Jack, 'UK university applications down for third year in a row', *Times Higher Education*, 15 February 2024.
https://www.timeshighereducation.com/news/uk-university-applications-down-third-year-row

25. 'Immigration: The UK's record rise', BBC *Panorama*, first broadcast 25 March 2024.
https://www.bbc.co.uk/iplayer/episode/m001xpqk/panorama-immigration-the-uks-record-rise

26. Nicola Kelly, X, 21 March 2023.
https://x.com/NicolaKelly/status/1638103630707322881?s=20

27. Richard Watson, 'Student visa system fraud exposed in BBC investigation', BBC *Panorama*, 10 February 2014.
https://www.bbc.co.uk/news/uk-26024375

28. Diane Taylor, 'English test scandal: Students and campaigners call on PM to end years of limbo', *Guardian*, 20 March 2023.
https://www.theguardian.com/uk-news/2023/mar/20/english-test-scandal-students-and-campaigners-call-on-pm-to-end-years-of-limbo?CMP=Share_AndroidApp_Other

    See also: Nicola Kelly, X, 21 March 2023.
https://x.com/NicolaKelly/status/1638103630707322881?s=20

9. Who Cares?

1. BBC News, 'David Cameron: "Swarm" of migrants crossing Mediterranean', 30 July 2015.
https://www.bbc.co.uk/news/av/uk-politics-33714282

2. Nicola Kelly, 'Migrant women charged up to £14,000 for NHS maternity services in England', *Guardian*, 9 June 2022.
https://www.theguardian.com/global-development/2022/jun/09/migrant-women-charged-up-to-14000-for-nhs-maternity-services-in-england

NOTES

3. Nicola Kelly, 'Home Office sued by asylum seeker over baby's death', *Guardian*, 23 April 2021.
   https://www.theguardian.com/global-development/2021/apr/23/home-office-sued-by-asylum-seeker-over-babys-death

4. Office for National Statistics, 'Exploring local income deprivation', 24 May 2021.
   https://www.ons.gov.uk/visualisations/dvc1371/#/E08000017

5. Alex Grove, 'Stabbings, drugs and overcrowding: Life on Yorkshire's most poverty-stricken estate', *Yorkshire Examiner*, 2 January 2021.
   https://www.examinerlive.co.uk/news/local-news/stabbings-drugs-overcrowding-life-yorkshires-19468892

6. Nick Fletcher transcript, nickfletcher.org.uk, 12 December 2023.
   https://www.nickfletcher.org.uk/news/rwanda-bill

7. Electoral Calculus. 'Don Valley: overview'.
   https://www.ons.gov.uk/visualisations/customprofiles/build/#E14000667

8. Doctors of the World report, 'They just left me', published March 2022.
   https://www.doctorsoftheworld.org.uk/wp-content/uploads/2022/04/DOTW-Access-to-healthcare-in-initial-and-contingency-accommodation-report-April-2022.pdf

9. Report from the Independent Chief Inspector of Borders and Immigration, 'A re-inspection of Napier Barracks', March 2022.
   https://assets.publishing.service.gov.uk/media/62bd4fefe90e075f2c8a83c9/A_re-inspection_of_Napier_Barracks__March_2022.pdf

10. Nicola Kelly, '"Unsafe" UK accommodation threatens asylum seekers' health – report', *Guardian*, 27 April 2022.
    https://www.theguardian.com/global-development/2022/apr/27/unsafe-uk-accommodation-threatens-asylum-seeker-health-doctors-of-the-world-report

11. Doctors of the World written evidence to the House of Commons Home Affairs Select Committee, 5 April 2023.
    https://committees.parliament.uk/writtenevidence/119904/pdf/

12. Ibid.

13. British Medical Association, 'Tackling COVID-19's effect on BAME doctors', 21 May 2020.
    https://www.bma.org.uk/news-and-opinion/tackling-covid-19-s-effect-on-bame-doctors

14. Nicola Kelly, 'If we fail, the NHS will fail: Tories' drive to cut migration leaves social care on a cliff-edge', *Guardian*, 18 December 2023.
    https://www.theguardian.com/global-development/2023/dec/18/if-we-fail-the-nhs-will-fail-tories-drive-to-cut-migration-leaves-social-care-on-a-cliff-edge

15. Gov.uk news story, 'Home Secretary underlines commitment to cut net migration', 30 January 2024.
https://www.gov.uk/government/news/home-secretary-underlines-commitment-to-cut-net-migration

    See also immigration rule changes:
    https://www.gov.uk/government/collections/immigration-rules-statement-of-changes

16. Vicky Gayle, Emiliano Mellino, Hajar Meddah and Charles Boutaud, 'Visa system forces care workers to stay silent on rape and abuse', The Bureau for Investigative Journalism, 11 March 2024.
https://www.thebureauinvestigates.com/stories/2024-03-11/visa-system-forces-care-workers-to-stay-silent-on-rape-and-abuse/

17. Ibid.

18. Matt Dathan, 'One in four foreign care workers abuse UK visa rules', *The Times*, 19 February 2024.
https://www.thetimes.com/uk/article/one-in-four-foreign-care-workers-abuse-uk-visa-rules-lpqzmsk6g

10. Advice Sharks

1. Screengrabs sent to the author of now-removed Facebook page.

2. 'Colombia: 1.5 million displaced post peace agreement', Norwegian Refugee Council, 21 November 2024.
https://www.nrc.no/news/2024/november/colombia-1.5-million-displaced-post-peace-agreement#:~:text=While%20more%20than%20130%2C000%20people,Norwegian%20Refugee%20Council%20(NRC)

3. Falsified documents shared with the author.

4. Gov.uk guidance, 'How to apply to the EU settlement scheme', last updated 21 May 2024.
https://www.gov.uk/settled-status-eu-citizens-families

5. Interview with the author, May 2024.

6. Presentation drew on a report from Refugee Action, 'Consumer barriers to complaints', published January 2022.
https://assets-global.website-files.com/5eb86d8dfb1f1e1609be988b/6204e62c7d994c661c694dcf_ConsumerBarrierstoComplaintsFinal.pdf

NOTES

7. 'Office of the Immigration Services Commissioner', report and accounts for 2022/2023, published 26 March 2024.
https://assets.publishing.service.gov.uk/media/6602c56ef1d3a09b1f32acb9/OISC_Annual_Report_and_Accounts_2022-23_certified.pdf

8. Jo Wilding, 'No access to justice: How legal advice deserts fail refugees, migrants and our communities', University of Sussex, 6 October 2023.
https://sussex.figshare.com/articles/report/No_access_to_justice_how_legal_advice_deserts_fail_refugees_migrants_and_our_communities/23490653

9. 'Immigration and asylum – legal aid deserts', The Law Society, 21 February 2024.
https://www.lawsociety.org.uk/campaigns/civil-justice/legal-aid-deserts/immigration-and-asylum

See also: Jo Wilding, Maureen Mguni and Travis van Isacker, '*A Huge Gulf: Demand and Supply for Immigration Legal Advice in London*', Justice Together, published June 2021.
https://www.phf.org.uk/assets/documents/A-Huge-Gulf-Demand-for-and-supply-of-immigration-advice-in-London-June-2021.pdf?v=1715614318

10. 'Ministry of Justice's Consultation: Legal aid fees in the Illegal Migration Bill. Response of the Immigration Law Practitioners' Association'.
https://ilpa.org.uk/wp-content/uploads/2023/08/07.08.23-ILPAs-Response-to-MoJ-Consultation-IMB-Legal-Aid-Fees.pdf

11. 'Public Law Project's response to the Ministry of Justice Review of Civil Legal Aid Call for Evidence', Public Law Project, February 2024.
https://publiclawproject.org.uk/content/uploads/2024/03/240207_RoCLA-Call-for-Evidence_Public-Law-Project.pdf

12. 'Review of Civil Legal Aid – Call for evidence', Ministry of Justice, last updated 19 January 2024.
https://www.gov.uk/government/calls-for-evidence/review-of-civil-legal-aid-call-for-evidence/review-of-civil-legal-aid-call-for-evidence

13. 'Ministry of Justice's Consultation: Legal aid fees in the Illegal Migration Bill. Response of the Immigration Law Practitioners' Association'.
https://ilpa.org.uk/wp-content/uploads/2023/08/07.08.23-ILPAs-Response-to-MoJ-Consultation-IMB-Legal-Aid-Fees.pdf

14. Ibid.

15. Ibid.

16. Jacqueline McKenzie, 'I'm an immigration lawyer, and now the target of a Braverman smear campaign. It will backfire', *Guardian*, 8 August 2023.
https://www.theguardian.com/commentisfree/2023/aug/08/immigration-lawyer-braverman-smear-campaign-rightwing-press-deported-to-rwanda?CMP=share_btn_tw

NOTES

17. Rajeev Syal, 'Target of Tory "lefty lawyer" dossier forced to review security after email', *Guardian*, 8 August 2023.
https://www.theguardian.com/politics/2023/aug/08/target-of-tory-lefty-lawyer-dossier-forced-to-review-security-after-email

18. Ibid.

19. Jacqueline McKenzie, 'I'm an immigration lawyer, and now the target of a Braverman smear campaign. It will backfire', *Guardian*, 8 August 2023.
https://www.theguardian.com/commentisfree/2023/aug/08/immigration-lawyer-braverman-smear-campaign-rightwing-press-deported-to-rwanda?CMP=share_btn_tw

20. Jemma Slingo, 'Patel lashes out at "lefty lawyers" in asylum speech', *Law Gazette*, 5 October 2020.
https://www.lawgazette.co.uk/news/patel-lashes-out-at-lefty-lawyers-in-asylum-speech/5105870.article

21. Jessica Elgot, 'Boris Johnson: UK must not return to status quo after Covid-19 pandemic', *Guardian*, 6 October 2020.
https://www.theguardian.com/politics/2020/oct/06/boris-johnson-uk-must-not-return-to-status-quo-after-covid-pandemic

22. Diane Taylor, 'Terror accused went to UK immigration lawyer's office with knife, court hears', *Guardian*, 11 March 2024.
https://www.theguardian.com/uk-news/2024/mar/11/cavan-medlock-trial-immigration-lawyer-harrow-knife

23. Ibid.

24. Ibid.

25. Gov.uk guidance, 'Fees for citizenship applications and the right of abode from 4 October 2023', last updated 10 April 2024.
https://www.gov.uk/government/publications/fees-for-citizenship-applications/fees-for-citizenship-applications-and-the-right-of-abode-from-6-april-2018

26. Gov.uk spousal visa fees, last updated June 2024.
https://www.gov.uk/uk-family-visa

27. Nicola Kelly, X, 28 February 2024.
https://twitter.com/NicolaKelly/status/1762834666157941109

28. Home Office press release, 'Government to build cases to prosecute rogue immigration lawyers', 8 August 2023.
https://www.gov.uk/government/news/government-to-build-cases-to-prosecute-rogue-immigration-lawyers

NOTES

29. Home Office news story, 'Three arrested in fake immigration law firm raid', 25 January 2024.
https://www.gov.uk/government/news/three-arrested-in-fake-immigration-law-firm-raid

30. Ibid.

31. James Tozer, 'Dramatic moment Home Office officials arrest three in raid for "posing as immigration lawyers to help with bogus asylum claims from office in suburban garage"', *Daily Mail*, 24 January 2024.
https://www.dailymail.co.uk/news/article-13001745/Police-arrest-raid-immigration-lawyers-asylum-claims-manchester.html

32. Tom Kelly and Izzy Lyons, 'EXCLUSIVE Lawyers charging £10,000 to make fake asylum claims: Special investigation exposes staff at immigration law firms briefing clients on how to LIE to the authorities to win the right to stay in Britain', *Daily Mail*, 27 July 2023.
https://www.dailymail.co.uk/news/article-12333013/Immigration-law-firms-LIE-authorities-win-asylum.html

11. Big Brother State

1. George Orwell, *1984*, Part 1, Chapter 1.

2. Garrett Nada, 'Iran's drone exports worldwide', United States Institute of Peace, 11 April 2024.
https://iranprimer.usip.org/blog/2022/nov/16/explainer-iran%E2%80%99s-drone-exports-worldwide

   See also: Kenneth McKenzie Jr, Damien Spleeters and Valerie Lincy, 'Iran's military drone program: Security implications and policy responses', The Washington Institute for Near East Policy, policy analysis, published 24 April 2023.
https://www.washingtoninstitute.org/policy-analysis/irans-military-drone-program-security-implications-and-policy-responses

3. Seth J. Frantzman, 'Iran's drones are clones. Now they're being used in multiple conflicts', Atlantic Council, 18 November 2021.
https://www.atlanticcouncil.org/blogs/iransource/irans-drones-are-clones-now-theyre-being-used-in-multiple-conflicts/

   See also: Garrett Nada, 'Iran's drone exports worldwide', United States Institute of Peace, 11 April 2024.
https://iranprimer.usip.org/blog/2022/nov/16/explainer-iran%E2%80%99s-drone-exports-worldwide

NOTES

4. Uzi Rubin, 'Russia's Iranian-made UAVs: A technical profile', Royal United Services Institute (RUSI), 13 January 2023.
https://rusi.org/explore-our-research/publications/commentary/russias-iranian-made-uavs-technical-profile

See also: Dan Sabbagh, 'Deadly, cheap and widespread: How Iran-supplied drones are changing the nature of warfare', *Guardian*, 2 February 2024.
https://www.theguardian.com/world/2024/feb/02/deadly-cheap-and-widespread-how-iran-supplied-drones-are-changing-the-nature-of-warfare

5. Khalid Abdelaziz, Parisa Hafezi and Aidan Lewis, 'Sudan civil war: Are Iranian drones helping the army gain ground?', Reuters, 10 April 2024.
https://www.reuters.com/world/middle-east/are-iranian-drones-turning-tide-sudans-civil-war-2024-04-10/

6. Wim Zwijnenburg, 'Is Ethiopia flying Iranian-made armed drones?', Bellingcat, 17 August 2021.
https://www.bellingcat.com/news/rest-of-world/2021/08/17/is-ethiopia-flying-iranian-made-armed-drones/

See also: Steven Feldstein, 'The larger geopolitical shift behind Iran's drone sales to Russia', Carnegie Endowment for International Peace, 26 October 2022.
https://carnegieendowment.org/posts/2022/10/the-larger-geopolitical-shift-behind-irans-drone-sales-to-russia?lang=en

7. Garrett Nada, 'Iran's drone exports worldwide', United States Institute of Peace, 11 April 2024.
https://iranprimer.usip.org/blog/2022/nov/16/explainer-iran%E2%80%99s-drone-exports-worldwide

8. Sebastien Klovig Skelton, 'English Channel surveillance used "to deter and punish migrants"', *Computer Weekly*, 3 March 2022.
https://www.computerweekly.com/feature/English-Channel-surveillance-used-to-deter-and-punish-migrants

9. Ibid.

10. Frontex press release, 'Frontex deploys its own plane in the Channel', 15 March 2022.
https://www.frontex.europa.eu/media-centre/news/news-release/frontex-deploys-its-own-plane-in-the-channel-cHkg9q

11. Written evidence submitted by Drone Wars UK, House of Commons Defence Committee, 'Inquiry into the role of the military in countering migrant crossings (Operation Isotrope)', 22 January 2022.
https://committees.parliament.uk/writtenevidence/43101/html/

NOTES

12. Morgan Meaker, 'Here's proof the UK is using drones to patrol the English Channel', *Wired*, 10 January 2020.
https://www.wired.com/story/uk-drones-migrants-english-channel/

    See also: 'TEKEVER drones to boost English Channel maritime surveillance', Sky News, 24 September 2020.
https://www.facebook.com/tekever/videos/657092675184882/

13. Oliver Harvey, 'Government's £420k "eye in the sky" drone designed to stop migrants meets embarrassing end as chaos in Channel continues', *Sun*, 20 July 2022.
https://www.thesun.co.uk/news/19253750/government-420k-migrant-spotting-drone/

14. Email exchange between Tekever and the author.

15. David Barrett, 'Jailed – the people smuggler who was tracked by drone: Iraqi, 36, was filmed by "eye in the sky" unmanned aircraft while he was at the helm of inflatable boat crossing from France', *Daily Mail*, 24 September 2020.
https://www.dailymail.co.uk/news/article-8766543/Jailed-people-smuggler-tracked-drone-Iraqi-36-filmed-eye-sky.html

16. Inzamam Rashid, 'Inside the control room that sends drones to catch people smugglers on the English Channel', Sky News, 24 September 2020.
https://news.sky.com/story/inside-the-control-room-that-sends-drones-to-catch-people-smugglers-on-the-english-channel-12079722

17. Katie Polglase, Livvy Doherty, Sarah-Grace Mankarious and Byron Manley, 'Britain's shadowy border', CNN, 31 July 2023.
https://edition.cnn.com/interactive/2023/07/uk/migrant-crossings-ai-small-boats/

    See also: Will Coldwell, 'A teenaged migrant piloted a dinghy that sank in the Channel. Then he was charged with manslaughter', *Prospect* magazine, 26 April 2024.
https://www.prospectmagazine.co.uk/politics/policy/immigration/65858/a-teenager-piloted-a-channel-dinghy.-after-it-sank-he-was-charged-with-manslaughter

18. Notes taken during court trial attended by the author, Canterbury Crown Court, February 2024. Checked with others present at the trial, solicitors and court clerk.

19. Katie Polglase, Livvy Doherty, Sarah-Grace Mankarious and Byron Manley, 'Britain's shadowy border', CNN, 31 July 2023.
https://edition.cnn.com/interactive/2023/07/uk/migrant-crossings-ai-small-boats/

NOTES

20. Notes taken during court trial attended by the author, Canterbury Crown Court, February 2024. Checked with others present at the trial, solicitors and court clerk.

21. Ibid.

22. Ibid.

23. Parliamentary business, legislative scrutiny, National and Borders Bill Part 3, published 1 December 2021.
   https://publications.parliament.uk/pa/jt5802/jtselect/jtrights/885/88508.htm

24. Notes taken during court trial attended by the author, Canterbury Crown Court, February 2024. Checked with others present at the trial, solicitors and court clerk. Prosecution opening statement sent to the author.

25. Ibid.
   See also: *https://twitter.com/NicolaKelly/status/1755616996207759756*

26. Nicola Kelly, 'Deaths in the Channel: Survivors and rescue teams feel targeted by plan to "stop the boats"', *Byline Times*, 14 December 2023.
   https://bylinetimes.com/2023/12/14/deaths-in-the-channel-survivors-and-rescue-teams-feel-targeted-by-plan-to-stop-the-boats/

27. Ibid.

28. Nicola Kelly, 'Can the DJ of Dakar stop people emigrating?', BBC News, 21 August 2016.
   https://www.bbc.co.uk/news/magazine-37129312

29. Home Office Twitter/X account, posted 23 February 2024.
   https://twitter.com/ukhomeoffice/status/1761090973520576879

30. Nicola Kelly, 'Facial recognition smartwatches to be used to monitor foreign offenders in UK', *Guardian*, 5 August 2022.
   https://www.theguardian.com/politics/2022/aug/05/facial-recognition-smartwatches-to-be-used-to-monitor-foreign-offenders-in-uk

31. Public Accounts Committee hearing, Electronic Monitoring programme, 21 October 2022.
   https://publications.parliament.uk/pa/cm5803/cmselect/cmpubacc/34/report.html

32. Nicola Kelly, 'UK plans GPS tracking of potential deportees by fingerprint scanners', *Guardian*, 13 January 2023.
   https://www.theguardian.com/uk-news/2023/jan/13/potential-deportees-fingerprint-scanners-gps-tracking-home-office-plans

NOTES

33. Dr Jo Hynes and Mia Leslie, '"Constantly on edge": The expansion of GPS tagging and the rollout of non-fitted devices', Medical Justice, Bail for Immigration Detainees and Public Law Project, December 2023.
https://publiclawproject.org.uk/content/uploads/2023/12/Constantly-on-Edge-Annual-Review-of-GPS-tagging-in-immigration-bail-2023.pdf

34. Ibid.

35. Nicola Kelly, 'UK plans GPS tracking of potential deportees by fingerprint scanners', *Guardian*, 13 January 2023.
https://www.theguardian.com/uk-news/2023/jan/13/potential-deportees-fingerprint-scanners-gps-tracking-home-office-plans

36. Home Office, 'Immigration bail conditions: Electronic monitoring (EM) expansion pilot', 23 June 2022.
https://assets.publishing.service.gov.uk/media/64956689831311001329625f/Immigration_bail_conditions_-_Electronic_Monitoring__EM__Expansion_pilot.pdf

37. Information Commissioner's Office, Home Office enforcement notice, 21 March 2024.
https://ico.org.uk/action-weve-taken/enforcement/home-office/

12. Raided

1. Arundhati Roy, Sydney Peace Prize Lecture, delivered 2004.
https://sydneypeacefoundation.org.au/peace-prize-recipients/2004-arundhati-roy/

2. Adam Toms, 'Immigration "raid" on Brixton restaurant sees 1 woman and 3 men arrested', My London News, 5 January 2024.
https://www.mylondon.news/news/south-london-news/immigration-raid-brixton-restaurant-sees-28392725

3. Rachel Burford, 'Restaurant and building trades targeted in more raids on illegal working, says Home Secretary James Cleverly', *Evening Standard*, 2 January 2024.
https://www.standard.co.uk/news/politics/raids-illegal-working-visas-migrants-restaurants-home-secretary-james-cleverly-b1129839.html#:~:text=The%20restaurant%20and%20building%20trades,112%2C000%20cases%20processed%20in%202023

4. 'Young people launch rally against immigration "terror" raids', Brixton Blog, 4 January 2024.
https://brixtonblog.com/2024/01/young-people-launch-rally-against-immigration-terror-raids/

NOTES

5. Charlotte Middlehurst, X post, 14 May 2022.
   *https://twitter.com/charmiddle/status/1525567020577742849?ref_src=twsrc
   %5Etfw%7Ctwcamp%5Etweetembed%7Ctwterm%5E1525567020577742849
   %7Ctwgr%5E8e9ca007b4f85364412c20fa4ce821c08715945c%7Ctwcon%5
   Es1_&ref_url=https%3A%2F%2Fwww.huckmag.com%2Farticle%2
   Fimmigration-raids-are-being-carried-out-with-impunity*

6. Leaflet seen by the author.

7. Amelia Gentleman, *The Windrush Betrayal* (Guardian Faber, 2019), p. 9.

8. Wendy Williams, 'Windrush lessons learned review', Home Office, 19 July 2018, ordered by the House of Commons to be printed on 19 March 2020.
   *https://assets.publishing.service.gov.uk/media/5e74984fd3bf7f4684279faa/
   6.5577_HO_Windrush_Lessons_Learned_Review_WEB_v2.pdf*

   David Lammy, 'Two years after Windrush, we're deporting people who've only known Britain as home', *Guardian*, 10 February 2020.
   *https://www.theguardian.com/commentisfree/2020/feb/10/windrush-
   deporting-people*

9. Home Affairs Select Committee, 'Compensation Scheme failures have compounded injustices faced by Windrush generation – Committee finds', report published 21 November 2021.
   *https://committees.parliament.uk/committee/83/home-affairs-committee/
   news/159118/compensation-scheme-failures-have-compounded-injustices-
   faced-by-windrush-generation-committee-finds/*

10. Amelia Gentleman, *The Windrush Betrayal* (Guardian Faber, 2019), p. 9.

11. Home Office immigration enforcement, 'About Us'.
    https://www.gov.uk/government/organisations/immigration-enforcement/about

12. House of Commons Public Accounts Committee, Immigration Enforcement, seventeenth report of session 2019–21, published 18 September 2020.
    https://committees.parliament.uk/publications/2633/documents/26242/default/

13. Ibid.

14. Mary Atkinson, 'Immigration raids don't work – they just leave communities scared and divided', *i*news, 20 May 2021.
    *https://inews.co.uk/opinion/immigration-raids-communities-scared-
    divided-1010449*

15. Rajeev Syal and Severin Carrell, 'Man detained by Home Office told he is being sent to Rwanda, says NGO', *Guardian*, 30 April 2024.
    *https://www.theguardian.com/uk-news/2024/apr/30/man-detained-by-home-
    office-told-he-is-being-sent-to-rwanda-says-charity*

NOTES

16. Darshna Soni, 'Over half the people earmarked for deportation to Rwanda to UK are "missing"', Channel 4 News, 30 April 2024.
https://www.channel4.com/news/over-half-the-people-earmarked-for-deportation-to-rwanda-to-uk-are-missing

17. Kate Ferguson, 'Illegal immigrant blitz on car washes & nail bars begins as Home Sec vows to "swiftly" deport law-breakers', *Sun on Sunday*, 20 July 2024.
https://www.thesun.co.uk/news/29362028/yvette-cooper-immigration-raids-labour-channel-migrants/

18. Carla Jenkins, 'Glasgow MPs condemn "inhumane" Maryhill dawn raid in letter to Home Secretary Priti Patel', Glasgow Live, 29 April 2021.
https://www.glasgowlive.co.uk/news/glasgow-news/glasgow-mps-condemn-inhumane-dawn-20491755

See also: Kirsteen Paterson, '"We are very afraid": Father, 67, taken to hospital after Home Office dawn raid', *National*, 2 April 2021.
https://www.thenational.scot/news/19260639.we-afraid-father-taken-hospital-home-office-raid-home/

19. Ibid.

20. Libby Brooks, '"A special day": How a Glasgow community halted immigration raid', *Guardian*, 14 May 2021.
https://www.theguardian.com/uk-news/2021/may/14/a-special-day-how-glasgow-community-halted-immigration-raid

21. Ibid.

22. Jemma Carr, 'Boris Johnson dons traditional headwear and samples classic Sikh cuisine as he visits temple in London on election trail', *Daily Mail*, 18 November 2019.
https://www.dailymail.co.uk/news/article-7695491/Boris-Johnson-dons-traditional-headwear-visits-Sikh-temple-London-election-trail.html

23. Robert Winder, *Bloody Foreigners* (Little, Brown, 2004), p. 299.

24. Channel 4 documentary series, 'Defiance: Fighting the far right', first broadcast 8 April 2024.
https://www.channel4.com/programmes/defiance-fighting-the-far-right

25. Ibid.

My London News, 'Defiance fighting the far right: Who was Gurdip Singh Chaggar?', 8 April 2024.
https://www.mylondon.news/news/tv/defiance-fighting-far-right-who-28959915

NOTES

26. Robert Winder, *Bloody Foreigners* (Little, Brown, 2004), p. 310.

27. Home Office immigration enforcement directorate, 'Operation Vaken evaluation report', published 31 October 2013.
https://www.gov.uk/government/publications/operation-vaken-evaluation-report

28. Home Office, 'Six London boroughs targeted in returns pilot', 22 July 2013.
https://www.gov.uk/government/news/six-london-boroughs-targeted-in-returns-pilot#:~:text=Voluntary%20returns%20are%20the%20most,28%2C000%20voluntary%20departures%20last%20year

29. Off-record interview with sources at the place of worship.

30. Nicola Kelly, 'Immigration officials target mosques, temples and churches to advise people to return home', *Independent*, 5 November 2022.
https://www.independent.co.uk/news/uk/home-news/immigration-mosques-hostile-environment-b2217603.html

31. Seen by the author during a visit to Southall, spring 2024.

32. Video seen by the author.

33. Nicola Kelly, 'Immigration officials target mosques, temples and churches to advise people to return home', *Independent*, 5 November 2022.
https://www.independent.co.uk/news/uk/home-news/immigration-mosques-hostile-environment-b2217603.html

34. Ibid.

35. Home Office data and documents shared with the author.

36. Diane Taylor, 'Homeless charity aided deportation patrols in search for rough sleepers', *Guardian*, 5 March 2018.
https://www.theguardian.com/uk-news/2018/mar/05/st-mungos-homeless-charity-helped-target-rough-sleepers-to-deport

37. Corporate Watch report, 'The Round-up: Rough sleeper immigration raids and charity', collaboration, 2017.
https://corporatewatch.org/wp-content/uploads/2017/03/CW%20rough%20sleepers%20investigation.pdf

38. St Mungo's report, 'A review into St Mungo's approach to working with Home Office enforcement teams 2010 to December 2017', published November 2019.
https://www.mungos.org/wp-content/uploads/2019/11/St-Mungos-review-into-its-approach-to-working-with-Home-Office-enforcement-teams-2010-2017-5-Nov-2019.pdf

39. Diane Taylor, 'Charity says sorry for giving rough sleepers' details to Home Office', *Guardian*, 5 November 2019.
https://www.theguardian.com/uk-news/2019/nov/05/charity-st-mungos-says-sorry-for-giving-rough-sleepers-details-to-home-office

13. When the State Gives Up

1. James Baldwin, *Nobody Knows My Name: More Notes of a Native Son* (Dial Press, 1961).

2. Gov.uk news story, 'Legacy backlog cleared as plan to stop the boats delivers', 2 January 2024.
https://www.gov.uk/government/news/legacy-backlog-cleared-as-plan-to-stop-the-boats-delivers

    See also: https://migrationobservatory.ox.ac.uk/resources/briefings/the-uks-asylum-backlog/

3. Gov.uk news story, 'Legacy backlog cleared as plan to stop the boats delivers', 2 January 2024.
https://www.gov.uk/government/news/legacy-backlog-cleared-as-plan-to-stop-the-boats-delivers

4. George Parker and Lucy Fisher, 'Rishi Sunak rapped by UK statistics watchdog over asylum backlog claim', *Financial Times*, 18 January 2024.
https://www.ft.com/content/98c48f15-e4e4-40cc-9a99-fe525b431d43

5. Ibid.

6. Nicola Kelly, 'The refugees turned out on to freezing streets to clear Rishi Sunak's asylum backlog', *Byline Times*, 19 January 2024.
https://bylinetimes.com/2024/01/19/the-refugees-turned-out-on-to-freezing-streets-to-clear-rishi-sunaks-asylum-backlog/

7. Ibid.

8. Email sent to the author from the Scottish Refugee Council with the latest figures from their database.

9. Diane Taylor, 'Thousands of refugees could face homelessness after Home Office policy change', *Guardian*, 15 August 2023.
https://www.theguardian.com/world/2023/aug/15/thousands-of-refugees-could-face-homelessness-after-home-office-policy-change

    See also: https://freemovement.org.uk/home-office-change-in-practice-increases-risk-of-homelessness-for-recognised-refugees/

NOTES

10. Nicola Kelly, 'The refugees turned out on to freezing streets to clear Rishi Sunak's asylum backlog', *Byline Times*, 19 January 2024.
    https://bylinetimes.com/2024/01/19/the-refugees-turned-out-on-to-freezing-streets-to-clear-rishi-sunaks-asylum-backlog/

11. Refugee Council report, 'Keys to the city: Ending refugee homelessness In London', April 2024.
    https://www.refugeecouncil.org.uk/wp-content/uploads/2024/04/Keys-to-the-City-2024-Ending-refugee-homelessness-in-London.pdf

12. Email exchange between the author and Gateshead Council.

13. Home Office, 'UK government support for resettled Afghans in bridging accommodation factsheet – September 2023'.
    https://homeofficemedia.blog.gov.uk/2023/04/24/uk-government-support-for-resettled-afghans-in-bridging-accommodation-factsheet-august-2023/

14. Local Government Association, 'Bridging hotels and homelessness for Afghan households research report', 7 September 2023.
    https://www.local.gov.uk/publications/bridging-hotels-and-homelessness-afghan-households-research-report

15. Video sent by WhatsApp to the author.

16. Ibid.

17. Liam Geraghty, 'Councils plead with Jeremy Hunt for urgent cash boost to keep families off the streets', *The Big Issue*, 1 November 2023.
    https://www.bigissue.com/news/housing/councils-homelessness-crisis-jeremy-hunt-funding-boost/

18. Ibid.

19. Robert Jenrick, written parliamentary question, answered 22 November 2023.
    https://questions-statements.parliament.uk/written-questions/detail/2023-11-14/2017/

20. Suella Braverman, X post, 4 November 2023.
    https://x.com/SuellaBraverman/status/1720730450556006714?lang=en

21. Ibid.

22. Nina Lloyd, 'Annual refugee cap to launch in January 2025, Home Office says', *Independent*, 20 October 2023.
    https://www.independent.co.uk/news/uk/government-home-office-robert-jenrick-local-government-association-steve-smith-b2433113.html

NOTES

23. Kiran Stacey, 'Tory social housing plan aims to prioritise "British homes for British workers"', *Guardian*, 24 January 2024.
   https://www.theguardian.com/politics/2024/jan/24/tory-social-housing-plan-aims-to-prioritise-british-homes-for-british-workers

24. Olivia Barber, 'Fourteen housing bodies sign letter opposing "British homes for British workers policy"', Housing Today, 29 January 2024.
   https://www.housingtoday.co.uk/news/fourteen-housing-bodies-sign-letter-opposing-british-homes-for-british-workers-policy/5127500.article

25. Kiran Stacey, 'Tory social housing plan aims to prioritise "British homes for British workers"',*Guardian*, 24 January 2024.
   https://www.theguardian.com/politics/2024/jan/24/tory-social-housing-plan-aims-to-prioritise-british-homes-for-british-workers

26. Nicola Kelly, 'It's impossible to self-isolate when you don't have a home', Vice News, 24 March 2020.
   https://www.vice.com/en/article/xgqpdq/homelessness-coronavirus-impact-uk

27. Ibid.

28. Gov.uk, '£3.2 million emergency support for rough sleepers during coronavirus outbreak', Ministry of Housing, Communities and Local Government press release, 17 March 2020.
   https://www.gov.uk/government/news/3-2-million-emergency-support-for-rough-sleepers-during-coronavirus-outbreak

29. Deborah Garvie, Hannah Rich, Charlie Berry and Robert Brown, Shelter report, 'Everyone in: Where are they now?', published August 2021.
   https://england.shelter.org.uk/professional_resources/policy_and_research/policy_library/everyone_in_where_are_they_now#:~:text=The%20ambition%20to%20get%20%27everyone,been%20helped%20under%20the%20scheme

30. Nicola Kelly, 'UK homeless charities call for suspension of "reckless" eviction of asylum seekers', *Guardian*, 13 November 2020.
   https://www.theguardian.com/global-development/2020/nov/13/uk-homeless-charities-call-for-suspension-of-reckless-eviction-of-asylum-seekers

31. Ibid.

32. Adam Bychawski, 'Home Office said sacked immigration watchdog was "excessively critical"', OpenDemocracy, 18 September 2023.
   https://www.opendemocracy.net/en/home-office-suella-braverman-david-neal-excessively-critical-independent-chief-inspector-borders/

33. Gov.uk official statistics, 'Rough sleeping snapshot in England: autumn 2023', published 29 February 2024.
https://www.gov.uk/government/statistics/rough-sleeping-snapshot-in-england-autumn-2023/rough-sleeping-snapshot-in-england-autumn-2023#main-findings

34. Figures given to the author.

14. Locked Up

1. Nicola Kelly, '"We share everything": Coronavirus fears inside a UK detention centre', *Guardian*, 29 March 2020.
https://www.theguardian.com/uk-news/2020/mar/29/inside-the-detention-centre-where-inmates-fear-coronavirus

2. Ibid.

3. Diane Taylor, 'Home Office releases 300 from detention centres amid Covid-19 pandemic', *Guardian*, 21 March 2020.
https://www.theguardian.com/uk-news/2020/mar/21/home-office-releases-300-from-detention-centres-amid-covid-19-pandemic

4. Nicola Kelly and Diane Taylor, 'Guards at Heathrow immigration detention centre try to quell protest', *Guardian*, 25 June 2023.
https://www.theguardian.com/uk-news/2023/jun/25/guards-at-heathrow-immigration-detention-centre-try-to-quell-protest

5. Ibid.

6. Ibid.

7. Callum Tulley, 'Undercover: Britain's immigration secrets', BBC *Panorama*, 4 September 2017.
https://www.bbc.co.uk/iplayer/episode/b094mhsn/panorama-undercover-britains-immigration-secrets

8. Ibid.

9. Nicola Kelly, X thread, 25 November 2021.
https://twitter.com/NicolaKelly/status/1463842696464941058

10. Brook House Inquiry, final report.
https://brookhouseinquiry.org.uk/main-page/launch/

See also: Diane Taylor, 'Physical and verbal abuse found in Brook House immigration removal centre inquiry', *Guardian*, 19 September 2023.
https://www.theguardian.com/uk-news/2023/sep/19/toxic-culture-brook-house-immigration-removal-centre-inquiry

NOTES

11. Jamie Grierson, 'Serco given £200m contract to run two more immigration removal centres', *Guardian*, 20 February 2020. https://www.theguardian.com/uk-news/2020/feb/20/serco-given-200m-contract-to-run-two-more-immigration-removal-centres

12. Leke Oso Alabi, 'Serco lifts profit guidance as demand for immigration services rises', *Financial Times*, 29 June 2023. https://www.ft.com/content/54a95040-342b-47d4-8fe7-9e68ded6a872

13. Medical Justice, 'Report: "If he dies, he dies": What has changed since the Brook House Inquiry?', published 11 December 2023. https://medicaljustice.org.uk/111223_embargo/

14. Ibid.

15. David Neal, 'I warned ministers about our disgraceful UK detention centres. Their solution? Stop the inspections', *Guardian*, 19 September 2023. https://www.theguardian.com/commentisfree/2023/sep/19/ministers-detention-centres-inspections-brook-house-suella-braverman-home-office

16. Home Office official statistics, published 29 February 2024. https://www.gov.uk/government/statistics/immigration-system-statistics-year-ending-december-2023/summary-of-latest-statistics

    See also: https://migrationobservatory.ox.ac.uk/resources/briefings/immigration-detention-in-the-uk/

17. Molly Blackall, 'Home Office operations to detain Rwanda migrants disrupted by protesters', *i*news, 1 May 2024. https://inews.co.uk/news/home-office-rwanda-detentions-disrupted-protesters-3035120

18. Dominic Casciani, 'Dozens of Rwanda detainees released on bail', BBC News, 12 June 2024. https://www.bbc.co.uk/news/articles/cp440pzp85ro

19. Victoria Taylor, 'Report: "No such thing as justice here"', University of Oxford, Border Criminologies and the Centre for Criminology, 25 February 2024. https://www.law.ox.ac.uk/content/news/report-launch-no-such-thing-justice-here

20. Ibid.

15. Say Goodbye

1. Star Bwoy, TikTok, posted 8 December 2023. https://www.tiktok.com/@star_bwoy_di_best/video/7310109250309737770

NOTES

2. Corporate Watch, '2022 UK charter deportations: A balance sheet', 15 March 2023.
   https://corporatewatch.org/2022-uk-charter-deportations-a-balance-sheet/

3. Ibid.

4. Rajeev Syal, 'Airline hired for UK's Rwanda deportations pulls out of scheme', *Guardian*, 21 October 2022.
   https://www.theguardian.com/uk-news/2022/oct/21/airline-hired-uk-rwanda-deportations-pulls-out-privilege-style#:~:text=The%20Mallorca%2D based%20carrier%20had,longer%20operate%20flights%20to%20Rwanda

5. Ibid.

6. Guardian News, Home Affairs Select Committee hearing clip, 'Amber Rudd says "we don't have targets for removals" during select committee questioning', 28 April 2018.
   https://www.youtube.com/watch?v=T8GkqD7slFE

7. *Hansard*, Home Office Removal Targets, volume 639, debated 26 April 2018.
   https://hansard.parliament.uk/commons/2018-04-26/debates/349BA8A9-1473-45F7-A0AB-24C8543CA468/HomeOfficeRemovalTargets

8. Heather Stewart, Amelia Gentleman and Nick Hopkins, 'Amber Rudd resigns hours after *Guardian* publishes deportation targets letter', *Guardian*, 30 April 2018.
   https://www.theguardian.com/politics/2018/apr/29/amber-rudd-resigns-as-home-secretary-after-windrush-scandal#:~:text=But%20Rudd%20 finally%20issued%20a,she%20drafted%20a%20resignation%20letter

9. Guardian News, Home Affairs Select Committee hearing clip, 'Amber Rudd says "we don't have targets for removals" during select committee questioning', 28 April 2018.
   https://www.youtube.com/watch?v=T8GkqD7slFE

10. Joe Churcher, 'UK to build prison in Jamaica for foreign criminals', *Independent*, 30 September 2015.
    https://www.independent.co.uk/news/uk/uk-to-build-prison-in-jamaica-for-foreign-criminals-a6672981.html

11. Amelia Gentleman, '"My life is in ruins": Wrongly deported Windrush people facing fresh indignity', *Guardian*, 10 September 2018.
    https://www.theguardian.com/uk-news/2018/sep/10/windrush-people-wrongly-deported-jamaica-criminal-offence

12. Diane Taylor, 'UK deportation flight with four onboard raises questions over viability', *Guardian*, 11 November 2021.
    https://www.theguardian.com/politics/2021/nov/11/uk-deportation-flight-four-onboard-raises-questions-viability-jamaica

NOTES

13. Ibid.

14. Diane Taylor, 'Jamaican man to be deported from UK after previous attempt was halted by fellow passengers', *Guardian*, 25 February 2024. https://www.theguardian.com/uk-news/2024/feb/25/jamaican-man-to-be-deported-from-uk-after-previous-attempt-was-halted-by-fellow-passengers

15. Ibid.

16. Mark Hookham and David Barrett, 'Farce of the gangster gunman we can't deport: Home Secretary berates plane mutiny "do-gooders" who thwarted the removal of thug jailed for blasting away at rivals in bloody street gun battle', *Mail on Sunday*, 14 January 2024. https://www.dailymail.co.uk/news/article-12960113/Farce-gangster-gunman-deport-Home-Secretary-berates-plane-mutiny-gooders-thwarted-removal-thug-jailed-blasting-away-rivals-bloody-street-gun-battle.html

17. Luke de Noronha, 'Life after deportation: "No one tells you how lonely you're going to be"', *Guardian*, 18 August 2020. https://www.theguardian.com/law/2020/aug/18/deportation-jamaica-britain-windrush-scandal-foreign-aid

18. Diane Taylor, 'Revealed: Five men killed in past year after being deported from UK to Jamaica', *Guardian*, 9 May 2019. https://www.theguardian.com/uk-news/2019/may/09/revealed-five-men-killed-since-being-deported-uk-jamaica-home-office

19. Home Office, 'Country Policy and Information Note Jamaica: Fear of organised criminal groups', published July 2022. https://assets.publishing.service.gov.uk/media/62e94a668fa8f5033896888d/JAM_CPIN_Fear_of_organised_criminal_groups__OCGs__July_2022.pdf

20. Notes taken by the author during the court hearing.

21. Home Office careers, Presenting Office job advertisement, 3 July 2023. https://careers.homeoffice.gov.uk/news/alar-june23

22. The Student Room, 'HEO presenting Officer Home Office 2023', forum discussion, posted March 2023. https://www.thestudentroom.co.uk/showthread.php?t=7329592

23. Home Office careers, Presenting Office job advertisement, 3 July 2023. https://careers.homeoffice.gov.uk/news/alar-june23

24. Oxford Migration Observatory, 'Deportation, removal, and voluntary departure from the UK', briefing published 14 February 2024. https://migrationobservatory.ox.ac.uk/resources/briefings/deportation-and-voluntary-departure-from-the-uk/

NOTES

25. Home Office, accredited official statistics, 'How many people are detained or returned?', updated 7 December 2023.
https://www.gov.uk/government/statistics/immigration-system-statistics-year-ending-september-2023/how-many-people-are-detained-or-returned#:~:text=2.1%20Enforced%20returns,the%20same%20period%20in%202022

26. Oxford Migration Observatory, 'Deportation, removal, and voluntary departure from the UK', briefing published 14 February 2024.
https://migrationobservatory.ox.ac.uk/resources/briefings/deportation-and-voluntary-departure-from-the-uk/

27. Oliver Wright and Chris Smyth, 'Small boats deal signals a new start with France, says Rishi Sunak', *The Times*, 10 March 2023.
https://www.thetimes.com/uk/politics/article/macron-rishi-sunak-latest-news-summit-migrant-asylum-channel-uk-france-2023-rrvnrvrlw

28. Jack Blanchard, 'Liz Truss: "Jury is out" on whether Macron is Britain's friend or foe', Politico, 25 August 2022.
https://www.politico.eu/article/uk-liz-truss-jury-is-out-on-whether-emmanuel-macron-is-britains-friend-or-foe/#:~:text=Asked%20directly%20at%20a%20hustings,him%20to%20deeds%20not%20words.%E2%80%9D

29. Matt Dathan and Bruno Waterfield, 'EU rejects new deal for return of migrants', *The Times*, 15 August 2023.
https://www.thetimes.com/uk/politics/article/eu-rejects-new-deal-for-return-of-migrants-7scbvsrw7

30. Rajeev Syal, 'Proportion of refugees granted UK asylum hits 32-year high', *Guardian*, 25 August 2022.
https://www.theguardian.com/uk-news/2022/aug/25/proportion-refugees-granted-uk-asylum-hits-32-year-high

31. Rajeev Syal, 'Priti Patel meets Albanian police over fast-track removal plan', *Guardian*, 30 August 2022.
https://www.theguardian.com/uk-news/2022/aug/30/priti-patel-meets-albanian-police-over-fast-track-removal-plan

32. Nicola Kelly, 'Albanian with British-born children faces deportation after decade in UK', *Guardian*, 26 August 2022.
https://www.theguardian.com/uk-news/2022/aug/26/albanian-british-born-children-faces-deportation-decade-uk

33. Ibid.

NOTES

Afterword: Home

1. 'Suella Braverman blames "Guardian-reading, tofu-eating wokerati" for disruptive protests – video', *Guardian*, 18 October 2022.
   https://www.theguardian.com/politics/video/2022/oct/18/suella-braverman-blames-guardian-reading-tofu-eating-wokerati-for-disruptive-protests-video

2. European Commission Eurobarometer poll, May 2024.
   https://europa.eu/eurobarometer/surveys/browse/all/series/4961

   See also: https://www.reuters.com/world/europe/economy-migration-war-top-voters-concerns-eu-election-survey-2024-06-10/

3. Oxford Migration Observatory, 'UK public opinion toward immigration: Overall attitudes and level of concern', 28 September 2023.
   https://migrationobservatory.ox.ac.uk/resources/briefings/uk-public-opinion-toward-immigration-overall-attitudes-and-level-of-concern/

4. Full Fact, 'The asylum backlog is far higher now than when Labour left government', 14 March 2023.
   https://fullfact.org/immigration/suella-braverman-asylum-backlog-labour/

5. Refugee Action, 'Ban on people seeking asylum from working will cost taxpayer £880 Million', 9 March 2022.
   https://www.refugee-action.org.uk/ban-on-people-seeking-asylum-from-working-will-cost-taxpayer-880-million/

6. Wendy Williams, 'Windrush lessons learned review', Home Office, 19 July 2018, ordered by the House of Commons to be printed on 19 March 2020.
   https://www.gov.uk/government/publications/windrush-lessons-learned-review

7. Joint Committee on Human Rights oral evidence, 'Safety in Rwanda (Asylum and Immigration) Bill, HC 435', Wednesday 17 January 2024.
   https://committees.parliament.uk/oralevidence/14124/html/

8. Rhys Clyne and Sachin Savur, 'Home truths: Cultural and institutional problems at the Home Office', Institute for Government, 25 May 2023.
   https://www.instituteforgovernment.org.uk/publication/home-office-problems
   https://www.instituteforgovernment.org.uk/sites/default/files/2023-05/cultural-and-institutional-problems-home-office_0.pdf

9. Emily Fielder, 'Break up the Home Office', Adam Smith Institute, 27 October 2023.
   https://www.adamsmith.org/news/break-up-the-home-office

10. Rhys Clyne and Sachin Savur, 'Home truths: Cultural and institutional problems at the Home Office', Institute for Government, 25 May 2023. *https://www.instituteforgovernment.org.uk/publication/home-office-problems*

   https://www.instituteforgovernment.org.uk/sites/default/files/2023-05/cultural-and-institutional-problems-home-office_0.pdf

Index

A
Abdul (Afghan) 204–6, 219
Abdul-Azim (Afghan) 192
Ade (Nigerian) 196–7
Afghan Citizens Resettlement Scheme 85
Afghanistan 61, 81–6
Afghans 5, 9, 72, 80, 8–5, 87, 191, 219–21, 241, 269
    See also individuals
agricultural sector 138–9
Ahmad, Tariq, Lord 86
Ahmed, Hussein Haseeb 67
aid workers 7, 9, 10, 66, 94, 133
Airbus 194
Albania 257
Albanians 9, 127, 136, 150, 236, 239–40, 257–8
Aldershot riot (2024) 117
Algeria 100, 224
Ali (Syrian) 103–4
Alternative for Germany party (AfD) 266
Amadou (project coordinator) 193
Amini, Mahsa 13
Amnesty International 132
Angelou, Maya 111
Angolans 151
Ann (asylum visitor) 245–6
anti-migrant protestors 49–50, 94, 265, 271
Anwar, Aamer 206
anxiety 155
Arab Spring 267
Arcturus fishing vessel 188–9
Arian (Iranian-Kurdish) 3–6, 12, 13–17, 112–14, 183–5, 274
Arnold, Matthew 19
al-Assad, Bashar 59–61
asylum applications
    backlog 89, 91–108, 215–16, 269, 270
    working during 271
Audibert, Lucie 197

B
Ba, Allaji 189, 190
Bah, Ibrahima 189–93, 242
Baldwin, James 215
Bangladesh 138
Bangladeshis 136, 138, 150
Barin (Rwanda) 45–6
Basam (Yemeni) 93, 94
Batoor (British mission Afghan) 80–3
Beachy Head, East Sussex 23
Bell, Jamie 259

327

INDEX

Benn, Tony 35
Bibby Stockholm barge, Portland 125–7
Biden, Joe 272
Bilal (Bangladeshi) 224
black market 131–46
Blair, Tony 35, 43–4, 58
Blix, Hans 58
Blunkett, David 50
Border Force 29–30, 29–34, 42, 188, 270
   boats 17, 22, 32, 55–6
Borena tribe, Ethiopia 133
Bower-Easton, Helen 267
Braverman, Suella 48, 58, 68, 77, 121, 143, 222, 240
Brazilians 136, 137, 199
Brexit 21, 76–7, 140, 167, 224, 266
bridging accommodation 219–20
Brighton 118, 227, 244
British Aerospace 123
British Council 81, 82
British Medical Association 157
British Red Cross 125
Brook House immigration removal centre 45
Brook House Inquiry (2019) 237–40
Brown, Gordon 50
Buddi Limited 195–6
Buerk, Michael 132
Bush, George W. 58
Byrne, Liam 86

C

Calais camps 8, 73–4
Calais Group 272
Cameron, David 36, 60, 148, 207, 250, 266, 267, 268
camps 8–10
Capita 194
caseworkers, charity 172, 176–7, 246
Chad 105
Channel, English 23
charity workers 7, 8, 72, 95, 243
children
   in boats 4, 5, 6, 32
   camp life 9
   deaths 87
   degrading tests 66, 119
   kidnapped from Brighton hotel 118–19
   processing centres 57
   separated from mother 7, 200
   Shewa and Hozan 9–10, 11, 51, 56, 62–4, 124–5, 275
   Syrian 61
   temporary accommodation 219
   treatment of 87, 119
   Ukrainian 78
   unaccompanied 66, 68, 273
   unconscious 25
   women protecting 73
   See also teenagers
China 75, 143
Chote, Sir Robert 216
Choudary, Anjem 39
Chris (Scouse cabbie) 111, 112, 113
Clarke, Charles 35
Clearsprings Ready Homes 122
Cleverly, James 158, 200, 251, 257
climate change displacement 134
coastguards
   British 5, 22–9, 270
   French 5, 27
Colnbrook detention centre, Middlesex 249
Colombians 163–6
Congolese 234
Conservative governments 36–41
   application backlog 95
   Bibby and 128
   cutting student route 143
   funding 'upstream' 88
   GPS tagging 197–8
   'lefty lawyers' 174–5
   Nationality and Borders Act 190
   NHS and 157

INDEX

small 'Small Boats Operational Command' 29
stopping the boats 86
Thatcher's 123
Conyers, James 169–70
Cooper, Yvette 41–2, 50, 203
Corbyn, Jeremy 58
Covid-19 pandemic 72–3, 94, 103, 152, 157, 225, 235–6, 249
  lockdowns 93, 95, 150, 226, 235
crossing numbers xi, 49–50, 75
CRS (Compagnies républicaines de sécurité) 8, 10, 11
custody officers 237–40

D

Da'esh 38–9, 61
data protection watchdog 198
deaths
  Aegean Sea 63–4
  English Channel 26–29, 50, 84, 185, 269, 272
  Mediterranean 29
  non-swimmers 32
decision makers, asylum 96–100
Deeda, Tume Yarco 133
Deliveroo 135–6, 137
Democratic Republic of Congo (DRC) 234
dependants 143, 159
deportations 45–6, 201–3, 212–13, 247–60
  self 208
  Windrush generation 38
  workplace 137, 139
  See also Rwanda scheme
depression 155
Detention Action 236
Dickens, Charles, *Hard Times* 123
dinghies 3, 6, 7, 29, 31, 75, 189
Doncaster 151–4, 271
Dorset Council 126, 128
Dover 19–21

Dover Castle 20–1
Dover Strait 22, 23–4
drones 94, 183, 184–8, 190
drug epidemics 238
Dublin 3 Regulation (EU) 256, 257, 272
Dunkirk camps 8

E

Eastern Europeans 148–50, 212
economic migrants 134
ECPAT (End Child Prostitution and Trafficking) 119
Ecuadorians 166
Egypt 105
Elira (Eastern European) 148–50
'Emergencies on Trial' course (coastguards) 29
enforcement teams, immigration 37–8, 137, 145–6, 199–213
English Channel disaster (2021) 26–29
English Channel disaster (2022) 188–9
English Defence League 124
English language tests 103, 142, 143–4
Eritrea 132
Eritreans 5, 8, 44
Ethiopia, Northern 131–3
Ethiopians 131–2, 275
ethnic cleansing 105
ETS (TOEFL Test Takers Educational Testing Service) 144
EU referendum (2016) 266
EU Settlement Scheme 167
Eurodac 77, 269
European Commission 266
European Convention on Human Rights 238
European Court of Human Rights (ECHR) 46
European Parliament 265–6
European Union (EU) 36, 49, 50, 76, 79, 256–7, 266–7, 272
Eurostar trains 89

INDEX

Evans (Ghanaian) 158–60, 162
'Everyone In' scheme 226, 271
Eves, Kate 238
evictions, camp 8, 10–11

F

far-right xii, 33, 94, 116–18, 127–8, 207, 265–6, 271
Farage, Nigel 21, 22, 33, 94, 266
FARC (guerrilla group) 165
Farruku, Leonard 127
fishermen 7, 27
Fletcher, Nick 153
food delivery riders 135–7
Foreign Affairs Select Committee xi, 83–6
Foreign, Commonwealth & Development Office (FCDO) 270
'foreign fighters', British 38
foreign national offenders 35–6, 195, 237–8
Foreign Office 43, 86, 103
Fowler, Nick 88
France 265–6
    asylum applications 10, 271
    British border officials 76
    police boats 31
    UK–France return deal 257
    UK funding for police officers 6, 31, 185
France, northern 3–4, 6, 76, 268
Freedom Party, Austria 266
Frontex 185–6

G

G4S 122, 194, 237–9
Gabriela (Colombian) 163–6, 168, 170
Gateshead Council 219
Gaza 84, 270
Gentleman, Amelia, *The Windrush Betrayal* 201–2

Georgia 257
Germany 266, 271
Ghanaians 158–60, 162
Ghani, Ashraf 82
Glasgow 204–6, 215–18, 224, 271
Glynn, Dr Fiona 152–4
Goan community, Southall 209
Grace (South African) 138–9
Grande-Synthe camp, Dunkirk 7
Greater London Authority 212–13
Greece 15, 63–4, 272
Greek coastguards 31, 64
Grenfell Tower fire (2017) 126
Guineans 189, 244

H

Hadi (Harmondsworth detainee) 235–6
Hague, William 267
Hamas 84
Hard Times (Dickens) 123
Harmondsworth immigration removal centre 233–7, 258–9
Harrington, Richard, Lord 141
Hawa, Ousmane 163–8, 170
hawala system 75
Hazem (Libyan) 216–18
health and social care visas 157–61, 268
healthcare, accessing 150–1, 153, 169
HMP Elmley 194, 242
Hollande, François 268
Home Affairs Select Committee 68, 77, 156, 250
Home Office 35–50, 86, 143–4, 273–4
    bullying allegations 42–3
    hostile environment policy 37–9
    immigration courses 255
    Marsham Street 35
    media handling 37–9
    press office 37–8, 48, 88, 102, 144–5, 155–6, 202
    rebellion in the 46–7
    social care system 161
    surgeries 210–13

INDEX

Home Office International Operations (HOIO) 87, 88
Hopper, Kay 96–100, 104
Hossain, Toufique 175
hotels, use of 111–25, 135, 269
   cost of 89, 270
housing shortage 116, 124, 221, 270
Human Rights Observers 10
Human Rights Watch 13, 132
humanitarian visas 50, 269–70
Hunt, Jeremy 221

I

Ilford, London 74–5
Illegal Migration Act (2023) 108, 240, 241, 256
immigration advisors, exploitative 168–71, 177–8
Immigration (Age Assessments) Regulations (2024) 66–7
Immigration Law Practitioners' Association (ILPA) 171, 172–3
immigration removal centres (IRCs) 45, 91–3, 233–7, 245, 272
Independence Party 266
India 257
Indians 5, 136, 143, 159, 206–13
International Development Select Committee 121–2
international students 142–4
Iran 183–5
Iranians 5, 13–14, 44, 87
Iraq 38, 58, 184
Iraqi-Kurds 44, 67
   See also Arian (Iranian-Kurdish); Qadir, Parwen and Dara
Iraqis 5, 44, 150, 236
Ireland 266–7
Iryna (Ukrainian) 78–9
ISIS 38–9, 61
Israel 84
Italy 15, 272

J

Jamaica 251–2
Jamaicans 247–9, 250–5, 259–60
Jamal (Afghan teen) 65–9, 71–4, 119, 275
Jarba, Ahmed 59–60
Javid, Sajid xi, 251
Jenrick, Robert 66, 226
Jeremy (British teacher) 78–9
Jerf, Naji 39
Johnson, Boris 88, 140, 141, 174–5, 207, 225
Johnson, Diana 68
Johnson KC, Mr Justice Jeremy 192–3
Joint International Irregular Migration Unit 272
Julianne (hotel manager) 116

K

Kachif, Fikri 106–7
Kemi (given birth) 151
Kent County Council 119, 120
Kent Intake Unit (KIU) 65
Kewser (Ethiopian) 131–2, 134, 135–6, 141–2, 275
Khamenei, Ayatollah 13, 185
Kidd, Andrew 84
Kinnock, Stephen 49, 50
Knowsley Suites Hotel disorder (2023) 112–13
Kurdistan 12–14
Kurds 9, 12, 13–17, 16, 44, 61, 119, 274

L

Labour governments 34, 76, 140, 268–9, 272
   New Labour 35, 266, 270
Langdon Battery, Dover 23, 24
law firm raids 178–9
Leak, Andrew (petrol bomber) 57–8
legal aid 171, 173, 176, 271

INDEX

Levelling Up, Department for 86
Lewis, Duncan 175
Liberated Territories 100
Libya 59
Libyans 216–17
lifejackets 26, 31, 56, 75
Lighthouse Reports 31
Lille, France 10, 72
Liverpool riots (2024) 118
local authorities 66, 120–1, 217, 220–2, 226, 229, 243, 271
Local Government Association 219, 223
lockdowns, Covid-19 93, 95, 150, 226, 235
Loon-Plage, Dunkirk 131
lorry crossings 71–2, 89
Loughton, Tim 77
Luiselli, Valeria 71
Lydd airport, Kent 186–7

M

Maan, Shakila Taranum 209–10
McKenzie, Jacqui 173–4
Macron, Emmanuel 31, 257, 265
Malan, Thia and Peter 103
Mandela, Nelson 233
Manston processing centre 67–9, 241
maritime law, international 30
marriages, sham 164, 165, 168
May, Theresa 36–7, 143–4
Mayday Rescue 103
Mears 118, 122, 154
Médecins Sans Frontières 129
media reporting 115, 156, 244, 262, 263–4
Medical Justice 240
Medlock, Cavan 175
men, elderly 25
mental health 141, 154, 235–7, 240, 245, 248, 252–3
Mercer, Johnny 220–1
Michael (Border Force) 29–34

Migrant Help 102, 114, 124–5, 154, 155
Miliband, Ed 50
militias, Middle East 184
Mina and Najwa (Batoor's family) 81, 82–3
mining 152–3, 271
Mohammed (Sudanese) 241–2
Morgan, Lawrence 251
Morocco 100, 101
Morrison, Herbert 272
Mustafa (son missing) 27–8

N

Napier barracks, Folkestone 93–5, 155
National Audit Office 129
National Coal Mining Museum 153
National Front 207
National Health Service (NHS) 156–7, 160, 169, 209, 273
Nationality Act (1948) 157
Nationality and Borders Act (2022) 44–5, 190, 242
Neal, David 48, 57, 120, 161, 227, 240
Neate, Polly 223
Netanyahu, Benjamin 84
New Horizons centre, London 228–9
Nigerians 125, 143, 169, 196–7, 224, 239
North Parade hotel, Skegness 116–17
Nubians 106–7

O

Oala, Nadgem Said 91
Obama, Barack 60–1
Office of the Immigration Services Commissioner (OISC) 171
Olympic Games, London (2012) 36
O'Mahoney, Dan 187–8
Omar (Sudanese) 243–6
Opal Coast, northern France 7
Open Arms shelter, Jamaica 252
Operation Isotrope 30
Operation Vaken (2013) 207–8

INDEX

Orwell, George 183
Oumar (Senegalese) 194
overseas aid budget 88, 121–2

P
Padgham, Mike 160–1
Pakistanis 225–6
Palestine 84
Palestinians 84, 270
Panorama (BBC) 143–4, 238
Parkes, Carralyn 126
Pasha (smuggler) 3, 4, 16–17
Patel, Priti 41–3, 46, 174, 252, 258
Patriotic Alternative 113
Patten, Chris 35
Philp, Chris 42
photographers 23
Poles 224, 226
population, UK asylum seeker xiii
Portes, Jonathan 134–5
post-traumatic stress disorder (PTSD) 154–5, 219
Powell, Enoch 156–7, 175
Preston, Lancashire 123–5
Privacy International 194
Privilege Style airline 249
processing centres 57–8, 67–9
'Professional Enablers Taskforce' 178
protests 29, 58–9, 61, 68, 112–13, 116, 126, 200–1, 271
Public Accounts Committee 195, 202
Punjabi community, Southall 206–9, 211
Putin, Vladimir 78

Q
Qadir, Parwen and Dara 9–11, 51, 55–8, 61–5, 68, 124–5, 275

R
RAF bases, former 128
Rahimpur, Hewa 74–6
raids, workplace 199–213, 258
Randall of Uxbridge, Lord 141
Rapid Support Forces 105, 107, 184
Read, John Kingsley 207
Refugee Action 169
refugee camps, Algerian 100–1
Refugee Convention (1951) 97, 105, 134
Refugee Tales 246
religion 39, 208–9, 211
reporting centres 203
resettlement schemes 85, 86, 269–70
Revolutionary Guard, Iranian 184–5
riot police 8, 10
Robbins, Tim 59
Robinson, Tommy (Stephen Yaxley-Lennon) 57
Romanians 237
Rotherham riots (2024) 117–18
rough sleepers 212–13, 215, 217–18, 222, 224–9
Roy, Arundhati 199
Royal National Lifeboat Institution (RNLI) 22, 33, 34, 270
Royal Navy (RN) 23, 29–30
Rudakubana, Axel Muganwa 117
Rudd, Amber 250, 272
Rutnam, Philip 42
Rwanda scheme 43–8, 50, 174, 203, 241

S
Sabah (Pakistani) 225–6
Safavi, Yahya Rahim 184–5
Safe in Scotland 224
safe routes 50, 80, 84, 86, 269
Safety of Rwanda Act (2024) 241, 256
Saharawis 100
St Cecilia's nursing home, Scarborough 158–62
St James' Estate, Doncaster 151
St Mungo's charity 212–13
Salter, Ann 154–5
Sanou (Borena tribe elder) 133

INDEX

Sarah (*Bibby* caterer) 127
Satchett, Bob 19–22
Savage, Dave 123–4
Scampton, Lincolnshire 128
Scarborough, North Yorkshire 157–8
Schengen Information System 269
Scotland 204–6, 215–18
Scottish Parliament 205
Scottish Refugee Council 217–18
seasonal worker visas 140
security guards 68, 93–4, 113, 122, 129
Senegal 193
Senegalese 189–93, 242
Serbia 257
Serco 114–16, 122, 124, 125, 239
Severoni, Dr Santino 147
sex workers 149
Shadi (Sudanese) 91–6, 105–8, 274–5
Shafak, Elif 3
Shaffi (British-Bangladeshi delivery rider) 136
Simon Community 215–18
Simon (drone pilot) 186
Singh, Gurdip 207
Singh, Navine 188–9
Sivanandan, Ambalavaner 247
Skegness 116–17, 270–1
slavery 61, 132, 138, 161, 250
Smith, Hannah Lucinda 87
smugglers 3–6, 15–17, 190–1
    Labour and 34
    migrants and 26, 28, 165
    networks 12, 195, 269
    pandemic and 73
smuggling networks 75–6
Soames, Rupert 239
social care system 161
social housing 112, 220–3, 223, 228
Solicitors Regulation Authority 178, 179
Somalis 152
South Africans 138–9
South Sudan 105

Southall Black Sisters charity 209–10
Southall, London 206–9, 211
Southport stabbings (2024) 117
spousal visas 78–9, 103, 143, 176
Stainforth, South Yorkshire 152–3
Starmer, Keir 174, 272
Steinbeck, John 163
Stephens, Polly 229
'Stop the War' events 61
Strachan, Raymond 188, 189, 190
student visas 143–6, 217
Sudan 105–7, 184
Sudanese 5, 44, 91–6, 105, 241–2, 243–6
suicide attempts 67, 155, 239–40
Suites hotel, Knowsley 111–14
Sunak, Rishi 6, 30–1, 95, 188, 215–16, 257
surveillance, state 194–5
surveillance technology 25, 31, 76, 185–6, 195–8
Sweden 271
Syria 38–9, 59–61, 267–8
Syrian Civil Defence 103–4
Syrian National Coalition 59, 61
Syrian refugee crisis (2015) 124
Syrians 44, 99, 103–4, 203

T

Taliban 61, 80, 81–2, 219
Tamworth riots (2024) 118
Tanvi (English language test) 145–6
Tava (smuggler) 73–4
teenagers 65–9
    age-disputed 68, 242–3
    education 82, 275
    evicted 228
    harassed by asylum seeker 111
    protesting 113
    rescued 57, 189–90
    rough sleepers 217
    smugglers and 73
    trafficked 148
    unaccompanied 9, 241–2

INDEX

Tekever 186–7
Telefonica 194
Tents 8, 9, 10
Thames Reach charity 212–13
Tigray People's Liberation Front 132
Tinashe (Zimbabwean) 227
Tinsley House immigration removal centre 239, 245
Titan Airways 249
Tomlinson, Michael 179
Tony (Dover coastguard) 22–6, 28–9
Tory–Lib Dem coalition 171
tourist visas 166
traffickers 149–50, 249
tribunal hearings 171–2
Trump, Donald 22
Truss, Liz 257
Tug Haven processing centre, Dover 57
Tulley, Callum 238
Turkey 14, 39, 75, 87–8, 103

U

Uber Eats 135–6
Ukraine 184
Ukrainians 78–9, 85, 221, 269
UN Refugee Agency UNHCR 85, 101
US 271, 272

V

Vietnam 257
Vietnamese 57, 72, 150
vigils 27–8
Vince, Gaia 131
visas
 centres 46–7, 79
 conditions attached to 223
 cost of 85, 176
 English language test 103
 expired 237–8
 extension 167
 health and social care 157–61, 268
 humanitarian 50, 269–70
 seasonal worker 140
 spousal 78–9, 103, 143, 176
 student 143–6, 217
 tourist 166
 waivers 80
 worker 104
voluntary returns programme 210–13

W

Warrington 119
'weapons of mass destruction' 58
weather conditions 16, 32–3
Western Heights, Dover 20–2, 25
Western Jet Foil processing centre, Dover 57
Western Sahara 100
Wethersfield, Essex 128, 129
Windrush generation 201–2, 250–1
Winston (Jamaican) 247–9, 250, 252–5, 259–60
Witney, Oxfordshire 147–8
women 4, 6, 73, 239
 pregnant 27, 67–8, 122, 129, 133, 150–1
 separated from children 7, 200
women, elderly 61
worker visas 104
Wright, Colin 40–3, 47–8

Y

Yarl's Wood immigration removal centre 91–3
Yaxley-Lennon, Stephen (Tommy Robinson) 57
Yemenis 93, 217

Z

Zanyar (missing migrant) 27–8
Zimbabweans 227
Zorgan (Saharawi) 100–1